Breaking the Cycle of Hurtful Family Relationships

Robert S. McGee, Pat Springle & Jim Craddock

with Learning Activities by Dale W. McCleskey

LifeWay Press
Nashville, Tennessee

ACKNOWLEDGEMENTS

Your Parents and You was originally co-published by Word, Inc. and Rapha Resources, Inc. and is available in its original version in Christian bookstores. We want to thank Rapha Hospital Treatment Centers for making this book available to the LifeWay Press for its use.

Rapha Hospital Treatment Centers is an independent, nationwide provider of adult and adolescent in-hospital psychiatric care and substance abuse treatment from a Christian perspective. For information about Rapha Hospital Treatment Centers you may contact Rapha at 1-800-383-HOPE or write to Rapha, 12700 Featherwood, Houston, Texas 77034.

Breaking the Cycle of Hurtful Family Relationships
Copyright © 1994 by Rapha Publishing, Reprint 2001

ISBN 978-1515028918

Sources for definitions in Breaking the Cycle of Hurtful Family Relationships : Webster's Ninth New Collegiate Dictionary (Springfield, Mass.: Merriam-Webster Inc., Publishers, 1991); Webster's New Twentieth Century Dictionary, Unabridged Second Edition (New York: Prentice Hall Press, 1983); W.E. Vine, The Expanded Vine's Expository Dictionary of New Testament Words (Minneapolis, MN: Bethany House Publishers, 1984); Francis Brown, S.R. Driver, and Charles A. Briggs, A Hebrew and English Lexicon of the Old Testament (New York, NY: Oxford Press, 1959).

Unless otherwise indicated, biblical quotations are from the New American Standard Bible. © The Lockman Foundation, 1960, 1962, 1963, 1968, 1971, 1972, 1973, 1975, 1977. Used by permission. Other versions used: From the Holy Bible, New International Version, copyright © 1973, 1978, 1984 by International Bible Society (NIV); the King James Version (KJV).

Printed in the United States of America

Table of Contents

About the Authors 4

Introduction 5

UNIT 1
    Identifying the Cycle 9

UNIT 2
    Substitutes for Relationships 28

UNIT 3
    Stages of Development 48

UNIT 4
    Emotional Healing 70

UNIT 5
    Analyzing Your Family 90

UNIT 6
    Bonding with God 106

UNIT 7
    Getting to Know God 124

UNIT 8
    Metamorphosis 143

UNIT 9
    Grieving and Healing 161

UNIT 10
    Modeling God's Character 182

UNIT 11
    Responding to Your Parents 199

UNIT 12
    Toward the Future 212

Course map ....Inside back cover

THE AUTHORS

Robert S. McGee is a professional counselor, lecturer, and author of the book, *Search for Significance* LIFE® Support Group Series Edition He also is founder of Rapha, a manager of inpatient psychiatric care and substance-abuse treatment from a distinctively Christian perspective in hospitals located nationwide.

Pat Springle is president of Baxter Press. He is former senior vice president for Rapha Resources and served on the staff of Campus Crusade for Christ for 18 years.

Jim Craddock is the founder and president of Scope Ministries International, a biblical counseling ministry which seeks to meet the spiritual and emotional needs of persons by helping them apply principles from the Bible.

Dale McCleskey is editor of LIFE® Support Group Series materials at LifeWay Christian Resources. He was a pastor for 15 years before joining LifeWay. He also wrote the leader's guide for *Breaking the Cycle of Hurtful Family Experiences.*

Graphics by Lori Putnam
Cover Design by Edward Crawford

The Study Begins

INTRODUCTION

Case in point

> **CAUTION: CYCLE AT WORK**
>
> Kathy's father was physically absent much of the time when Kathy was a child. Even when he was physically present, he was emotionally absent. He never expressed feelings of love or affirmation. The only emotion he displayed was anger. Her mother was hypercritical of her and never seemed to be interested in hearing about Kathy's feelings.
>
> Kathy left home when she was 16. She had to get away. She managed to get a job and went to the community college. She was determined to build a life that was different from the family in which she grew up. She met Edwin at a church social. He seemed to be all the things she wanted in a husband.
>
> Kathy and Edwin both came from painful family backgrounds. They determined that they would not repeat the patterns they experienced in their childhood homes. Now, with teenage children, Kathy finds herself right back where she said she never would be. Her husband is obsessed with work and is emotionally distant. Her children say and do the same things Kathy said and did around her parents. Worst of all, Kathy finds herself acting and sounding just like her mother. Kathy is stuck in a repeated cycle of family dysfunction. She wants things to be different with her children, but she doesn't know where to start to break this painful cycle.

Can you identify with Kathy's dilemma? Does your family history contain painful experiences that you want to avoid repeating? Do you see others in society today making the same destructive choices and the same mistakes over and over? *Breaking the Cycle of Hurtful Family Experiences* will help you to understand, identify and, to the degree that the cycle is at work in your family, begin to change this process of reproduced family dysfunction.

We learn much of life from our first and primary role models—our parents, who are imperfect people. They model beliefs and behaviors they learned from their own imperfect parents. And on and on and on the cycle goes. When those ideas about life, ourselves, others, and God are faulty, both we and our relationships suffer. What's more, we continue this faulty and sometimes damaging cycle for future generations.

Breaking the Cycle of Hurtful Family Experiences helps you identify these harmful patterns so that you may make Christ-honoring and life-enhancing changes. It will help you learn how God, by speaking to us through His Word, can help us replace false perceptions of Him and His Word so we can experience His love, forgiveness, and power in all of life's circumstances.

After you complete a study of *Breaking the Cycle of Hurtful Family Experiences*, you will have the means to identify the ways that past experience is damaging

Course goal

your present family or the family of someone you love. You will be equipped to begin a healing process which will bring you a clear sense of identity and a healthy relationship to the lordship of Christ built on a positive experience of His unconditional love.

To help you to accomplish this goal, *Breaking the Cycle of Hurtful Family Experiences* will help you to learn—

- the causes and symptoms of the cycle of destruction in families;
- some of the things we substitute for healthy family relationships;
- the stages of human development and how they affect both our lives and our parenting;
- how to develop healthy and Christ-honoring relationships;
- to analyze your family and understand your family;
- to build a strong and healthy relationship with God;
- to model God's character to your children;
- to respond in a positive and Christ-honoring way to your parents.

A wide variety of individuals will profit from studying *Breaking the Cycle of Hurtful Family Experiences*. Individuals will learn how to understand themselves better and how better to relate to the hurting or difficult people in their lives. *Breaking the Cycle of Hurtful Family Experiences* is an ideal course for adults of all ages, including expectant parents or new parents who want to avoid repeating painful patterns from previous generations as they begin the child-rearing process.

Breaking the Cycle of Hurtful Family Experiences was written to include both those who came from a dysfunctional family background and those who did not but who wish to understand and minister to hurting people. For that reason you will see the following boxed statement appearing in the margin periodically:

> *The material and activities you are reading may or may not apply to your particular family. If you have experienced the painful family situations described, apply the learning activities to your situation. If you have not experienced the situations, the activities will help you to understand and minister to others.*

How this course fits in

Breaking the Cycle of Hurtful Family Experiences is not merely designed for you to understand concepts. The purpose of this material is life change. *Breaking the Cycle of Hurtful Family Experiences* is part of the LIFE® Support Group Series. The LIFE® Support Group Series is an educational system of discovery-group and support-group resources for providing Christian ministry and emotional support to individuals in the areas of social, emotional, and physical need. These resources deal with such life issues as chemical dependency, codependency, recovery from sexual abuse, eating disorders, divorce recovery, and how to grieve the losses of life. People using LIFE® Support Group Series courses will be led through recovery to discipleship and ministry by using these materials.

Breaking the Cycle of Hurtful Family Experiences is a discovery-group course that can be basic to any biblically-based support-group ministry. A discovery group studies dysfunctional family issues and other problem areas that individuals face. A group leader guides discussion of the topics and helps group members consider applications to life. Because it deals with issues common to large numbers of people, *Breaking the Cycle of Hurtful Family Experiences* is an ideal course for a church to use to begin a support-group ministry among its members.

What's in it for you?

Breaking the Cycle of Hurtful Family Experiences is an integrated course of study. To achieve the full benefit of the educational design, prepare your individual assignments and participate in the group sessions. The principles behind *Breaking the Cycle of Hurtful Family Experiences* represent a lifelong learning process. This is not a course which you will study and then forget. It represents an opportunity to understand and change basic areas which have generated pain in your life. For many people participating in an *Breaking the Cycle of Hurtful Family Experiences* group will be the beginning of a journey. The journey is not always easy, but it leads to a whole new world of healing and usefulness. When you complete *Breaking the Cycle of Hurtful Family Experiences*, we will suggest some possibilities from which you may wish to choose to continue your growth and study.

Study Tips. Five days a week (which compose a unit) you will study a segment of content material. You may need from 30 to 60 minutes of study time each day. Even if you find that you can study the material in less time, spread the study out over five days. This will give you more time to apply the truths to your life. Study at your own pace. Your group may decide to take a longer time to study each unit. The leader's guide to *Breaking the Cycle of Hurtful Family Experiences* will give you some helps on other formats for study. Do not become discouraged if you or your group members are unable to complete *Breaking the Cycle of Hurtful Family Experiences* in 12 weeks. Remember that the purpose is life change, not speed reading. Take the time necessary to work the truths deeply into your life.

This book has been written as a tutorial text. Study it as if the authors are sitting at your side helping you learn. When they ask you a question or give you an assignment, you will benefit most by writing your response. Each assignment is indented and appears in boldface type. When you are to respond in writing, a pencil appears beside the assignment. For example, an assignment will look like this:

✎ Read Psalm 139:13. Write what the verse tells about God's care for you.

Of course, in an actual activity, a line would appear below each assignment or in the margin beside the assignment. You would write your response as indicated. Then, when you are asked to respond in a non-written fashion—for example, by thinking about or praying about a matter—a ➥ appears beside the assignment. This type of assignment will look like this:

➥ Pause now to pray and thank God for unconditionally accepting you.

In most cases your "personal tutor" will give you some feedback about your response—for example, you may see a suggestion about what you might have written. This process is designed to help you learn the material and apply the concepts more effectively. Do not deny yourself valuable learning by skipping the learning activities.

Set a definite time and select a quiet place where you can study with little interruption. Keep a Bible handy for times in which the material asks you to look up Scripture. Memorizing Scripture is an important part of your work.

Set aside a portion of your study period for memory work. Make notes of problems, questions, or concerns that arise as you study. You will discuss many of these during your discovery-group sessions. Write these matters in the margins of this textbook so you can find them easily.

Discovery-Group Session. You will benefit most from *Breaking the Cycle of Hurtful Family Experiences* if once each week you attend a discovery-group session. A group session is designed to help you discuss the content you studied the previous week, practice your memory work, share insights, look for answers to problems encountered, and apply the material to your life.

The discovery group adds a needed dimension to your learning. If you have started a study of *Breaking the Cycle of Hurtful Family Experiences* and you are not involved in a group study, enlist some friends or associates to work through this material with you. A large group of people is not necessary; three or four individuals studying the material together can be highly beneficial. *Breaking the Cycle of Hurtful Family Experiences Leader's Guide* (0805499822) provides guidance and learning activities for these sessions. (Send orders or inquiries to LifeWay Church Resources Customer Service, 127 Ninth Avenue, North; Nashville, TN 37234-0113; FAX order to (615) 251-5933; PHONE 1-800-458-2772; EMAIL to CustomerService@lifeway.com; ONLINE at www.lifeway.com; or visit the LifeWay Christian Store serving you.

A key decision

Breaking the Cycle of Hurtful Family Experiences is written with the assumption that you already have received Jesus Christ as your Savior and that you have Him guiding you in the healing process. If you have not yet made the decision to receive Christ, you will find guidance in unit 2. You will benefit far more from *Breaking the Cycle of Hurtful Family Experiences* if you have Jesus working in your life and guiding you in the process.

Beware of Parenting Guilt

In Breaking the Cycle you will study God's ideal plan for the family. Because we all are damaged by sin, NO family ever lives up to God's purpose totally. No child has or had perfect parents. No parent does or did a perfect job of rearing children. All of us who are parents have memories and regrets that haunt us with guilt.

This study is to help you to understand and relate better to your childhood and your parents and to help you to be a more effective parent. Please do not let your feelings of anger toward parents or your feelings of inadequacy and guilt about your own parenting stand in the way of the growth God has planned for you.

➥ As you begin this study, would you please pray the following prayer?

Dear God, consistently you deal with me in your wonderful and unimaginable grace. You forgive me always. You cleanse, accept, and have patience with me. As I work better to know myself and my family, please give me the ability to forgive and accept my family members and myself with something of the grace that You display. Lead me to feel and express appropriately my guilt and my anger, Lord. Then lead me on to your forgiveness and to your love.

UNIT 1

Identifying the Cycle

Case in point

> ### A LEGACY OF DYSFUNCTION
>
> "Dad was a driver. He worked long and diligently, and he expected his children to do the same," Steve said. "If I didn't do something exactly the way he wanted it done—though I really tried to do a good job—he'd let me have it. I can remember only one time when I was growing up that he put an affirming hand on my shoulder. But he put his hand on my backside a few more times than that!"
>
> "Did you ever spend much time with his father, your granddad?" I asked.
>
> Steve responded instantly with a look of revelation. "You know, I did, and he was a crotchety old goat. He always seemed to have something to say about everybody, and it wasn't very complimentary! He even gave his grandchildren a pretty rough time."
>
> Steve went on to say: "I don't like to admit it, but I treat my children the same way my father treated me and the same way his father treated him. I hate it! And I feel so guilty about it!" (You will read more about Steve on page 10.)

What you'll learn

This week you will
- begin to identify the concept of a cycle of hurtful family experiences;
- describe how parents shape their children;
- explain how hurting parents pass their hurts, needs, and distorted perceptions to their children;
- describe how the absence of a parent affects a child;
- identify results of emotionally distant, abusive, or perfectionist parents.

What you'll study

The Cycle Begins	Shaping a Child	Your Parents and You	The Absent-Parent Syndrome	Distant or Abusive Parents
DAY 1	DAY 2	DAY 3	DAY 4	DAY 5

Memory verse

This week's verse of Scripture to memorize

I am the Lord your God, who brought you out of the land of Egypt, out of the land of slavery.

—Exodus 20:2

DAY 1

The Cycle Begins

The Lord, the Lord God, compassionate and gracious, slow to anger, and abounding in lovingkindness and truth; who keeps lovingkindness for thousands, who forgives iniquity, transgression and sin; yet He will by no means leave the guilty unpunished, visiting the iniquity of fathers on the children and on the grandchildren to the third and fourth generations.
—Exodus 34:6-7

You read part of Steve's story on page 9. The members of his family, from his grandfather to his children, are experiencing the reproductive legacy of destruction called sin. We all have seen the cycle in action, though we may not have been able to understand and put the process into words. People we know—and sometimes we, if we have enough courage and insight to see it—are stuck in a repeating generational cycle of dysfunction and pain. You've probably heard people make statements like these that emphasize this type of cycle:

- Why does she always pick such jerks?
- He's just like his father!
- Why do they treat their children that way?
- Didn't he learn anything from that last experience?
- Why do the same things keep happening to them?

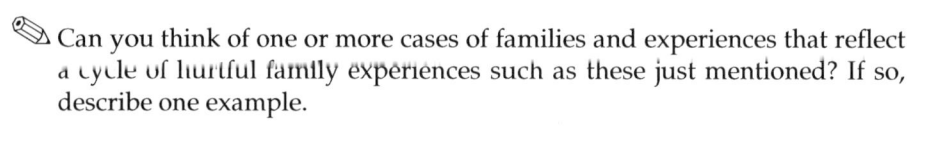

✎ Can you think of one or more cases of families and experiences that reflect a cycle of hurtful family experiences such as these just mentioned? If so, describe one example.

_____

_____

You may have described one of a great many examples of this vicious cycle at work in families. Tragically, we repeat the same behaviors we have experienced. If you could not think of an instance, you will gain insight as this study continues.

> Note: Often in this book we will mention the word *sin*. At the mention of this word many people feel shame. Our discussion of sin in this book is not intended to create or increase your feelings of guilt or shame. We mention sin to emphasize "missing the mark"—the type of actions that lie behind these harmful cycles of behavior. As you continue today's study, you will learn the true meaning of *sin*.

The Lord, the Lord God, compassionate and gracious, slow to anger, and abounding in lovingkindness and truth; who keeps lovingkindness for thousands, who forgives iniquity, transgression and sin; yet He will by no means leave the guilty unpunished, visiting the iniquity of fathers on the children and on the grandchildren to the third and fourth generations.
—Exodus 34:6-7

✎ Read the Scripture verses that appear in the margin. In the three paragraphs that follow, underline the statements that accurately reflect the meaning of the Scripture.

The Bible records a disturbing truth about a reality of life: the consequences of sin are reproduced in a family for generations. The effects of a father's or a mother's sins—bitterness, unbridled anger, neglect, abuse, passivity, harmful communication patterns, or manipulation—will be passed down to the children, grandchildren, and great-grandchildren. The parents' behaviors affect the way they relate to everyone in their lives—from neighbors to spouses to children to friends. This truth may seem harsh and cruel, but it is an accurate reflection of sin's terrible consequences.

Note that the emphasis in the passage is on God's constant and dependable love. The Bible does not say that God is waiting to pounce on sinners and punish them or to blast their descendants. It says that our sin affects us and infects others, and although God always desires to bring healing and forgiveness, He will not compromise either our freedom or His holiness to ignore our sin.

God always desires to bring healing and forgiveness.

Many people have understandings of sin that are far too limited. They think of sin only as the violation of certain moral laws. For them sin means only acts like lying, stealing, and committing adultery. The biblical view of sin is much broader than that. *Sin* means *missing the mark*. It means falling short of being all that God created us to be. Our first ancestors chose to rebel against God, and we have followed their example. This broken relationship with God has warped us spiritually, and we live in a world that is damaged in the same way. Sin has touched every relationship and every aspect of our existence. Although sin harms all of us, some families and individuals have experienced far greater harm than others.

Missing the mark

✏ Check the following responses that accurately reflect the meaning of Exodus 34:6-7 and the explanation in the previous paragraphs.
- ❏ 1. Only certain specific actions are sins.
- ❏ 2. Specific sinful behaviors or groups of behaviors are passed from one generation to the next.
- ❏ 3. Sin spreads in the life of a person and of a family.
- ❏ 4. Every person on earth is warped and harmed by sin, but some families and individuals have suffered greater damage than others.

All of the answers except the first reflect the meaning of the passage and paragraphs.

Two biblical models for thinking about our sin problem will help us as we seek to understand and break the cycle of hurt in our family experiences. In the first passage in the margin the apostle Paul spoke of sin as if it were a living entity, like a disease, living in his body and prompting him to do what he hated.

That which I am doing, I do not understand; for I am not practicing what I would like to do, but I am doing the very thing I hate. So now, no longer am I the one doing it, but sin which indwells me.
–Romans 7:15,17

In the second passage in the margin the prophet Isaiah spoke of what we might term the sociological aspect of sin. He connected sin to the nation, community, and family in which he lived.

Woe is me, for I am ruined! Because I am a man of unclean lips, And I live among a people of unclean lips; For my eyes have seen the King, the Lord of hosts.
–Isaiah 6:5

We often fail to recognize these aspects of evil at work in our lives. Sin is like a disease—we need to treat the roots of the problem. Sin carries with it a component of learned behavior, learned primarily from our family. We need to identify and change harmful patterns of thought and action.

The Great Challenge

Since sin is so destructive and since its effects last for generations, the challenge becomes clear. We need to break the cycle. Through God's grace and

You can overcome the fear, shame, and habits that create and maintain the cycle of hurtful family experiences.

> *The material and activities you are reading may or may not apply to your particular family. If you have experienced the painful family situations described, apply the learning activities to your situation. If you have not experienced the situations, the activities will help you to understand and minister to others.*

power we need to stop the destruction and pain of reproduced personal and family dysfunction. In the pages ahead you can make major strides in this life task. You can learn to identify the cycle of hurt at work in your family and in families around you. By learning to recognize and experience God's truth and grace, you can overcome the fear, shame, and habits that create and maintain the cycle of hurtful family experiences.

In this study you will explore how a cycle of hurtful family experiences begins, develops, and continues. You will learn ways you can work to break the cycle and to replace destructive patterns with positive, Christ-honoring patterns.

Jesus often used the phrase "He who has ears to hear, let him hear." Jesus recognized that we do not naturally or automatically see, hear, and understand the processes that motivate and control our lives. As you read and especially as you do the written work in *Breaking the Cycle*, you will develop the ability to see your parents and yourself more objectively. As you participate in a discovery group, you will give and receive insight and support for the journey.

➥ Take time to pray. Ask God to give you the courage and strength to do the work in this process of discovery. Thank Him that His purposes for you are good. Tell Him you are willing to do the difficult work necessary as you realize that this study requires courage and perseverance.

✏ To get the most from your experience with **Breaking the Cycle**, you will need two things. You will need to complete your daily written work, and you will need to participate in a discussion-and-sharing group. Set aside a certain time each day to devote to the daily assignments. Record this time below as well as the time your group will meet.

My daily preparation time/place will be _____

My group will meet _____

If you are not participating in a discovery group, consider inviting some friends to share this experience with you or contact your church about the possibility of forming a group to study and grow together.

✏ In the margin write the unit memory verse from page 9 and begin memorizing it. Consider the fact that the God who brought the Israelites out of slavery also wants to deliver you from the behaviors that enslave you.

SUMMARY STATEMENTS

- Many people are stuck in a repeating generational cycle of dysfunction and pain.
- We need to identify and change harmful patterns of thought and action.
- Through God's truth and grace, you can overcome the fear, shame, and habits that create and maintain the cycle of hurtful family experiences.

DAY 2

Shaping a Child

Train up a child in the way he should go, even when he is old he will not depart from it.

—Proverbs 22:6

Children are supremely moldable. They each have their own God-given personalities and learn to make their own choices, but like a potter shapes lumps of clay, parents shape the confidence and self-concept of children.

✎ In the following paragraph underline the parental influences that shape a confident, secure child. Circle the parental influences that result in an insecure, guilt-riddled, angry, or lonely child.

If children feel loved, valued, and protected and if they are encouraged to try without the threat of condemnation when they fail, then they will usually be shaped into confident, secure adults. If, however, children feel condemned by harsh, perfectionist parents or neglected by parents who are too preoccupied with their own selfish interests, then they usually will be shaped into adults who are plagued by insecurity, guilt, fear, anger, loneliness, and withdrawal. They likely will be driven to accomplish goals and to please others in an attempt to win the love and acceptance they crave. This effort, they hope, will fill the emptiness in their lives.

You may have underlined such words as *feel loved, valued,* and *protected.* You may have circled such words as *condemned, harsh, perfectionist,* and *neglected.*

✎ No family is perfect. All of us fall short of God's glory, and no family is 100 percent distorted. On the scale below place an X on the spot that most nearly represents how you felt about your childhood home.

Loved
Protected
Supported

By watching what their parents get excited or angry about, children learn what is important.

Many authorities agree that young children form their concept of reality by looking at their parents. By watching what their parents get excited or angry about, children learn what is important. By seeing how their parents relate to others and each other, children learn about love and hate. By observing their parents, they learn about every significant issue in life. The child also ascribes godlike characteristics to the parents: what they say is truth; what they demand is law; and how they treat the child is love. If the parents' words and actions are loving, protective, and compassionate, then the child likely will experience good emotional, relational, and spiritual health. But if parents' words and actions are harmful and confusing, the child's concept of life will be characterized by pain and distortion. The accuracy of these early concepts and the warmth of the family environment contribute significantly to the child's development in the critical areas of self-concept, relationships with others, and view of God.

✎ Review the paragraph you just read and describe how children form their concept of reality.

_____

What becomes the child's basis for recognizing and understanding truth?

_____

What becomes the child's basis for understanding law?

_____

How does the child grow to know and understand love?

_____

The paragraph explains that we get our concept of reality primarily from the values and actions of parents. What they say becomes truth. What they demand becomes our understanding of law, and we believe that how they treat us is love.

A Child's Self-esteem

Consistent affirmation and loving discipline help children know that they are valued and secure.

If children experience consistent affirmation and loving discipline, they likely will grow up believing that they are valued and secure. They will be able to take appropriate social and business risks without fearing failure, and they will be able to enjoy relationships without fearing intimacy.

If children's needs for love and acceptance are not met because the parents are condemning or neglectful, the children may conclude that something is wrong with them. Most children think that their parents are always right, so the fault must be theirs, not the parents'. Consequently, the children learn to condemn themselves for not being worthy of love, and they either deny their needs for love and acceptance or try to win that love by their performance. If this self-condemnation is not stopped by consistent love, it slowly can evolve into a deeply rooted self-hatred.

✎ Using the information in the paragraphs above, describe what might happen in each of the following situations.

A child grows up in a family in which she experiences discipline but little affirmation.

_____

_____

A child grows up being told that he is loved, but his parents impose no limits on his behavior.

_____

_____

A child grows up with neither affirmation nor discipline.

You may have given any of a variety of answers to the previous questions. Possibly the child without affirmation may see herself as having little value. She might attempt to work hard enough to earn value—becoming the family "hero" or a workaholic. She might become a people-pleaser and a professional "doormat." The child who experiences no limits may never learn self-discipline. He may be insecure because he never learns to rely on anyone or anything. He might become very skilled at manipulating others to get what he wants. The child without either affirmation or discipline may experience all of the problems described. This person may go through life with a deep sense of inadequacy and self-condemnation.

Relating to Others

Curt is the rejected son of his family. His father made no secret of his preference for Curt's older and more athletic brother. Curt has few or no friends. He wants so desperately to be liked that he pushes people away by attempting to control and smother those who would be his friends. He is a very lonely young man.

In a secure and loving environment children learn to give and receive love.

In a secure and loving environment children learn to give and receive love. They learn to experience the deep joy and pain of intimate relationships with other people. In an environment characterized by severe criticism or manipulation, children learn to condemn and manipulate others. They typically whine until they get their way. Even as adults, they may whine and complain until others either give in to them or withdraw from them. They may become master manipulators, subtly and intricately using praise and condemnation to change others' behavior to suit themselves. People then become objects used to meet the children's needs instead of individuals to be loved.

✎ Based on the information given, why do you believe Curt has problems with relationships?

You may have noted that Curt apparently did not learn to give and receive love. Since his needs were not met, Curt attempts to demand what can only be freely given. His needy, demanding behavior destroys the relationships he so desperately needs and desires.

We have a very strong tendency to emulate our parents' attitudes, behavior, and relationships, good or bad. In other words, we tend to treat and relate to people the way our parents have treated and related to people—the way they related to us. Although it is true that some people attempt to be as unlike their parents as possible, this response usually is limited to behavior. For instance, a child of an alcoholic may refuse to touch alcohol. Even people who consciously choose to be different from their parents may discover, if they are able to be honest and objective, that they have assimilated the very personality traits they despise in their parents. Parental modeling is a powerful, if sometimes complex, force in shaping children's lives.

A Child's View of God

Parents represent God to their children.

For better or for worse, parents represent God to their children. Parents provide the emotional and spiritual foundation for their children. Most important of all, parents should model God's love and strength to their children. They are responsible for portraying God's reliability, His unconditional love, His acceptance, and His purposeful discipline. In the next lesson we will consider in greater detail the origin of our concept of God.

SUMMARY STATEMENTS

- Children's confidence and self-concept are primarily shaped by their parents.
- If children experience consistent affirmation and loving discipline, they will likely grow up believing that they are valued and secure.
- Parents are to model God's love and strength to their children.

✎ In the margin write twice the unit memory verse, Exodus 20:2. Check your memory work on page 9.

DAY 3

Your Parents and You

The tongue of the wise makes knowledge acceptable, But the mouth of fools spouts folly.

–Proverbs 15:2

Your relationships with your parents have shaped your belief system and relational abilities significantly. If your parents were (and are) loving and supportive, then you probably believe that God is nurturing and affirming. You probably are a fairly secure and confident person who is able to relate easily to other people. But maybe your parents treated you harshly and demanded a lot from you in exchange for their approval. If so, you probably believe that God also is that way and that you never can do enough to please Him. Feelings of insecurity resulting from that misconception may prompt you either to withdraw or to be defensive in your relationships with others.

Your parents have played a major role in forming your concept of God.

Whether they have been loving or aloof, kind or harsh, supportive or condemning, attentive or neglectful, your parents have played a major role in forming your concept of God, your self-concept, and your ability to relate to others. The results can be wonderful or tragic.

Some parents are too self-absorbed to give their children what they need. If they are too busy or if they are abusive, condemning, or neglectful, their children will believe that God is condemning instead of forgiving, cruel instead of loving, and neglectful instead of attentive.

✎ The following paragraph describes two problems resulting from parents with unmet needs. Underline the references to the first problem. Circle the references to the second problem. Then describe the two problems in the activity that follows the passage.

When parents have unmet needs, they generally are unable to meet their children's needs.

When parents have unmet needs or significant unresolved problems, they generally are unable to meet their children's needs. This situation promotes at least two problems. One is that the parents' distortions, hurts, and needs likely will be passed from one generation to another. Secondly, and maybe more importantly, their children will lack the fundamental resources of perception, affirmation, and strength necessary for coping with the many and varied problems of life. In healthy human development, parents normally impart these resources to their children. But when parents have unresolved issues from their childhood, their ability to impart these qualities to their children is hindered to one degree or another. Not only do children then develop distorted concepts of God, themselves, and others, but also the very mechanisms that enable them to conceptualize become distorted.

Distorted concepts, distorted mechanisms

✎ In your own words describe the two problems.

_____

_____

_____

_____

The first problem is that parents pass on the same distortions, hurts, and needs to their children. The children then develop distorted concepts of God, themselves, and others.

The second problem is more subtle, damaging, and difficult to change. The children lack the fundamental resources necessary for coping with the problems of life. The mechanisms that enable them to conceptualize become distorted. The children do not develop the ability to perceive—to see, hear, and understand—correctly. For example, since they do not see problems like a parents' alcoholism or rage being acknowledged and addressed, they not only do not learn to solve the problem, but they also do not learn to perceive the problem. What would be bizarre to most people seems normal to the child who has experienced it.

Diana's story

When Diana finally understood this issue of perceptions, she explained it with this analogy: "I was born in Mexico. Even though my family moved back to the States when I was three years old, I have an ear for Spanish. The issue is more than understanding the meaning of Spanish words. I have the developed ability to hear Spanish words distinctly and to reproduce the sounds easily, but when I hear other languages, I cannot distinguish between or make the sounds. Likewise, we need the ability to distinguish and understand—to perceive—concepts like truth, honesty in relationships, and healthy behavior. Our early home life must develop these abilities, but since mine did not, my perceptions are distorted."

Assimilating truth

This ability to perceive reality accurately is the reason that while teaching the truth is important, we also need to help people learn how to assimilate that truth so that they can apply it to their lives. Otherwise, desired growth and change probably will not occur.

People may know a lot; they may even be excellent teachers of the truth; but deep changes in their hearts—those that would affect their lives—still may elude them. Real, substantive change can occur only when both the truth and the ability to perceive and apply that truth are firmly planted in a person's life. This is why it is so important for us to be involved in strong, vibrantly healthy relationships. In the context of loving relationships we can learn to be honest with ourselves and others; we can learn to perceive life accurately; and we can receive comfort and encouragement in the slow and often painful process of growth. Perhaps a mature friend, a pastor, a counselor, or a small group can provide an environment of affirmation for you as you seek to grow and change.

We need strong, vibrantly healthy relationships.

The tongue of the wise makes knowledge acceptable, But the mouth of fools spouts folly.
—Proverbs 15:2

✎ Carefully review the two paragraphs you just read and compare them with Proverbs 15:2, which is printed in the margin. Which of the following responses most clearly relates the content of the paragraphs to the idea of making knowledge acceptable?

❑ 1. Soften the truth so that it will be easier to swallow.
❑ 2. Teach the truth and also help a person develop the mechanism to perceive and apply the truth.
❑ 3. Teach the truth with such clear argument and solid reasoning that the person will be compelled to accept it.

What does the paragraph suggest is necessary to develop the mechanisms to perceive life accurately?

❑ 1. strong and authoritative teaching
❑ 2. clear, indisputable logic
❑ 3. nurturing relationships

In the first exercise number 2 most clearly expresses the idea of the paragraph and of Proverbs 15:2. Nurturing, affirming relationships with a mature person or group are necessary to develop the skills of perception (answer number 3).

An Example of Warped Perceptions

I asked Carol to describe her home life. "It was OK," she said, not exactly giving the kind of full description I was looking for.

"Tell me how your parents got along."

"Well, they argued a lot. My father was a Sunday School teacher, but he was a bear at home."

"How did he treat you, Carol?"

Carol's head dropped slowly. "OK, I guess."

"How did he show that he loved you?"

"He didn't!" she exploded. "He doesn't love me at all. He always teased me and picked on me or let my brothers pick on me."

"How do you relate to him now?"

"I stay away from home unless I absolutely have to go there."

"As little as possible. I stay away from home unless I absolutely have to go there. When I must go, I stay for only a day or two. I can't stand any more than that."

Carol's difficulties were painfully obvious. Her parents had not communicated love and acceptance to her. They had not given her the freedom to fail when she was a child, so she withdrew from them, unwilling to risk further rejection.

Carol's relationship with God mirrored her relationships with her parents. She believed that she could never do enough to please Him, and yet she felt guilty if she did not try. Her parents' belittling her led her to feel that God did the same. She had begun to put herself down and to fear relating to anyone.

In addition, Carol's focus was directed primarily toward herself: *Have I done enough today? What did my boss think of me when I said that? I wonder if I should have said no to Bill? Why do I feel this way? There must be something wrong with me!* Carol's introspection was morbid and paralyzing. Her immobility created tremendous guilt for her. She knew that God wanted her to be obedient to Him and felt that she knew what she should do, but a deeply rooted fear of rejection prevented her from doing it. As motivators for behavior, fear and guilt are a lethal combination!

✎ Carol's story illustrates the cycle of hurtful family experiences. Describe what you think will happen when Carol becomes a parent.

_____

_____

_____

Carol's unmet needs will affect her parenting.

Though it may work itself out in a number of ways, Carol's unmet needs will affect her parenting. She may duplicate her parents' actions and become harsh, judgmental, and perfectionistic in her own family. She may seek to change the outward behavior and vow never to be like her parents. She then may become a smothering parent who violates her children's boundaries. In whatever way the cycle operates, Carol will grow only if she works purposefully to build healthy, Christ-honoring behaviors in place of the dysfunctional messages of her childhood.

✎ Below write Exodus 20:2 from memory if you can. Then describe in your own words how the passage can apply to people stuck in the cycle of hurtful family experiences.

_____

_____

_____

> **SUMMARY STATEMENTS**
>
> - Your parents have played a major role in forming your concept of God, your self-concept, and your ability to relate to others.
> - The mechanisms that enable children to conceptualize become distorted when parents have unresolved issues from their own childhood.
> - Real, substantive change can occur only when both the truth and the ability to perceive and apply that truth are firmly planted in a person's life.

DAY 4

The Absent-Parent Syndrome

Teach them [God's teachings] to your children, talking about them when you sit at home and when you walk along the road, when you lie down and when you get up.
—Deuteronomy 11:19, NIV

The command above from the Book of Deuteronomy makes clear one fact of God's intention for family life. He intended for parents to spend time with their children. In this lesson we will examine some of the results when parents are emotionally or physically unavailable to children.

Unaffectionate Parents

Susan's story

If you met Susan on the street, you might think that she sang in her church choir or taught Sunday School. In reality, she has slept with three different men this past week and has been with 12 others over the past month. How did she develop such a lifestyle? Her problem started a long time ago.

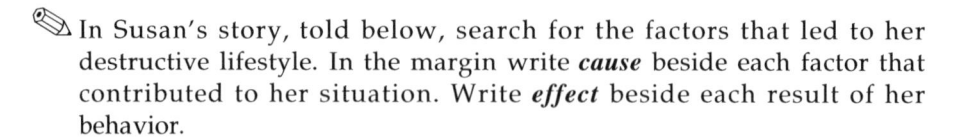

✎ In Susan's story, told below, search for the factors that led to her destructive lifestyle. In the margin write **cause** beside each factor that contributed to her situation. Write **effect** beside each result of her behavior.

At the age of 8 Susan said to herself: *Something must be wrong with me. My daddy won't hug me or touch me or spend time with me. I guess I'm not what I ought to be. If I were, Daddy would love me!*

Her father was a decent man, but he had grown up in a home in which parents did not touch children to show affection. Such children, as they mature, often relate physical affection to sexual intimacy. Much to the detriment of their children they tend as fathers to be non-touchers.

By the time Susan was 13, she tried to find in other men the love that her father had withheld from her. Her promiscuity caused her to be popular with older boys and even with older men.

20 Unit 1

She later married, not because she deeply loved her husband but to get the affection she had always wanted but never had received from her father. As you can imagine, the couple had serious problems. After a while, one man could not meet Susan's insatiable desire for affection. Apart from the grace of God, such a marriage had no chance to succeed!

Shocked but helpless

Susan realized something was wrong within her, but she could not pinpoint what it was. It was as though she looked at her conduct through a window and was shocked by it but was unable to change it. She stumbled through life confused, hurting, and acting out her craving for fatherly love.

Only through hours of counseling did Susan recognize that her life was a complex set of needs, combined with problems created when those needs were not met. She had a deep need to be loved and to love in return. Consequently, she developed many behavioral patterns to try to gain that love from others—especially from men—but her behavior led to complicated consequences and a lot of heartache.

As a result, Susan struggled not only with how she felt about herself but also with how she related to others, especially to God. She found it almost inconceivable that God really could comfort her or meet her emotional needs. Susan's situation at home typifies a relatively predictable phenomenon we call the absent-father syndrome.

✎ Check each of the following that contributed to Susan's predicament.

❑ 1. She was born with a natural need for affection.
❑ 2. Her father's passivity left her longing for love.
❑ 3. Her father had an unmet need from his own childhood.
❑ 4. In her childlike thinking Susan assumed she was at fault.
❑ 5. Susan's relationship with her husband was based on hidden needs.
❑ 6. Susan's behavior did not bother her.

You could have written *cause* beside many parts of Susan's story. Her father's unmet need for affection, her assumed blame, her search for love from other boys and men, and her escalating desire to fill the need all added to the problem. The results included self-blame, her shocked but paralyzed attempts to change, and her slavery to the habits her responses had created. In the checklist all the responses except 6 contributed to the situation.

When a Parent Is Absent

The absent-parent syndrome is present in a large percentage of American homes. It is not a sickness but a social disease that robs parents of the enjoyment that should be theirs. Its effects, sometimes devastating children, last for a lifetime.

Absent parents do not provide their children the time and emotional support they need.

This syndrome occurs when father or mother is absent from home due to death, career, divorce, prolonged withdrawal, or disinterest. The result is that they do not provide their children with the time and emotional support they need. Perhaps this is because they simply do not know how. Maybe the parents' parents did not provide those needs for them. Perhaps divorce or any number of possible problems between two parents prevent one parent from meeting the children's emotional requirements. Some fathers simply perceive

The child is the big loser; nobody can take the father's place in the family.

the home as the wife's domain. Rather than provide any real input there, they withdraw to pursue other activities, like business, sports, or the church, which enable them to feel more successful. For whatever reason, the absent-parent syndrome occurs when the father or mother is physically and/or emotionally absent from his child's life. The child is the big loser; nobody can take the missing parent's place in the family.

✎ The material you are studying may hit some very sensitive spots for you. You may begin to feel angry with your parents and then feel disloyal because of the anger. You may feel guilt over real or perceived deficiencies in the way you have parented your own children. Feeling your feelings is appropriate. We need to assign or accept appropriate responsibility. If your parents mistreated or neglected you when you were a child, they are responsible for that behavior. But we are responsible for our behavior today.

↪ Take time to pray about the matter of blame. Parents generally do the best they know how with their children. Ask God to help you look objectively at this material with a view to change and grow. Ask Him to give you the courage not to blame yourself or your parents.

Results of the absent-parent syndrome vary. The daughter whose father is absent may reject her appearance and sometimes even her femininity. She may reason that if she cannot attract her father, then she cannot attract anyone. She may feel at a disadvantage with men, no matter how attractive she is. She probably craves attention and affection. She often wants to be held and never seems to get enough. This may leave her vulnerable to sexual activity with young men who gladly will exchange embraces for other pleasures. Many fathers have been astounded to learn of their daughters' sexual activities, when actually they set up their daughters for them.

The exception to this pattern is the woman who resents all men so deeply that she desires no attention from them whatsoever. She may not understand how someone ever could love her. She may become a "rejection sponge" and interpret the smallest inconsistency in her husband or friends as complete rejection. This sensitivity to rejection not only may be linked to her husband but also may influence all of her relationships. Looking for a "dad," she might find herself attracted to older men and may marry an older man. This may result in sexual dysfunction as she finds herself unable to "sleep with Dad." Also, since her father was a passive figure, she may develop an attraction for passive men.

✎ List as many possible results of the absentee-father syndrome in a daughter's life as you can remember. Then review the previous paragraphs to fill in the results you omitted.

_____

_____

_____

Your list may have included the daughter's rejection of her appearance or even her femininity, her feeling at a disadvantage with men, her craving attention and affection, her vulnerability to sexual promiscuity, her deep resentment of men, a tendency to become a "rejection sponge," a hyper-sensitivity to rejection, her looking for a "dad" to marry, possible sexual dysfunction, or her attraction to passive men.

Difficult to trust God

A woman who is a product of the absent-father syndrome probably finds trusting God to be difficult. Because she formed her misconceptions about the father's role early, she may experience a great deal of insecurity and loneliness if she is unable to trust even God the Father.

✎ In the following description of the effects of the absent-father syndrome on a son, circle all the possible results in a son's life.

Sons also are affected by the absent-father syndrome. Having lost their male role model, they either depend on their mother or are forced to look to the world for a role model. Looking to the world, they often attempt to be a "macho man," usually as an act to hide their insecurity in not being able to identify with men. Sons who look to the mother as the role model may adopt her mannerisms and pattern themselves after her. Like the daughters, the sons also find themselves craving masculine attention and affection, which can cause vulnerability to homosexual interaction. They often mistake sex for love and, like the daughters, become "rejection sponges." Since the mother was the dominant figure in the home, they too may have great difficulty trusting the Heavenly Father.[1]

The material and activities you are reading may or may not apply to your particular family. If you have experienced the painful family situations described, apply the learning activities to your situation. If you have not experienced the situations, the activities will help you to understand and minister to others.

You may have circled such results as seeking to hide insecurity by acting macho, being unable to identify with men, adopting feminine mannerisms, craving masculine attention, growing vulnerable to homosexual interaction, mistaking sex for love, becoming a "rejection sponge," and having difficulty trusting the Heavenly Father.

Physical abandonment by fathers seems more common than by mothers in our society, but mothers can also be physically or emotionally absent. Those who have experienced abandonment by their mothers will assure you that the results are no less painful and damaging.

✎ This activity will require some courage and honesty. If either of your parents was an absentee parent—even partially, such as emotionally absent or always working—describe below the results you have experienced in your life.

_____

_____

_____

↪ Thank you for the courage and honesty even to attempt the learning activities above. Now please take a few moments to pray. Tell God your feelings about the material on which you have worked today. You may feel strong emotions, including hurt and anger at God. In the margin write a prayer to Him and honestly express your feelings to Him.

✎ Review the unit memory verse. If you are having difficulty remembering the verse, write it on a card to carry with you. Review it several times every day.

Unit 1   23

> **SUMMARY STATEMENTS**
>
> - God intended for parents to spend time with their children.
> - Absent fathers do not provide their children the time and emotional support they need.
> - The child is the big loser; nobody can take the father's place in the family.

DAY 5

Distant or Abusive Parents

We were gentle among you, like a mother caring for her little children. We loved you so much that we were delighted to share with you not only the gospel of God but our lives as well, because you had become so dear to us.
—1 Thessalonians 2:7-8, NIV

Parents sometimes emotionally withdraw from their families when they feel overwhelmed by life's pressures and activities. Children then feel abandoned. Young children usually believe that the parent's withdrawal must be the child's fault. This misperception often is confirmed by the withdrawing parent who, feeling guilty for not being loving and responsible, blames the child.

As abandoned children enter other relationships, they tend to hold back and want to protect themselves from being abandoned again. Unfortunately, this kind of "protection" actually results in more pain and a lack of intimacy in relationships because of their inability to commit themselves to others.

People whose parents have been inactive or withdrawn usually find accepting love to be difficult.

People whose parents have been inactive or withdrawn usually find accepting love to be difficult. These persons reason that because they could not evoke the love of their parents, something must be wrong with them. They resist accepting the others' love at face value. They feel lonely, guilty, and condemned.

Finally, children of withdrawn parents also see God as distant and uninvolved. When they hear of others' vibrant relationships with Him, they often conclude that their relationship with God is not like those they hear about because they are "such poor Christians."

✎ Describe in your own words three possible results of experiencing distant relationships with parents.

_____

_____

_____

You may have summarized the three results as fear of abandonment, difficulty believing that they are worthy of love, and a limited relationship with God—for which they often blame themselves.

Unit 1

✎ Check any of the results of distant relationships with parents that you identify in your life.

❑ fear of abandonment
❑ blaming myself for lack of relationship with God
❑ difficulty accepting love
❑ other: _____
❑ none of the above

Abusive Parents

Patricia's story

Patricia volunteered to serve in a Christian organization. During her orientation a speaker gave a series of lectures titled "God, Our Father." Every time he started a lecture, Patricia got up and left the room.

Patricia had a problem! Her relationship with her father had been the opposite of what Susan (whose story you read in day 4) had experienced. Patricia's father repeatedly had molested and humiliated her during her childhood. She lived in constant dread of his presence in the home. This particularly bothered her at night. She was afraid to tell her mother what was taking place. Consequently, Patricia's childhood was shrouded in lonely, silent fear.

Patricia could not bear the suggestion that God was like a father to her! Her category for the word *father*, shaped by her relationship with her dad, was too vile to be applied to God. As a result, she did not have a positive concept of God as Father, and the very mention of it created trauma for her.

She explained to a friend: "I don't want a relationship with God the Father. I have one with Jesus, and that's enough for me!"

Since Patricia could not trust her own father, what sort of a relationship could she establish with her Heavenly Father? For her, worshiping God was impersonal. No emotion, no affection, no trust could exist between her and God the Father.

Strange as it may seem, the reason Patricia had chosen to enter a Christian vocation was related directly to her problem. You see, thinking of God as a person—a friend—was not possible for her. She followed a cold and impersonal set of rules and sought to relate to God by serving Him. She wanted to appease Him by living sacrificially as His volunteer in a religious organization. Intimate times of prayer with Him were impossible. The best she could attempt was to read from devotional books—and to slave away at the task of pleasing the harsh, and false, God in her head.

✎ Describe what you believe to be the moral of Patricia's story.

_____

_____

Children who are abused believe that something must be wrong with them. They reason that even though their parents were wrong, they must have provoked the situation somehow. The shame is overwhelming, and their ability to relate to others—even to God—is disturbed severely.

Perfectionist Parents

Perfectionists may make great employees, but they are ineffective parents unless they can change their natural responses to their children. Perfectionist parents' standards are so high and rigid that even they cannot attain them, and certainly their children can't.

Children are shattered when they feel that they cannot measure up in their parents' eyes.

Often, perfectionist parents rationalize that they are encouraging their children to experience the most in life, but the parents may be pushing their children over the emotional edge. Children are shattered when they feel that they cannot measure up in their parents' eyes. The children feel like failures. Trying desperately to please their parents, they probably later in life will fight the depression associated with repressed hurt and anger. Or they simply may rebel. Rebellious children often have perfectionist parents. The children also may avoid relating to peers who succeed. Instead, they tend to associate with those who are prone to failure and who therefore are not threatening.

✎ Which characteristics of a child with perfectionist parents do you see at work in your life?

❑ high, rigid, and unattainable standards
❑ feeling that you do not measure up
❑ feeling like a failure
❑ trying desperately to please your parents
❑ depression, possibly related to repressed hurt and anger
❑ rebellion
❑ associating with those who are prone to failure
❑ others _____

Whether they rebel or play the performance game, children of perfectionist parents struggle with their perception of God. They just cannot do enough for Him. Sometimes they participate in ritualistic church activities. Sometimes they drop out completely. In either case, they feel God is distant and condemning.

Objectivity and Loyalty

Some people feel guilty when they begin to evaluate their parents' lifestyles and influence, as though they were becoming disloyal, unloving children. That is not the case! Taking an honest look at your heritage does not mean that you must respond with vindictiveness or that you harshly judge your father and mother. It simply means that you recognize that they have limitations and that they gave you the best they could give at the time! Whether their parenting was good or bad, they tried their best. Be benevolent as you think about the way your parents reared you.

At the same time, work to become the generation that ends the further passage of negative consequences. In order to accomplish that, you will need to develop objectivity and understanding about what has taken place in your family. Your story is being written as you read these pages. What will it be like? For Susan and Patricia, life was filled with confusion, pain, and struggle. Yours can be different. The process may be painful and difficult, but change is possible. As you continue, think about what your life would be like if we included it in this material.

In this first unit you have worked to understand the process of repeated thoughts, feelings, and behaviors that make up the cycle of hurtful family experiences. You have also begun to explore how this cycle has affected your life.

Each unit includes the unit review you find below. You may choose to complete it when you complete your day 5 material. Many people in other discovery groups have found that they benefit by doing the review at a separate time—perhaps even on another day. Whatever your choice, sorting out the significance and impact of each unit's study in your life is very important. Do not neglect it.

Unit Review

✎ Review the five lessons in this unit. Find one statement in the text that helped you better understand the importance of relationships. Circle this statement in your text and rewrite it in your own words.

_____

_____

_____

✎ Review your written work and prayer responses throughout the unit. What exercise meant the most to you during this week? Identify the exercise and explain your choice.

_____

_____

_____

✎ Review the memory verse. Find it in your Bible and check your memory. Then close your Bible and write the verse in the left margin. How have you applied this passage during your study of this unit? Below record your thoughts.

_____

_____

_____

Notes
[1] Jim Craddock, *The Absent-Father Syndrome* (Houston: Rapha Publishing, 1986).

UNIT 2

Substitutes for Relationships

Case in point

FILLING THE EMPTY HOLE

Since she was a little girl, JoAnne had been aware of a great, empty hole in her life. She wanted her father to love her and to tell her she was special. She wanted to feel secure—that she was part of a family in which she was accepted. Instead, her father was gone most of the time. When he was home, he criticized JoAnne for her looks, her grades, her weight, what she ate, and what she did.

Whenever JoAnne's father went on an extended business trip, her older brother took his place. He constantly told JoAnne that she was fat, that she was clumsy, that she was stupid. JoAnne's mother was no help. She was lost in a fantasy world with her romance novels.

When JoAnne was 14 years old, she learned that she could fill the emptiness in her life—at least temporarily—in several ways. She found that she could control her weight by purging with laxatives or by throwing up. When she purged, she felt in control. She discovered that when boys or men took an interest in her, the loneliness went away for a while. She learned that alcohol made her feel that she belonged. JoAnne became an expert at finding substitutes for relationships. (You will read more about JoAnne on page 41.)

What you'll learn

This week you will
- explore the influences that mold secure, healthy individuals and ineffective, unhealthy people;
- evaluate the results of a fractured childhood;
- describe seven false solutions to which people often turn in an attempt to stop the pain of the cycle of hurtful family experiences;
- have an opportunity to choose Jesus Christ as your Savior and as your role model to break the cycle of family dysfunction;
- describe the reparenting/rechildhooding process.

What you'll study

Looking for Love	Relationships Make the Difference	Empty Solutions	Your Role Model	Applying the Solution
DAY 1	DAY 2	DAY 3	DAY 4	DAY 5

Memory verse

This week's verse of Scripture to memorize
Truly I say to you, unless you are converted and become like children, you shall not enter the kingdom of heaven.

–Matthew 18:3

DAY 1

Looking for Love

Godliness actually is a means of great gain, when accompanied by contentment. And if we have food and covering, with these we shall be content.
–1 Timothy 6:6,8

In unit 1 you became familiar with the cycle of hurtful experiences in family life. You identified some roots from which the hurtful cycle grows and read some examples of the process in action. You even began the process of examining how this cycle of hurtful family experiences may function in your own life and family.

In this unit you will explore a basic drive we all share—the drive to love and to be loved. God made us to require loving relationships; but since we are damaged by sin, we often seek substitutes like power or success in place of healthy relationships. The true stories in unit 1 demonstrate the powerful influence relationships have on us. Relationships, especially our relationship with God, are the keys to life. They are intended to be our foundation for stability and fulfillment. But those who have not experienced love and affirmation often turn to success and possessions for their security and significance. When individuals have accepted these counterfeits, they often make statements like the following.

- "The good life is achieving one's goals."
- "Happiness means having plenty of money to do whatever you wish."
- "A quality life requires you to have a good job, a good spouse, and good health."
- "The best life? It begins when you can take long vacations, own your own business, live in a beautiful home, and drive expensive cars."

✎ What possession(s) or accomplishment(s) are you tempted to believe would make your life meaningful?

Relationships, especially our relationship with God, are the keys to life.

We all sometimes fall into the trap of thinking, *I would be happy if only I had this or if only I had accomplished that.* According to John 8:44, Satan is the father of lies, and his goal is to make us believe his lies. One myth he tells us is that success and possessions determine our quality of life. But that simply is not true. God has made us so that success, pleasure, and possessions cannot ultimately satisfy us. Relationships (and especially our relationship with Him) provide real fulfillment.

> You are of your father the devil, and you want to do the desires of your father. He was a murderer from the beginning, and does not stand in the truth, because there is no truth in him. Whenever he speaks a lie he speaks from his own nature; for he is a liar and the father of lies.
> –John 8:44

✎ In light of John 8:44 and every person's tendency to fall for Satan's lie that possessions and approval bring happiness, what do you think the apostle Paul meant in 1 Timothy 6:6 when he said, "Godliness actually is a means of great gain, when accompanied by contentment"?

The apostle Paul understood that real meaning and purpose in life come from quality relationships—with God and with other people. All of the substitutes in the world never will bring contentment.

✎ As you read the stories of Sarah and Eric, look for the influences that nurtured true contentment and emotional wealth or for the hurtful cycle of emotional poverty. In the margin draw a plus mark beside the indications of positive influences and a minus sign beside statements of negative influences.

Sarah's story

Sarah's father was a tailor, and her mother was a Swedish immigrant. Her father had no money when the couple married in 1923. He worked 18-hour days to save enough to invest in his own business. In 1927 he finally reached his objective. He prospered, bought a home, and hired several employees. Then in 1931 the Great Depression left him in poverty. Unable to cope with the loss of all he had worked for, he became severely depressed.

Sarah remembers her father during that bleak period. He slept on the couch while she tiptoed around the house, quietly playing with her dolls. She vividly remembers when their fine home was lost in a foreclosure and auctioned for a fraction of what it had cost to build. They moved to a tiny apartment—and then to another and another.

But love remained in that family, no matter where they lived. Sarah's two older brothers and mother constantly showed affection to her. Even Sarah's father emerged from his depression and became very affirming of her. Although she recognized that their food had become very plain, they always had enough. A lengthy family time always followed the evening meal with open communication and laughter. Sarah particularly looked forward to the honest interaction that took place in her family then.

Love is not expensive!

In a poverty-filled house Sarah learned to love God. Their finances had nothing to do with the amount of faith and trust in God that existed in her home. Love is not expensive! Its value cannot be weighed with the same scale as gold.

Today Sarah is the wife of a pastor and the mother of three sons. Her oldest brother is the president of a seminary, and her other brother is a missionary among teenagers in France. Her father died penniless, but he enriched the world by introducing his three children to the Lord.

Eric's story

Eric was the product of a night of passion between a couple who enjoyed living in the fast lane. They did not want children, and they accepted his presence with thinly veiled resentment. His father, an attorney, and his mother, a designer, had inherited millions of dollars. Their posh residences in New York and Palm Beach were designed for parties. Each room was filled with expensive and fragile antiques. This created a world in which Eric felt out of place. His parents shouted at him: "Don't touch that!" "Leave it alone!" "Be careful!" When Eric was only three years old, his father severely beat him for damaging a treasured vase. His parents constantly reminded him of his own worthlessness and of the high value of things.

Eric's parents seldom told him they loved him. They rarely hugged him or encouraged him in his studies or sports. His governesses came and went. Some tried more diligently than others to befriend him.

Eric remembers the night he deliberately snapped the hood ornament off his father's favorite Rolls Royce. Eric was eight years old at the time. He later said: "I enjoyed the beating I got. It was worth every bit of it to see his rage over that stupid thing's being broken."

Eric became increasingly destructive. On one occasion he deliberately poured black paint on his parents' expensive Persian rugs. His mother sent him to a psychiatrist for help with "his problem."

Eric spent his school years in private boarding schools. He dreaded holidays and vacations. When he was 18, he left the United States to roam around Europe. He sank into the drug scene, became evasive and withdrawn, and spent several months in prison.

When Eric was 30 years old, he had his first encounter with Christians in a free clinic in London. Several weeks passed before a trusting relationship developed between Eric and the workers there. Finally, Eric said: "My parents always told me that they didn't want a child. The last words I heard from my mother's lips were another reminder that I was an accident. I never want to see them again as long as I live."

The last words I heard from my mother's lips were another reminder that I was an accident.

✎ In your opinion why did Sarah and her siblings develop into secure, healthy, effective individuals in spite of difficult circumstances?

_____

_____

Why do you think Eric developed into an angry man with severe problems?

_____

_____

You may have noted that Sarah's parents let her know that she was loved, even though economic circumstances were difficult. They affirmed her. They modeled God's character by interacting honestly with one another. Eric's parents, on the other hand, valued their possessions and pleasures while they rejected and devalued Eric.

✎ Write your own moral to the stories of Sarah and Eric.

_____

_____

_____

You may have written one of many morals to the stories. Some examples include: "Love is more powerful than money." "Parents shape children more by their relationships than by their commands." "What you own is not as important to your child as who you are." The bottom line is the title of tomorrow's lesson: relationships make the difference.

Unit 2   31

✏️ Most of us can identify in some ways with both Sarah and Eric. Describe ways your experience growing up resembled that of Sarah.

_____
_____

In what ways did your experience resemble that of Eric?

_____
_____

> Truly I say to you, unless you are converted and become like children, you shall not enter the kingdom of heaven.
> –Matthew 18:3

✏️ To begin memorizing this week's Scripture verse, Matthew 18:3, copy the passage twice.

_____
_____
_____
_____

SUMMARY STATEMENTS

- God made us to require loving relationships; but since we are damaged by sin, we often seek substitutes like power or success in place of healthy relationships.
- God has made us so that success, pleasure, and possessions cannot ultimately satisfy us.
- Love's value cannot be weighed with the same scale as gold.

DAY 2

Relationships Make the Difference

Truly I say to you, unless you are converted and become like children, you shall not enter the kingdom of heaven.
—Matthew 18:3

If a child is born into a family which bountifully provides affirmation and love, he or she probably will develop a healthy self-image. If the family gives affirmation as a reward for success and if love becomes a reward for behaving properly, the child likely will develop an insecure, competitive spirit. In each case relationships in the home shape the child.

How does alcoholism shape a child? What is the impact of a mother who does not want her child? What happens to a child thrust into a schoolroom with a teacher who ridicules every mistake? What is the consequence of placing a teen in a drug-infested school, where violence in the hallways is a common occurrence?

✎ Below you will see a list of factors that cause problems for a child. Rank the list by writing a 1 by the factor you see as the most damaging, a 2 by the next, and so on to the least damaging.
___ affirmation given only as a reward for success
___ love given as a reward for proper behavior
___ parent's unavailability because of alcoholism or another addiction
___ rejection by a parent who did not want him or her
___ rejection and ridicule by a teacher
___ attendance at a drug-infested, violent school
___ other: _____

> *The material and activities you are reading may or may not apply to your particular family. If you have experienced the painful family situations described, apply the learning activities to your situation. If you have not experienced the situations, the activities will help you to understand and minister to others.*

All of the factors above can have a powerfully negative effect on a person. No right or wrong order exists for estimating the impact of these factors. The first two behaviors in the list—using love and affirmation to control and reward—may be the least dramatic, but they do great harm in many people's lives.

✎ In the list above, underline any issues you have experienced or are dealing with in your life. Then read the following paragraph, which describes the results of a fractured childhood. Circle any results with which you identify.

Two extremes

A fractured childhood produces a variety of painful results. Some people experience intense guilt, anger, and bitterness. Driven to succeed to prove their worth, these people often are thwarted in their efforts to develop close associations with others because they have not experienced warm, affirming relationships. Others respond differently. Instead of being driven to succeed, they try to avoid the pain of rejection and failure by withdrawing from risks—socially, professionally, and in every other way. Many of us combine these two extremes. We are driven to succeed in the relationships and tasks in which we are likely to do well, but we become passive when the risks seem to be too great.

✎ In what areas are you too much of a risk-taker?

_____

_____

_____

In what areas are you too much of a risk-avoider?

_____

_____

_____

Many of us particularly avoid risks that might expose us to rejection. Some people do not attempt to make friends or to meet others because they fear rejection. Others do not apply for new jobs or attempt to follow creative dreams because they fear rejection.

↪ Take a few moments to pray about the material you have studied. Thank God for giving you the insights you have experienced. Ask Him to enable you to recognize the truth about your family and your present situation. Many of us struggle because as we begin to understand the cycle of hurtful family experiences, we feel guilty about our relationships with our own children. Ask God to help you lay aside blame. Remember that the goal of this process is not to assign fault or blame but to see reality clearly and to make healthy, Christ-honoring changes.

✎ In the case study that makes up the remainder of this lesson, look for factors, such as unmet needs in a person's life, that contribute to the cycle of hurtful experiences.

Case study

A few tortured souls leave family and friends behind, hoping to find love and acceptance elsewhere. Their search turns to misery when they take the wrong path. For example, the wife of a missionary and mother of three small children came to her counselor and declared, "God has told me to leave my husband and to marry another man!" This young wife had been a committed Christian who had seemed totally devoted to her husband and calling. What made her willing to give up everything for another man?

She explained that this man had become her closest friend, that they could talk about anything and pray about everything together, and that life with him was an adventure she had never experienced with her spouse.

During counseling sessions several things became apparent. She felt just as committed to Christ as she had before the affair began, and she did not view her third-party involvement as sinful or immoral. The counselor learned that her father had left the family when she was a small child and that she never had established a close relationship with her stepfather. She married her husband not because of her deep love for him but because she felt that he would be good for her. In fact, she had been far more infatuated with another man before she married her husband.

Problems of adjustment started immediately after the wedding. Instead of getting better, the problems grew worse. She felt frustrated, angry, and disillusioned. *Surely*, she thought, *marriage should be better than this.*

She felt as though her husband centered on their physical relationship. He always wanted to have sex—"as though that would make everything right." A strange feeling began to emerge in her. She tried to be a dutiful wife, but her feelings of revulsion toward sex grew stronger. As she described her feelings toward her husband, her counselor recognized that young girls often use these same words to describe sexually abusive fathers or stepfathers.

Her husband became confused and angry. Rather than admit that his marriage was failing, he tried to promote his masculinity through sexual aggression. This only increased the tension between them.

Then she met a man at church who treated her more respectfully. She was attracted to him instantly, although he was almost 15 years her senior. He not only showed her the attention and consideration she was seeking but also showed understanding and sympathy.

Their relationship started with conversation. Soon she was sharing her frustration and sadness with him, and he was confiding in her about his marital problems. Of course, as he understood her problems, she understood his. It felt so good just to be held. . . .

✎ What unmet need in this woman's life did she expect her husband to fill?

_____

What action did she repeat that she had seen one of her parents model?

_____

This woman tried to make her husband meet her longing for a father's love. She repeated the same behavior she had seen in her family of origin—leaving her husband and children just as her father had abandoned the family.

You may recall reading this statement in day 2 of unit 1: "Although it is true

> Major-issue alert: Beware of shame, guilt, and blame at this point in the process. If you are experiencing situations similar to some of the case studies in this book, we urge you to deal with the situation one step at a time. At this time the point is to understand the cycle of hurtful family experiences. Later, you will explore how you can accomplish major life changes. The solution for the wife in this example is not simply to change her behavior. The solution includes recognizing the needs that drive her life and finding a healthy, legitimate means for God and others to meet those needs.

that some people attempt to be as unlike their parents as possible, this response is usually limited to behavior." Although parents may have habits we reject, we still have a frightening tendency to duplicate their attitudes and relationships.

We have a frightening tendency to duplicate our parents' attitudes and relationships.

✎ What behavior did one or both of your parents practice that you have rejected?

_____

_____

What deeper attitudes or relationships that your parents exhibited do you still find in yourself?

_____

_____

Genuine life change goes much deeper than changing a single behavior.

Genuine life change—breaking the cycle of hurtful family experiences—goes much deeper than changing a single behavior. Many people have avoided alcohol because a parent drank, refused to express anger because a parent raged, or stayed with their family because a parent abandoned the family. These people have changed specific behavioral factors, only to discover that in many other ways they remained in bondage to the parent's modeled behavior.

> Truly I say to you, unless you are converted and become like children, you shall not enter the kingdom of heaven.
> –Matthew 18:3

✎ Write your own paraphrase of this unit's Scripture-memory verse, which appears in the margin.

_____

_____

_____

SUMMARY STATEMENTS

- Children are shaped by relationships in the home.
- A fractured childhood produces a variety of painful results.
- Although parents may have habits we reject, we still have a frightening tendency to duplicate their attitudes and relationships.

Empty Solutions

DAY 3

> *Why do you spend money for what is not bread, and your wages for what does not satisfy? Listen carefully to Me, and eat what is good, and delight yourself in abundance.*
> –Isaiah 55:2

Children whose parents have given them affirmation, encouragement, protection, loving discipline, and time usually feel confident and secure as adults. Generally, they are able to relate well to the Lord and to other persons. They are willing to try new things, take chances, and even laugh at their mistakes.

The amount of love and positive modeling people receive greatly influences their emotional, spiritual, and relational health. A lack of these essentials for wholeness produces a vacuum in their lives. When this is true, virtually everything they do is designed to meet their need for approval and acceptance and to avoid pain.

> *A lack of love and positive modeling produces a vacuum in people's lives.*

We devise all kinds of ways to fill this vacuum—to win approval and to avoid pain. Today we will examine some of these alluring, but ultimately empty, alternative solutions.

A Knight in Shining Armor

If only I had James, then I'd be really happy! Some of us are waiting for someone to gallop into our lives on a handsome horse (or in a new red Porsche!) and to give us the attention and affection we want. We may be waiting for a spouse or a friend to meet our deepest needs and to make us really happy. Occasionally, someone comes along who seems to be "that special person." Our expectations (and demands) climb sky-high; but sooner or later, that

36 Unit 2

person falls off his horse, and we drop him. Then we start looking for someone else to make us happy.

Many marriages begin this way. One partner expects the other to provide happiness, contentment, and excitement. After a few weeks, a few months, or a few years, these unrealistic expectations are shattered. In many cases the couple divorces, and the partners look for someone else to make them happy.

✎ Imagine that you have entered a relationship—a romance or a friendship—with a person you really care about. After a while you realize that this other person has completely unrealistic expectations of you. He or she expects you to give all of your time to the relationship and to solve all of his or her problems. From the following list check all the feelings you might feel toward the person.

❑ betrayed: I didn't know you were going to be this way.
❑ smothered: I don't have room to breathe.
❑ repulsed: why are you so needy?
❑ angry: I can't be all the things you want me to be.
❑ confused: what do you expect of me?
❑ shamed: I thought I could meet your needs, but I guess I'm a failure.
❑ disappointed: I'm losing respect for you.
❑ other: _____

A person in a relationship with someone who is looking for "a knight in shining armor" might report any or all of the feelings listed above.

✎ Do you now struggle or have you ever struggled with the illusion that the ideal person could make life wonderful?   ❑ Yes ❑ No
If so, describe what effect your thinking has had on your relationships.

_____

_____

The Ostrich Syndrome

All of us have psychological defense mechanisms we use to avoid pain and anxiety, but some of us use these mechanisms to an extreme. Like the proverbial ostrich with its head in the sand, we escape from reality by withdrawing; denying the truth in our lives; and becoming passive, indecisive, and numb. Avoiding emotional pain, however, can have negative consequences. When we block out pain this way, we also block out intimacy, warmth, and affection. Avoiding the pain of rejection causes us to miss the pleasures of healthy relationships, too.

When we block out pain by withdrawing, we also block out intimacy, warmth, and affection.

Denial

Denial—an unwillingness or inability to see problematic issues in life—can lead to either of two seemingly unrelated responses. Some people get clinically depressed as they suppress their pain and anger. Others become idealistic and claim that everything is "just fine" and "getting better" without objectively seeing the good, the bad, and the ugly in life. Such objectivity is too painful for them, so they hide behind their idealism.

✎ In what ways have you seen others use denial to avoid facing painful reality?

Denial might be called selective blindness by choice. People use denial in an amazing number of ways. Spouses or parents sometimes cannot see a family member's wrongful behavior. Similarly, they sometimes cannot see a person's strengths or good behavior.

Denial might be called selective blindness by choice.

✎ In what ways can you recognize denial in your past or present perceptions and actions?

The Rambo Defense

Some of us divide people into two groups—for us or against us. Those who are for us can do no wrong; but we brand those who disagree with us as terrible people. We may attack or criticize them for being stupid, narrow, or mean. These "Rambo" attacks, however, are not reserved entirely for others. We may reserve our harshest attacks for ourselves. We call ourselves horrible names and berate ourselves terribly. This anger is a form of self-hatred.

We may reserve our harshest attacks for ourselves.

✎ Do you sometimes find yourself thinking in the extremes of totally for you or completely against you? ❏ Yes ❏ No

What names do you call yourself when your performance does not measure up to your expectations?

The 007 Technique

Some of us attack others openly; but some of us attack in secret, behind another's back. We may covertly get others on our side. We form alliances and turn people against the object(s) of our scorn. Gossip often is the main weapon we use secretly to condemn others and elevate ourselves. This 007 approach is a terribly destructive practice.

✎ Do you sometimes find yourself criticizing those you perceive to be a threat to you? ❏ Yes ❏ No
In the margin describe your most recent example.
✎ How do you feel about yourself when you criticize or gossip about a person because you feel threatened?

- ☐ ashamed: I hate having done that.
- ☐ discouraged: I said I wouldn't do what my parent did, and now I sound just like him or her.
- ☐ justified: that person deserves it.
- ☐ hopeless: I can't seem to change.
- ☐ other: _____

At times some of us have used all of the terms above to describe our feelings about our behavior. We find ourselves doing the very things we dislike about others' actions.

Rat on a Treadmill

Some of us are driven. We race to accomplish goals and try to succeed, gain favorable attention, and avoid any reflection on the emptiness in our lives. We are busy from the moment we get up until we go to bed. This frantic pace characterizes even our devotions, if we have them. We read this chapter or that one, pray through our list, close our Bibles, check off "quiet time," and continue racing through the day.

Mary and Martha characterize the contrast between being reflective and driven. When Jesus visited these women, Mary ...

> ... was listening to the Lord's word, seated at His feet. But Martha was distracted with all her preparations; and she came up to Him, and said, "Lord, do You not care that my sister has left me to do all the serving alone? Then tell her to help me." But the Lord answered and said to her, "Martha, Martha, you are worried and bothered about so many things; but only a few things are necessary, really only one: for Mary has chosen the good part, which shall not be taken away from her."
>
> –Luke 10:39-42

"You are worried and bothered about so many things; but only a few things are necessary."

Many of us are obsessive-compulsive about our schedules; that is, we think obsessively about all we have to do and drive ourselves compulsively to get it all done. Like rats on a treadmill, we always are running but never arriving.

✎ What areas of your life do you carefully and meticulously control?

_____

_____

Many of us think that we must keep some area of our lives such as our clothes, our cars, or our desktop perfectly in order. No one can do everything perfectly, so we neglect other areas of our lives.

✎ What areas of your life do you consider unimportant and allow to be imperfect?

_____

_____

Puppet on a String

Unit 2   39

In both function and purpose, many of us are like puppets. We do whatever others want us to do, say what they want us to say, and try to be what they want us to be. Our primary purpose in life is to please others, to impress them, and to perform well enough to win their approval.

✎ Rate the degree to which you act like a puppet in relation to the following persons. Think about whether you say or do what you think they want you to. Rate each on a scale of 1 to 10, with 1 meaning you do not worry about impressing them and 10 meaning you disregard your own feelings and values trying to gain their approval.

___ mother
___ father
___ spouse or romantic interest
___ children
___ boss
___ pastor
___ teachers
___ others: _____

The material and activities you are reading may or may not apply to your particular family. If you have experienced the painful family situations described, apply the learning activities to your situation. If you have not experienced the situations, the activities will help you to understand and minister to others.

Some of us are fairly effective puppets because we have a finely tuned sense of perception. We are able to sense how our words, actions, attitudes, and tone of voice affect others. We then change our behavior to please them. Like puppets, we respond to every pull others make on our emotional strings.

The Escapist

Painful relationships lead many people to alcohol and drugs, which are effective and reliable in numbing the pain, if only for a short time. The fact that people use these methods repeatedly while recognizing their destructiveness only demonstrates how desperate some are to end their pain. Abusing chemical substances only compounds people's problems. It adds another layer of "protection" from seeing and dealing with reality.

✎ On the following list check each means you have used at some time in your life to escape the pain of relationships.

❑ alcohol or other mood-altering chemicals
❑ daydreaming
❑ food: compulsive eating, self-starvation, or controlling food by bingeing and purging
❑ pornography
❑ romance novels: fantasy
❑ acting out sexually
❑ gambling
❑ religious language or activity
❑ perfectionism
❑ controlling or rescuing others
❑ other: _____

We orchestrate our lives to win approval and avoid pain.

Most of us combine more than one empty solution. We orchestrate our lives for two primary purposes: to win approval and avoid pain. But no matter how diligently we try, we experience only limited relief from the gnawing fear of rejection and failure.

JoAnne, whose story you read on page 28, finally realized that her life was out of control. Using most of the escape methods in the previous list, she realized that the means of escape she had used to control the emptiness were now controlling her. She is getting help through therapy and a Christ-centered support group.

✎ From all of the substitutes for healthy relationships in this lesson, name the ones you use most frequently.

_____

_____

We need to see the truth.

We need to see the truth. Reality may be painful, but without it we never will achieve growth and health in our lives. The other alternatives are not cute. They are not clever. They are seductive and pathological. They rob us of intimacy, strength, and hope. The sooner we begin to realize how empty these alternatives are, the sooner we will begin to experience the refreshment of God's truth, God's Spirit, and God's people.

➥ Stop and pray about what you have studied in today's lesson. Honestly tell God what you have learned about yourself. Ask for His power and strength to face what He shows you about your situation.

SUMMARY STATEMENTS

- The amount of love and positive modeling people receive greatly influences their emotional, spiritual, and relational health.
- Avoiding the pain of rejection causes us to miss the pleasures of healthy relationships.
- We need to see the truth. Reality may be painful, but without it we will never achieve growth and health in our lives.

DAY 4

Your Role Model

Hear, my son, your father's instruction, and do not forsake your mother's teaching.

–Proverbs 1:8

In ancient Israel the parents' first responsibility was to guide their children. This awareness saturated the Jewish culture. The Book of Proverbs, for example, contains potent teachings King Solomon shared with his son. The prophet Isaiah wrote, "fathers tell their children about your faithfulness" (Isaiah 38:19, NIV). God intends for parents to experience His faithfulness and then to communicate that faithfulness to their children.

In Deuteronomy Moses talked to Israel's fathers about their earlier deliverance from Pharaoh's army at the Red Sea. He insisted that they share with their children, who had not been present, this experience of God's faithfulness.

> *Fix these words of mine in your hearts and minds; tie them as symbols on your hands and bind them on your foreheads. Teach them to your children, talking about them when you sit at home and when you walk along the road, when you lie down and when you get up. Write them on the doorframes of your houses and on your gates, so that your days and the days of your children may be many in the land that the Lord swore to give your forefathers, as many as the days that the heavens are above the earth.*
>
> –Deuteronomy. 11:18-21, NIV

Nothing has changed! A child's development in all areas—social, intellectual, physical, emotional, spiritual—still is the responsibility of the father and the mother. Many factors affect a person's emotional health. These factors include economics, extended-family relationships, social context, physical health, and peer relationships; but when parents offer their children a healthy balance of love and discipline, they usually produce healthy, well-balanced young adults. When parents are unattached to God and relate poorly to their offspring, their offspring generally create much pain and sadness for them.

Relationships Provide Our Role Models

We pattern our actions after the people who are close to us.

From the first day of life we pattern our actions after the people who are close to us. Children instinctively copy the attitudes and actions of those they are exposed to most. God's design is that they model themselves after loving and protective parents, but many parents do not cooperate with this plan.

A parent gave her three-year-old child a science-fiction videotape to occupy him while she pursued her own interests. Unattended, the youngster watched it seven times. In the movie a man with a patch over one eye rode a motorcycle while killing and maiming several persons each minute. The child later went into his bedroom and improvised a costume like the one worn by the man in the movie. Wearing a patch over one eye, he began riding his tricycle around the neighborhood and viciously clobbering children with a small baseball bat. Several were badly cut or bruised.

✎ Compare the two previous paragraphs. What lesson can be learned from the example of the child and the inattentive parent?

_____

_____

This child simply was copying his role model. Lacking the judgment to select a worthy model, he copied what his mother had endorsed when she gave him a videotape as an electronic baby-sitter. You may have written something like "Children copy their role models, whether the role models are good or bad, real or imaginary."

We become like those we are exposed to most.

We too unconsciously pattern ourselves after our role models, whether good or bad, and become like those we are exposed to most, even if those persons are cruel to us. Almost invariably, husbands or wives who batter their spouses or children have grown up in homes in which violence was commonplace. On the other hand, positive role models provide powerfully positive results. Have you ever met a couple who has been happily married for years and now even looks like brother and sister? Or have you ever met a young man who walks, talks, and speaks like an older person he admires?

How about you? Who is your role model? How powerfully has this individual influenced you? Do you talk, walk, think, and reflect this person in your mannerisms? What are you like today because of your father, your mother, or the lack of one of them? We adopt our life patterns without thought. We select from this person and that one the ways we deal with life. Seldom is any of it intentional. It just happens.

Changing Role Models

Breaking the Cycle of Hurtful Family Experiences is not merely about self-understanding. It is about life change. Throughout this study you will learn additional ways to cooperate with God to change your life and the lives of others.

One of the first steps—and the central step—in life change has to do with your primary role model. Jesus Christ—God's only Son and God Himself in fully human form—became human for a number of reasons.

- He came to demonstrate the depth of God's love for us (see Romans 5:8).
- He came to suffer the penalty of our sin and to pay the price for our sin (see 1 Peter 2:24).
- He came to redeem us from the penalty our sins deserved (see Revelation 5:9).

Jesus can be the perfect parent none of us ever had and none of us can ever be for our children.

Jesus also came to show us a perfect role model. He can be the perfect parent none of us ever had and none of us can ever be for our children.

The process of *Breaking the Cycle of Hurtful Family Experiences* requires growing and maturing. It involves identifying the missing elements in your growth and maturity. Then it means going through the maturing now that ideally you would have done many years ago.

An essential link in breaking the cycle of family dysfunction involves exchanging our imperfect parents for God—the holy and complete Father. This exchange does not mean abandoning or rejecting our earthly parents. It means that you must make a decision: *Do you want to continue the pattern of dysfunction and pass on to your children the cycle of hurtful experiences? Or do you want to attach your life to God the Father, who loves you and who can be the Father you need to grow and mature?*

When the fulness of the time came, God sent forth His Son, born of woman, born under the Law, in order that He might redeem those who were under the Law, that we might receive the adoption as sons. And because you are sons, God has sent forth the Spirit of His Son into our hearts, crying, "Abba! Father!"
–Galatians 4:4-6

✎ Read Galatians 4:4-6, which appears in the margin. In the following list check each statement that accurately reflects the passage's meaning.
❏ 1. We were all "under the Law"—guilty before God and deserving punishment.
❏ 2. We were alienated from God, enemies rather than children.
❏ 3. Jesus paid the penalty of our rebellion and sin so that we could be reconciled to God.

Unit 2   43

❏ 4. This made it possible for us to be adopted into God's family—given the full rights as children.
❏ 5. When a person receives the gift of salvation or adoption that God offers, God Himself—the Holy Spirit—comes into that person's life.

All five responses accurately reflect the teaching of the passage. Other Scriptures expand on each statement, but this passage contains the essential truth of all the statements.

The single most important step is the decision to have God as Father.

The single most important step in the life change necessary to break the cycle of hurtful family experiences is the decision to have God as Father. You can make that decision by personalizing the truths in the previous learning activity. You choose to—
- admit that you are guilty of sin—rebelling, ruling your own life, and trying to be God for yourself;
- acknowledge the truth that apart from Jesus Christ you are an alienated enemy of God;
- believe that Jesus paid for your sin by dying on the cross;
- believe that God wants you as His beloved child;
- ask God, in the power of the Holy Spirit, through the shed blood of Jesus Christ, to forgive you of your sins and to receive you into His family.

✎ Have you come to a time in your life when you made the decision to accept God's gift of forgiveness and salvation—when you received Jesus Christ as your Savior and Lord? ❏ Yes ❏ No

If the answer was yes, REJOICE! That does not mean you do not still need to grow and mature, but it does mean that you have the essential place to begin—a relationship with God the Father.

If your answer was no, thanks for your honesty. If you want to begin the process of life change and growth, you can receive Jesus Christ now by inviting Him into your life. Read the promise of John 1:12 appearing in the margin.

To all who received him, to those who believed in his name, he gave the right to become children of God.
–John 1:12, NIV

If you are not 100 percent sure that you would spend eternity with God if you died today and if you are willing to trust Christ and accept His payment for your sin, tell this to God in prayer right now. You may use this sample prayer to express your faith.

Dear Father, I need You. I want Jesus to be my Savior and my Lord. I accept His death on the cross as payment for my sin, and I now entrust my life to Your care. Thank You for forgiving me and for giving me a new life. Please help me grow in my understanding of Your love and power so that my life will bring glory and honor to You. Amen.

_____ (signature) _____ (date)

Trusting in Christ does not guarantee that you will be delivered instantly from the cycle of hurtful family experiences or from any other problem in life. It means that you are forgiven; that you are restored to a relationship with Him that will last throughout eternity; and that you will receive His unconditional love and acceptance, as well as His strength, power, and wisdom, as you grow.

Baptism

Water baptism is the biblical way of showing on the outside what Christ has done for you on the inside. The act of baptism symbolizes being dead, buried, and raised with Christ. Through baptism we identify ourselves publicly with Christ and with His people. I encourage you to go to a Bible-believing church, to make a public profession of your faith in Christ, and to demonstrate that faith through water baptism.

The journey to a changed life begins with a positive commitment to God.

The journey to a changed life—free from the cycle of hurtful family experiences—begins with a positive commitment to God. As our Father, He gives us unconditional love and always models the character we need to develop.

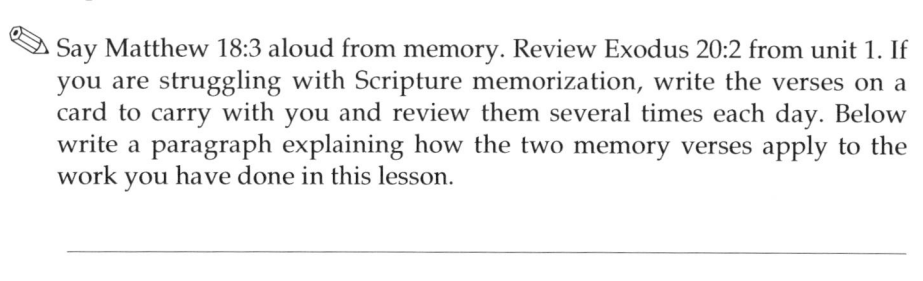

✎ Say Matthew 18:3 aloud from memory. Review Exodus 20:2 from unit 1. If you are struggling with Scripture memorization, write the verses on a card to carry with you and review them several times each day. Below write a paragraph explaining how the two memory verses apply to the work you have done in this lesson.

___

___

___

Through Jesus, God delivers us from sin—including slavery to repeated, hurtful family experiences. We begin to experience His healing by becoming like little children. We literally begin the process of growing up all over again, this time with God as our Father and with the body of Christ, the church, as our surrogate family.

SUMMARY STATEMENTS

- A child's development in all areas—social, intellectual, physical, emotional, spiritual—is the responsibility of the father and the mother.
- We too unconsciously pattern ourselves after our role models, whether good or bad, and become like those we are exposed to most.
- An essential link in breaking the cycle of family dysfunction involves exchanging our imperfect parents for God—the holy and complete Father.

DAY 5

Applying the Solution

I will make up to you for the years that the swarming locust has eaten.
—Joel 2:25

Joel 2:25 tells about a remarkable desire of God. To understand the verse, you need to know the background of the passage and the goal of healthy parenting.

Unit 2   45

God's purpose is not to punish His children but to train them in effective living.

Wise and caring parents want their children to develop responsibility and good character. Therefore, they set boundaries for the children, and they allow the children to experience the results of their misbehavior. In the same way, God disciplines His children. The root of the word *discipline* means *to teach*. God's purpose is not to punish His children but to train them to live effectively.

In the Book of Joel God's people were disobeying God and destroying themselves. God set boundaries and let the people experience the results of their disobedience. Joel saw a plague of locusts as God's judgment on the people. Joel called for the people to return to God. Then God said He wanted to "make up" to the people "for the years that the swarming locust has eaten."

✎ What could God's desire in this passage mean to you?

_____

_____

_____

God desires to make up for your lost growth, health, and maturity.

Whatever your past experience, in whatever way the hurtful cycle in your family has been expressed, God desires to make up for your lost growth, health, and maturity.

✎ Do you really believe that God has your best interest at heart—that He desires to give you the guidance, assurance, and strength you need to build a healthy, effective, Christ-honoring life? ❑ Yes ❑ No

✎ How do you feel about the prospect of growth and change?

❑ Doubtful: can this really work?
❑ Hopeful: maybe God really does care.
❑ Excited: this is what I've been praying for.
❑ Sad: I've lost so much.
❑ Fearful: what will all this mean?
❑ Overwhelmed: I don't think I can do any more.
❑ Other: _____

↪ Remember that God values your honesty. He does not want you to give Him lip service. He does not want you to say one thing and believe another. Please write a paragraph that honestly tells God how you feel about His enabling you to break the cycle of hurtful family experiences.

_____

_____

_____

_____

We normally experience a variety of feelings as we consider growth and change. If you have committed yourself to Jesus Christ, you have taken the essential first step. In the remainder of this study you will build on that decision.

- When you identify gaps in your childhood experiences, you will learn to allow God to be your positive parent.
- You will grow and mature in ways you missed in the past.
- You will begin to replace the substitute and counterfeit solutions of the past with genuine relationships with God and healthy believers.

✎ Write from memory the Scripture verses for units 1 and 2 below. If you need to look back to the unit pages to check the verses, you may do so. If you are having difficulty memorizing the Scriptures, begin now to make regular, consistent efforts to complete the memory assignments.

_____

_____

_____

_____

Unit Review

✎ Review the five lessons in this unit. Find one statement that helped you better understand the importance of relationships. Circle this statement in the text and rewrite it in your own words.

_____

_____

_____

✎ Review your written work and prayer responses throughout the unit. What exercise meant most to you this week? Identify the exercise and explain your choice.

_____

_____

_____

UNIT 3

Stages of Development

Case in point

> HELPING OR CONTROLLING?
>
> As Sharon described to me her present life and family background, I noticed that she seemed to have a problem determining what her responsibilities were. She tried to take care of others' problems, but she did not do a very good job of solving her own. In fact, she expected others to take care of her problems for her. When others would not or could not do so, she thought they were being selfish. She spent her life being responsible for others' feelings and behaviors, and she expected them to take care of her.
>
> Some people come into our lives to control and "fix" our problems. They give us "helpful advice." They make decisions for us. They "serve us" tirelessly. Some may say that they are "just trying to help" us, but they may condemn and belittle us in the process so that we will say and do what they want. These kinds of people invade our personal boundaries to manipulate and control us. One tries to control through kindness; the other, through condemnation. (You will read more on page 63 about what Sharon and others need to change these destructively helpful patterns.)

What you'll learn

This week you will
- identify the stages of human development;
- describe the bonding, separateness, adolescence, and maturity stages of development;
- explore the results when development is blocked in each stage of development.

What you'll study

Stages of Development	Bonding and Separateness	From Separateness to Maturity	Blocked Development, Part 1	Blocked Development, Part 2
DAY 1	DAY 2	DAY 3	DAY 4	DAY 5

Memory verses

This week's verses of Scripture to memorize

When the fullness of the time came, God sent forth His Son, born of a woman, born under the Law, in order that He might redeem those who were under the Law, that we might receive the adoption as sons.

–Galatians 4:4-5

DAY 1

Stages of Development

When I was a child, I used to speak as a child, think as a child, reason as a child.
—1 Corinthians 13:11

The Bible does not use the language of 20th-century psychology, but it deals with many of the same life issues. In the verse above, the apostle Paul recognized that children think and reason as children. Many educators and psychologists have observed patterns in human development from birth to adulthood. Some of these authorities explain this developmental process in minute detail, especially in infants. Others define it more broadly.

A basic understanding of the stages of human development can help us gain valuable insights into our emotional, relational, and spiritual progress—or lack of it. Four broad stages of development build on one another. They are:
- Bonding (birth through 2 years old): the need to be loved
- Separateness (2 through 11 years old): the need to set personal boundaries, including what a person is and is not responsible for
- Adolescence (12 through 18 years old): the need to develop adult relationships, gender behavior, and identity
- Maturity (19 years of age and older): the need to continue growing in adult relationships, gender behavior, and identity

The ages given for each of these stages are somewhat arbitrary because, for a wide variety of reasons, people develop at different rate. In fact, using only four stages to outline human development simplifies a very complex process. Each could be divided into many smaller, more defined stages that describe the subtle (and not-so-subtle) changes in people's lives as they grow and mature. Also, many aspects of development, such as bonding and separateness, are repeated in different contexts and relationships throughout the growth process. The treatment of these stages in this unit only introduces the developmental process at the most rudimentary level. The important idea, however, is that each stage serves as the foundation for the one that follows it.

Each stage of development serves as the foundation for the one that follows it.

✎ Because an understanding of the basic developmental tasks is very important, please review the preceding paragraphs as necessary while you complete the following activity. Fill in each blank with the appropriate stage of human development.

One learns to establish boundaries in the _____ stage of development.
One learns to accept love in the _____ stage of development.
One begins to develop adult relationships and gender identity in the _____ stage of development.
One begins to develop the ability to form loving relationships in the _____ stage of development.
One continues to grow in adult relationships throughout the _____ stage of development.

At each stage of life we need to grow in these basic developmental tasks. The responses to the learning activity are: separateness, bonding, adolescence, bonding, and maturity.

Unit 3   49

Are Developmental Stages Biblical?

The Scriptures do not outline stages of emotional, relational, and spiritual development in a systematic way. However, they speak clearly and strongly about the needs to be addressed in these stages. For example, our need for bonding, or attachment to another, is found in passages that portray love, compassion, value, warmth, and affection.

Passages about direction, discipline, and instruction describe the need for a child to have a sense of separateness—what he is and is not responsible for.

The need for a young person to develop adult relationships, goals, and behavior appears in passages such as those in Psalms and Proverbs that address "young man" and "my son."

> Each of the seven Scripture passages appearing in the margin deals with one of the first three stages of human development. Beside each passage in the margin write *B* for ***bonding,*** *S* for ***separateness,*** or *A* for ***adolescent.***

All Scriptures apply to all stages of life, but you may have noted that Psalm 103:13; Isaiah 49:15; and 1 Thessalonians 2:7-8 deal with the particular issues of bonding. Deuteronomy 6:6-7 and Proverbs 22:6 deal with the issues of separateness and responsibility. Psalm 119:9 and Proverbs 1:10 apply to adolescent issues.

Besides the first three stages of development, the need to continue growing in relationships, goals, and behavior during the maturity stage can be found in teachings like the Sermon on the Mount (Matthew 5—7), the instruction to the twelve (Matthew 10:5-42), and Christ's promise and commission to His disciples (Matthew 28:18-20).

Many scriptural passages deal with adolescence-and-maturity issues like values, choices, goals, motives, conflict, and spiritual warfare. (People do not encounter these issues only in these stages, of course, but they need a firm foundation of bonding and separateness to cope with adolescence-and-maturity issues.)

All Scriptures are for all of God's people, and the distinctions between adolescence and maturity often are blurred. However, the Bible encourages a strong foundation of emotional, spiritual, and relational health so that a person can respond more freely and fully to the Lord.

The chart that appears in the margin on page 51 overviews the stages of development. Notice the growth through the four stages of life.

Why Is This Information Important?

From the information in this lesson you can see that some fairly predictable results occur when a person does not grow and mature through each developmental stage. In later lessons you will explore these results more fully. You then can use this information to understand and ultimately break the cycle of hurtful experiences in your life and family.

These words, which I am commanding you today, shall be on your heart; and you shall teach them diligently to your sons and shall talk of them when you sit in your house and when you walk by the way and when you lie down and when you rise up.
    –Deuteronomy 6:6-7

Just as a father has compassion on his children, So the Lord has compassion on those who fear Him.
    –Psalm 103:13

How can a young man keep his way pure? By keeping it according to Thy word.
    –Psalm 119:9

My son, if sinners entice you, Do not consent.
    –Proverbs 1:10

Train up a child in the way he should go, Even when he is old he will not depart from it.
    –Proverbs 22:6

Can a woman forget her nursing child, And have no compassion on the son of her womb? Even these may forget, but I will not forget you."
    –Isaiah 49:15

We proved to be gentle among you, as a nursing mother tenderly cares for her own children. Having thus a fond affection for you, we were well pleased to impart to you not only the gospel but also our own lives, because you had become very dear to us.
    –1 Thessalonians 2:7-8

✎ Recalling what you have read thus far match the four stages of development with the possible results if growth is blocked.

___ 1. Developing a poor self-image and the inability to make choices that differ from one's peer group's
___ 2. After experiencing some hurt or difficulty, regressing to an earlier stage
___ 3. Being attracted to abusive or destructive relationships
___ 4. Being unable to tell where one's responsibilities begin or end
___ 5. Having great difficulty forming an attachment to another person or to God

a. bonding
b. separateness
c. adolescence
d. maturity

Describe additional results you might expect if development is blocked at the bonding stage of development.

_____
_____

Describe possible results of blockage at the separateness stage.

_____
_____

Possible answers to the matching activity are: 1. c; 2. b, c, or d; 3. a; 4. b; 5. a. You may have given other valid answers, and you may have noted many possible additional results. Blockage at the bonding stage results in an inability to form loving attachments or a tendency to attach to abusive or destructive relationships. Blockage at the separateness stage may result in all kinds of boundary problems—like attempting to control other people's lives or allowing others to control our lives.

✎ This unit's Scripture-memory verses appear in the margin. Note that God was willing to be incredibly patient in waiting for the proper time to send Jesus. Write your own paraphrase of the verses. Begin to memorize this week's passage.

_____
_____

> When the fullness of the time came, God sent forth His Son, born of a woman, born under the Law, in order that He might redeem those who were under the Law, that we might receive the adoption as sons.
> –Galatians 4:4-5

SUMMARY STATEMENTS

- Each stage of development serves as the foundation for the one that follows it.
- Blockage at the bonding stage results in an inability to form loving attachments or a tendency to attach to abusive or destructive relationships.
- Blockage at the separateness stage may result in boundary problems.

DAY 2

Bonding and Separateness

He went down to Nazareth with them and was obedient to them. But his mother treasured all these things in her heart. And Jesus grew in wisdom and stature, and in favor with God and men.
—Luke 2:51-52, NIV

To become mature, every person must grow through a developmental process. God designed us so that we must complete certain tasks or have certain needs met in each stage of our growth. In this lesson we will examine the first two stages, bonding and separateness.

Bonding: The Need to Be Loved

From birth to 1½ or 2 years of age a child's greatest need is to bond with parents. *Bonding* means *forming an attachment.* Its purpose is to convey feelings of warmth, love, value, worth, closeness, and trust. Parents initiate this process by tenderly holding their baby, talking to him, making eye contact, playing with him, feeding him, changing his diapers, and giving him a lot of time and attention.

The father of a three-year-old girl had made a habit of holding her often and talking to her softly since she was an infant. One day, as he held her in his lap, he told her, "I love you, Honey."

She looked up at him, smiled, and said, "I know that, Daddy."

"How do you know that?" he asked.

"'Cause you tell me that all the time!" was her reply.

Bonding takes time, attention, and genuine love for the child.

Bonding—communicating warmth, affection, and value to a child—takes time, attention, and genuine love for the child. It cannot be faked, and it cannot be accomplished in a few hurried minutes from time to time. Bonding is well worth the effort, however, because it forms a solid foundation for the second stage of development.

✎ To what extent did you feel loved, valued, and special to your parents when you were a child? Place an *X* on the chart to respond.

Loved	Unloved

Why did you feel that way? Describe two incidents from childhood that illustrate your feelings.

_____

_____

_____

52   Unit 3

✎ To what extent do you feel loved, valued, and special to people now?

❑ I consistently feel loved, valued, and special.
❑ I sometimes feel loved, valued, and special.
❑ Circumstances determine whether I feel loved, valued, and special.
❑ I seldom or never feel loved, valued, and special.

Describe why you feel the way you do. Be specific.

_____
_____

Describe some relationships you have had in which you felt loved and free to be yourself.

_____
_____

The purpose of these activities is not to cause you distress or to trigger angry feelings toward others. Objectivity is the goal. Until you describe your feelings, you probably never will begin to deal with them, and you will remain stuck in the cycle of hurtful experiences.

Separateness: The Need to Set Personal Boundaries

At about 1½ years of age a child learns a new word: *no!* She is learning to set limits and to assert her individuality. Bonding has to do with feeling loved; separateness has to do with healthy independence. For the next 10 years or so the child learns to be comfortable with her thoughts and desires. She learns who she is and who she is not. Following are some of the issues children begin to work through during this stage.

- I am responsible for this. I am not responsible for that.
- This is what I feel. I do not feel that way.
- This is who I am. That is who you are.
- I am in control of my life. You are in control of your life.
- I believe this. I do not believe that.
- I want to be this way. You can be that way.
- I can see both sides of an argument. I do not have to be one-sided in my opinions.
- I make my own choices. You make your own choices.

Bonding has to do with feeling loved; separateness has to do with healthy independence.

✎ Review the list of separateness statements you just read. Place a check mark beside each statement that causes you trouble in your life today.

Many of us find that we struggle with many separateness issues. One person said: "I have difficulty with the matter of responsibility. I think that I am responsible for everything that happens—especially everything that goes wrong." Another person said: "I struggle with extremist thinking—I tend to think that only one opinion exists and that everyone either must agree with me or they are opposed to me. As a result, my children say I try to control their lives for them."

During this second stage of development the concept of oneself begins to emerge. It lays the groundwork for developing identity in later adolescence. If this budding concept of self is nourished and strengthened in a positive environment, children gradually learn to be perceptive, to think well, to experience their emotions, and to relate to others.

✎ To live effectively, one must develop the ability to practice healthy, positive obedience to God. Here are some benefits that grow from a positive concept of self. Check each characteristic we need to have relationships with God and with others.

❑ To be perceptive ❑ To experience our emotions
❑ To think well ❑ To relate to others

Unless we successfully develop a sense of separateness, we cannot have effective relationships.

Unless we successfully develop a sense of separateness, we cannot have effective relationships. All four benefits that grow from separateness are essential to good relationships.

Establishing boundaries during the separateness stage is much like setting physical boundaries on a piece of property. The book *Untangling Relationships* illustrates this concept.[1] The idea is that if each of us owned a ranch, we would be responsible individually for setting its boundaries and then caring for it and protecting it. As caretakers, we also would be responsible for choosing whom to allow on our property. If invited to another person's ranch, we could go there for a visit. However, we would not try to run anyone else's ranch, nor would we allow anyone else to run ours.

In the same way, we have individual personalities (thoughts, feelings, and behavior), and we are responsible for setting our personal boundaries, that is, for establishing what part of ourselves we will share—and with whom. We may choose to allow certain others to share themselves with us. But we must avoid trying to run other people's lives, just as we should not allow others to run ours.

Self versus selfishness

Many people confuse the term *self* with the concept of selfishness or with rebellion against God. They therefore think that the term *self* automatically means something evil or wrong. They confuse the term *self* with biblical references to the flesh, as in Galatians 5:19: "The deeds of the flesh are . . .." In this instance *flesh* refers to our fallen nature, but *self* refers to who we are. In this discussion the term *self* means one's individual existence.

God created us to be distinct individuals. Genesis 1:28 says we are to reproduce and to manage nature. Genesis 2:24 says we are to leave our parents and to join ourselves to our mates. Genesis 2:17 commands us to obey God in our choices. All of these functions require an awareness of ourselves. Jesus said, " 'If any one wishes to come after Me, let him deny himself, and take up his cross, and follow Me' " (Matthew 16:24). Before we can deny ourselves (our selfishness) and follow Christ, we must recognize our identity as separate individuals. Establishing boundaries—separateness—is not disobedience. Establishing boundaries is the key to obedience and self-denial.

Your ranch

We need to have valid boundaries without putting up impenetrable walls.

✎ Check the response that most nearly describes how you care for your "ranch."

❑ 1. I maintain poor boundaries. I tend to allow anyone on my ranch.
❑ 2. I am a caretaker. I spend my time fixing other people's ranches.
❑ 3. I allow someone else to run my ranch for me, and I resent him or her for it.
❑ 4. I patrol my borders with automatic weapons. Nobody comes on my land!
❑ 5. I allow certain others on my ranch, but I choose who and when.

The desired result of the combination of bonding and separateness is a healthy independence for oneself, not selfishness; a recognition of one's individuality, not isolation or self-indulgence. Ideally, we grow toward the fifth answer. We need to have valid boundaries without putting up impenetrable walls.

Unfortunately, a number of us still struggle with our individuality, or separateness, from others. Recently, while having lunch with several couples, Jim asked Bill what he thought about a program in which the group was involved. Bill articulately expressed his ideas. Then Jim asked Bill's wife, Jane, for her opinion. Jane's ideas were very different from her husband's. After she finished, Bill spoke again, changing his opinion to fit his wife's. The next day Jim asked Bill if he realized that he had changed his mind after Jane had expressed a dissenting opinion. Bill answered: "Well, yeah. I guess I did."

"How often do you do that?" Jim asked.

"Well, pretty often, I guess."

Bill was letting his wife's opinions and desires control him to a great degree. He had not learned to be separate—to have his own emotions, ideas, and behavior. He was letting Jane run his ranch.

Some people, however, are able to maintain a healthy sense of separateness from others. Dan was working on a committee for a civic club. Brian, a friend who was also on the committee, said to him: "Dan, the project we're working on is really important to me. I need you to stay late tonight and finish it." Dan had told his wife that he would take her out to dinner that night. How would he respond to Brian? Would Dan give in? If he gave in, what would he say to his wife?

Dan was comfortable and confident about his decision. He calmly replied: "I'm sorry, Brian, I can't stay tonight. I already have something important planned. Please let me know a little sooner next time."

✎ Do you sometimes encounter similar situations?   ❑ Yes ❑ No

How much difficulty do you have standing up for yourself and calmly setting boundaries?

❑ I have great difficulties. I usually cannot stand up for myself.
❑ I am able to do as Dan did. I calmly but firmly enforce my boundaries.
❑ I give in and then become angry later.
❑ I do not stand up for myself—and I hate myself for it.
❑ I enforce my boundaries, but I often do so with anger.

Describe a time when you have faced a decision similar to Dan's. What did you do? If you could respond differently, how would you respond?

_____

_____

Because he had learned to be separate and to set limits when he was growing up, Dan was calm and confident as he expressed his decision to his friend.

The stages of bonding and separateness lay a strong foundation for the development of an adult identity during adolescence.

✎ Practice memorizing this week's Scripture passage, Galatians 4:4-5, by writing it in the margin. Check your work on page 48.

SUMMARY STATEMENTS

- God designed us so that we must complete certain tasks or have certain needs met in each stage of our growth.
- Bonding—communicating warmth, affection, and value to a child—takes time, attention, and genuine love for the child.
- During the separateness stage the concept of oneself begins to emerge, laying the groundwork for developing one's identity in later adolescence.

DAY 3

We learn and grow little by little in age-appropriate bits.

From Separateness to Maturity

To whom would He teach knowledge? And to whom would He interpret the message? Those just weaned from the milk? Those just taken from the breast? For He says, "Order on order, order on order, Line on line, line on line, A little here, a little there."

–Isaiah 28:9-10

This passage from Isaiah applies to God's careful method of training His people. God recognized that we learn and grow little by little in age-appropriate bits. In this lesson you will continue to examine the areas of separateness and adolescence.

✎ Because objectivity requires careful self-examination, indicate the degree to which you agree with the following statements by marking each statement with **N** for *not at all,* **S** for *somewhat,* or **D** for *definitely. Then explain your answer to each question.*

If people are not happy, I *need* to do something to cheer them up. _____

_____

_____

56   Unit 3

If someone needs something, I *need* to help him or her. _____
_____
_____

If others are happy, I tend to be happy; if they are sad, I tend to be sad. ___
_____
_____

When I say no, I usually feel guilty. _____
_____
_____

I try to please others so that they will approve of me. _____
_____
_____

I find making decisions that affect other people to be difficult. _____
_____
_____

I make decisions impulsively, without reflecting on the consequences. ___
_____
_____

I often see people and situations as right or wrong, black or white. _____
_____
_____

I tend to be overly responsible. _____
_____
_____

I tend to be irresponsible or passive. _____
_____
_____
_____

When I help people, I feel like a hero. _____

_____

_____

When I help people, I get angry with them for using me and for not appreciating what I have done for them. _____

_____

_____

Appropriate limits   This inventory deals with setting appropriate limits. Responses of *somewhat* or *definitely* to the statements indicate difficulty with the issues of separateness. Your answers do not mean that something is wrong with you. However, your responses indicate that you may need to work on the issues related to separateness.

Adolescence: The Need to Develop Adult Behavior and Identity

The years from 12 to 18 are difficult and awkward for everyone; yet some people are able to make the transition from childhood to young adulthood much more easily than others. Why? Among the many reasons is the degree to which individuals have developed their sense of bonding and separateness. If they have a sense of inherent worth, believing that they are loved and lovable, they will be better able to reach out to others and build good relationships. Also, if they have learned to be comfortable with their own thoughts, feelings, and behavior, they will be less influenced by the tremendous peer pressure all adolescents encounter. On a firm foundation of love and limits, an adolescent can develop effective life skills.

On a firm foundation of love and limits, an adolescent can develop effective life skills.

✎ The following statements point to maturing life skills in four areas, which we begin to develop during adolescence. Beside each one rank yourself on a scale of 1 to 10, with 1 indicating that you still struggle greatly with the issue and 10 indicating that you are very comfortable with the statement.

- Adult identity: I recognize
  ____ what I am good at doing;
  ____ what I am not good at doing.
  ____ I accept my strengths without a sense of pride.
  ____ I accept my weaknesses without a sense of shame.
- Adult behavior: I am able to determine
  ____ what are good choices;
  ____ what are unwise choices;
  ____ how I can deal with ambiguity and avoid considering everything black or white;
  ____ what risks I should take and what consequences I am willing to endure.
- Adult goals: With relative ease I can decide
  ____ what is worth my time and affection;
  ____ what is really important to me;
  ____ what is unimportant.
- Adult relationships: I am able to

___ experience both intimacy and separateness in relationships with others;
___ identify and experience real love;
___ identify artificial or contrived love;
___ deal with conflict;
___ let others fail and still love them.

Resolving crucial issues like these begins in adolescence and continues for the rest of our lives as we mature in each area. None of us have the issues in the list completely resolved. If you answered 9 or 10 to most of the items, we would like to nominate you for sainthood—or for a severe case of denial! Most of us find that we still struggle more with certain areas, such as accepting our strengths, dealing with ambiguity, or dealing with conflict.

Maturity: The Need to Continue Growing in Adult Behavior and Identity

One mark of maturity is realizing how little we really know and how much more we have to learn.

This side of heaven, no one ever "arrives." We all have a lot to learn about God, ourselves, and others. In fact, one mark of maturity is realizing how little we really know and how much more we have to learn. As we mature, we gradually shed the cockiness of youth and develop a depth that does not require having all of the answers neatly packaged and expressed. With maturity comes more insight and less hurry, more honesty and less pretense, more real joy and fewer shallow substitutes, more genuine love and fewer hollow words. We can be assertive and still be submissive. We can be wise but not demanding. We can be strong but gentle, caring yet willing to let others fail so that they can learn their own lessons.

With maturity comes more insight, more honesty, more real joy, and more genuine love.

This kind of maturity is rare in our fast-paced, shallow culture, but some people possess it. Can you think of someone in your church who is compassionate but strong, someone who is not in a hurry and is not self-promoting but is willing to listen patiently and to whom others go for wise counsel?

Take time to look for a man or a woman like this; he or she may not stand out in a crowd. Then spend time asking questions and listening. Look into his eyes. Listen to the depth of her experience. You may hear of pain, loss, and heartache, as well as hope, warmth, and wisdom. Developing a relationship with a person like this will be well worth your time; it could change your life.

✎ To estimate your progress toward maturity, describe how you are growing in the following areas of your life.

Adult identity: _____

_____

_____

Adult behavior: _____

_____

Adult goals: _____

Adult relationships: _____

You may have described your growth in terms of an increasing awareness of your identity in Christ and of your resulting worth as a person (identity). You could have written about choices you are facing (behavior), about directions and plans for your life (goals), and about the ongoing challenges of developing and maintaining healthy relationships. In whatever way you see yourself in these areas, you may be assured of one thing—these are areas of continued challenge throughout life. None of us "arrive."

Continued challenges

What happens when a person does not progress through the four broad stages of human development? How is a person affected by abuse, divorce, neglect, alcoholism, or other family disorders? The next lesson will examine blockages in our emotional, relational, and spiritual development.

✎ Repeat aloud from memory the Scripture-memory verses for this unit, Galatians 4:4-5.

SUMMARY STATEMENTS

- We learn and grow little by little in age-appropriate bits.
- On a firm foundation of love and limits, an adolescent can develop effective life skills.
- One mark of maturity is realizing how little we really know and how much more we have to learn.
- We face continued challenges throughout life.

Blocked Development, Part 1

DAY 4

The naive believes everything, but the prudent man considers his steps.
—Proverbs 14:15

A person's emotional, relational, and spiritual growth can be blocked at any point in the developmental process; but generally, the earlier it happens, the greater the damage. For example, people who do not develop personal boundaries almost certainly have problems in the adolescence and maturity stages. And people who have had bonding problems likely will develop difficulties in all of the subsequent stages as well.

In addition, an emotional blow can be so severe that it not only blocks

An emotional blow can be so severe that it not only blocks development but also actually reverses it.

development but also actually reverses it and returns you to an earlier stage. Examples of an emotional blow of this nature might be abuse from a parent, sibling, or spouse; the loss of a parent, sibling, spouse, or close friend; the commission of an act so shameful that it drastically alters your life; involvement with the wrong crowd at school; deep hurt by a coach or a teacher; or any of a myriad of other possibilities.

✎ Reread this lesson's Scripture verse, Proverbs 14:15. In light of the material you have studied, what might be a reason a naive person would believe everything?

_____

_____

You might have observed that a person who did not experience positive growth through the separation stage of development will have difficulty determining responsibility. Therefore, if someone says to such a person, "It's your fault that I (got drunk, failed, hit you . . .)," the person naively may accept inappropriate responsibility. You may have described any of a host of other possibilities involving the bonding, separation, or adolescence stages of development.

An isolated, traumatic incident is not usually the thing that damages human development the most. The consistently subtle, yet extremely powerful, message that says: "you're not loved," "you're not good enough," "I'm ashamed of you," "I don't value your feelings or opinions," does far greater damage. A person who is steeped in this environment believes not only that something is terribly wrong with him but also that all of these hurtful communications are "normal" and never will be different. This insidiously powerful situation, unfortunately, is common to many families. Parental modeling is among the most influential forces in human development. The way parents use their authority contributes either to a child's health and stability or to insecurity and instability. We will examine the causes and symptoms of hindered or reversed growth in each developmental stage.

Parental modeling is among the most influential forces in human development.

> Our goal in presenting this material is not to blame others or to evade responsibility. The purpose is to understand how people develop healthy self-concepts and relationships and what may have hindered this process in our lives. Understanding these issues may prove to be painful, and we may realize some unpleasant things about our parents; but understanding is not the same as condemnation. In a later chapter we will see how important it is to forgive those who have hurt us. At this point we are simply trying to see if and how we have been hurt.

When Development Is Blocked in the Bonding Stage

One of at least three significant events occurs in a child's life during the bonding stage:
- He or she develops an attachment to a loving role model.
- He or she develops an attachment to an abusive role model.
- He or she is unable to form a significant bond with a role-model figure.

The absence of bonding presents tremendous problems in every area of human development. Jenny was reared by emotionally troubled parents. They became so absorbed in their own personal and relational problems that they had no time or energy left to give her. They lived together in the same house; but emotionally, her parents were absent.

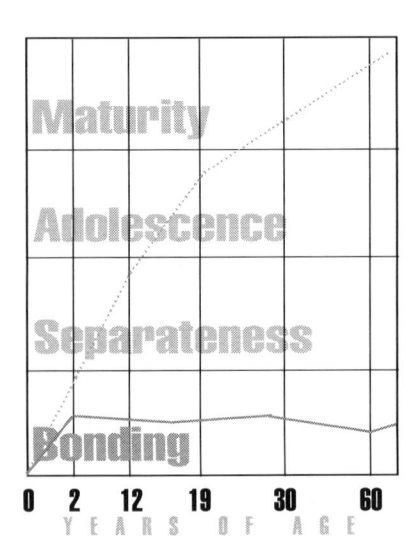

Steve has an alcoholic father and a demanding, manipulative mother. His father spent very little time with the family, and his mother expected Steve to meet the emotional needs her husband failed to meet. In response to her demands, Steve's primary concern became pleasing his mother and trying to win her approval. He consequently developed an unhealthy bond with his mother and had problems establishing limits and a sense of separateness from her and others. The result was a rescuing, codependent relationship with his mother, which carried over into all of his relationships.

Bonding problems primarily result from abandonment (physical and/or emotional neglect) and abuse (emotional, physical, sexual, verbal, and so on). The symptoms those who have not experienced a deep sense of being loved and valued show are tragic, especially when contrasted with those that result from healthy bonding.

✏️ The graphs below represent the range of results from healthy bonding to the results of bonding problems. On each graph place an *X* on the point that most nearly represents your feelings.

Results of Healthy Bonding   Results of Bonding Problems

Valued	Worthless
Lovable	Unlovable
Open	Withdrawn

valued, loveable, and open, but many people have overcome and are overcoming these difficulties. We want to encourage you that these feelings can be changed. Bonding problems often contribute to addictions to drugs, success, pleasing people, food, or other substances or behaviors. They also can leave us with a fear of closeness, a fear of being known, loneliness, denial, and an inability to perceive and experience reality.

All of us exhibit some negative feelings and behaviors from time to time but not to the extent that those with bonding difficulties do. As people at a seminar examined these stages, Karen commented: "I have felt lonely. Do I have bonding problems?" After more discussion Karen realized that people who are stuck in the bonding stage often have a pervasive and oppressive sense of loneliness (if they are in touch with their emotions). The feeling is not a temporary one.

When development is blocked in the bonding stage, people have difficulty believing that God or anyone else possibly could love them. But a compounding problem is that they often do not even know what love is. They then are unaware of the nature and depth of both their need and the defense mechanisms they have unconsciously incorporated to block the pain.

When Development Is Blocked in the Separateness Stage

Sharon seemed to have a problem determining what her responsibilities were. She tried to take care of others' problems, but she did not do a very good job solving her own. In fact, she expected others to take care of her problems for her. When others would not or could not do so, Sharon thought they were being selfish. She spent her life fixing other people's "ranches," and she expected others to take care of hers.

Some people trespass on our ranches to fix them. They give us "helpful advice." They make decisions for us. They "serve us" tirelessly. Some may say that they are "just trying to help" us, but they may condemn and belittle us in the process so that we will say and do what they want. These kinds of people trespass on our ranches to manipulate and control us. One tries to control through kindness; the other, through condemnation.

Often, parents are unable to find a healthy balance between advising and correcting their children and giving them the freedom and affirmation they need to assume their own thoughts, feelings, and identities. They may nurture the children a lot as infants; but by failing to teach them how to make their own decisions and develop their own unique personality traits, they fail to help them move from bonding to separateness. Their form of love sustains an infant's development but smothers a child in grade school. It harms even more a child approaching adolescence.

✎ In the following paragraph circle the words or phrases that best describe your relationships with your parents when you were a child.

Most parents lean toward one end of a spectrum. Some are highly controlling and refuse to allow their children to work through the process of making their own decisions and developing their own thoughts and feelings. Other parents are relatively uninvolved in this important childhood process, so their children have to try to figure out things entirely on their own. Both smothering and neglect block the development of healthy independence in children.

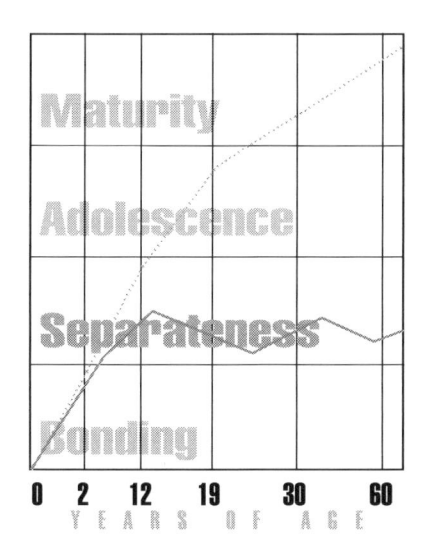

Both smothering and neglect inhibit the development of healthy independence in children.

✎ Which of the following traits did your parents tend to exhibit as you were growing up?

❏ Control: they refused to permit me to make my own decisions and have my own feelings.
❏ Neglect: I had to figure out things on my own.
❏ Balance: they let me have my feelings and make my decisions, but they were usually available for support when I needed it.

Describe how you feel about your response to the previous question.

_____

_____

Remember that your feelings are your own. You may feel any combination of many emotions about this issue. Some feel intense guilt—as if they betray the family by admitting their experience. Others feel deep sadness because of all they have missed. As you continue this process, pray that you will see that openness and honesty clear the path to understanding, forgiving, and breaking the cycle of hurtful family experiences.

➡ Stop and take all the time you need to pray. Tell God how you feel about this process and about what you are learning. Be sure to share with Him your feelings of grief, anger, and guilt.

✎ The following list contains typical problems we encounter when we still struggle with separation issues. Place a check mark beside those that sometimes are problems for you. Then circle the three areas that cause you the most difficulty.

❑ Feeling responsible for making others happy and successful
❑ Assuming others' thoughts, feelings, and behavior instead of developing your own
❑ Being unable to say no without feeling guilty
❑ Saying yes to please others and to win their approval
❑ Being manipulated (controlled) by others
❑ Trying to manipulate others
❑ Being unable to make decisions because of a fear of rejection or failure
❑ Having difficulty distinguishing between good and bad, acceptable and unacceptable, behavior
❑ Impulsively making decisions by perceiving different factors as black or white with very little ambiguity; seeing people and situations as all good or all bad
❑ Rescuing, fixing, enabling (codependency)
❑ Being overly responsible/competitive
❑ Being irresponsible/passive
❑ Frequently demonstrating anger, bitterness, resentment
❑ Living in denial, unable to see your problems with establishing limits

The material and activities you are reading may or may not apply to your particular family. If you have experienced the painful family situations described, apply the learning activities to your situation. If you have not experienced the situations, the activities will help you to understand and minister to others.

People who have problems establishing limits make decisions for others while letting others make decisions for them.

Again, the ranch illustration can help us visualize some of these difficulties. People who have problems establishing limits trespass on other people's ranches and make decisions for them, while they let others trespass on their ranches and make decisions for them. They may get angry if the others become too bossy or domineering, but they will not tell them to leave. After all, they are busy tending to somebody else's business.

Many people with separation difficulties actually have set limits—very rigid limits—in one or more specific areas of their lives. These might include rearing their children or managing a job, finances, or certain relationships. They may let others tell them what to think, feel, and do about many other parts of their lives but not this one! If they feel threatened in this area (and they often do), they defend this area with tenacity and vengeance. They often use either passive or aggressive behavior to do so.

John's story

John typifies many people who have problems with setting limits. John's father believed that rearing children was a woman's job. He therefore poured most of his time and energy into his work, so that he had very little of either left to give to his son or his wife. John's mother was a domineering woman who was accustomed to getting her way in the home.

When John was growing up, his parents rarely gave him opportunities to make his own decisions; when he did, he often felt as though he had been placed in a double bind. His mother might give him options, but she withheld affection from him when he chose to do something that she really did not want him to do. John learned how to read his mother well and became devoted to making her happy in all that he said and did.

John, an exceptionally bright student, excelled in math and science. He became a physician, started a private practice, and married a woman much like his mother. John transferred his devotion and approval-seeking skills to his wife. He allowed her to run their home; but if she tried to give him any input on how to run his practice, he became very agitated. His response was either to argue with her defensively or to act as if he had listened to every word—and then dismiss all she said.

Throughout his married years John poured almost all of his available time and energy into his practice. He worked late and remained on call on most weeknights and weekends. Helping his patients as he did gave John the feeling that he was a hero, despite the negative influence his wife's domination had on him.

Helping his patients as he did gave John the feeling that he was a hero.

John had allowed himself to be driven from most of his ranch, but he still clung to a shed (his medical practice) in "the back 40." When he felt threatened by his wife's inquiries or suggestions about his work, he responded with defensiveness or withdrawal. He pretended to hear her but ignored her words.

Those who defend a particular area of their lives may make demands, whine, complain, criticize, or condemn the ones posing the perceived threat. Or they may make black-or-white responses and believe that others are for them or against them. They may try to get others on their side against the perceived attackers. Again, those who have problems establishing and maintaining limits commonly tell others how to run their lives and then are offended when others do not take their advice.

We need to remember that defensive people are seeking to avoid reinjury.

We easily may become frustrated and angry with people who are so defensive, but we need to remember that the root of their defensiveness is hurt. Seeing them as hurting people who act defensively to avoid reinjury helps us feel compassion for them.

✎ Repeat Galatians 4:4-5 from memory; then write the verses in the margin. Check your work on page 48.

SUMMARY STATEMENTS

- A person's emotional, relational, and spiritual growth can be blocked at any point in the developmental process; but generally, the earlier it happens, the greater the damage.
- When development is blocked in the bonding stage, people have difficulty believing that God or anyone else possibly could love them.
- Both smothering and neglect inhibit the development of healthy independence in children.

DAY 5

Blocked Development, Part 2

A wise son accepts his father's discipline, but a scoffer does not listen to rebuke.
—Proverbs 13:1

The most significant hindrances to development are in the bonding and separateness stages. If growth occurs properly in these stages, the child then will be ready for the challenges of adolescence. If the child does not successfully complete the bonding and separateness stages, adolescence will prove to be extremely difficult and awkward.

When Development Is Blocked in the Adolescence Stage

An emotionally strong and happy young man named Jim moved to a new town with his family when his father was transferred to a new job. As Jim entered his new high school, he experienced all of the normal anxieties teenagers do when meeting people in a new school. He was tense and apprehensive, but his parents tried to encourage him.

"Hang in there. Things will work out," they said. They regularly asked Jim questions and listened carefully when he talked, without always trying to change his negative feelings or to provide answers to his problems.

Jim had played football at his previous high school, so he tried out for the team. But instead of being a starter, he was placed on the second team. Then he learned that the girl he wanted to date already was going with another guy. He was doing well in his classes—until algebra came along. No matter how diligently he tried, he could not seem to understand it.

After a couple of months of this pressure, Jim's confidence and happiness slowly began to erode. He experienced no single turning point but rather a number of seemingly minor tensions and setbacks. Jim began to doubt himself. He grew increasingly depressed and started spending time with some boys who were not really bad—just sarcastic and cynical.

The next summer Jim and his family visited the town they had left almost a year before. Their former neighbors and friends could hardly believe the changes in Jim. The confident, happy boy they had known before had become a sullen, withdrawn, and angry young man.

Problems in the adolescence stage may be caused by experiencing peer pressure, developing bad habits, or making bad choices. These problems could lead to distortions in one's self-concept, a tendency to avoid risks because of the fears of failure and rejection, and rigid performance motivation.

✎ The list at the top of the next page contains symptoms of arrested development in the adolescence stage. All of us struggle with these issues to some degree. Evaluate yourself by writing a number from 1 to 10 beside each symptom, with 1 meaning that you experience little struggle with the issue and 10 representing an issue that causes you ongoing difficulty.

66 Unit 3

Poor self-concept:
___Uncertainty about my personal strengths and weaknesses
___Pride about my strengths
___Shame about my weaknesses
___Self-condemnation
___Anger, bitterness

Making unwise choices:
___Unwillingness to take risks
___Taking impulsive risks
___Unwillingness to accept responsibility and consequences
___Inability to make different choices from my peer group's

Immature relationships:
___Becoming too dependent on one person or group
___Becoming isolated
___Inability to deal with conflict
___Condemning others when they fail
___Being easily susceptible to peer pressure

You would not be human—or at least would not be honest—if you did not indicate difficulty with some of these issues. For example, you may be secure in some areas of your life while you feel shame about certain weaknesses. You might be willing to accept responsibility very well while you fear conflict and tend to condemn those who fail. We all need to continue growing in our relationship skills, in our ability to make wise choices, and in our self-concept.

When Development Is Blocked in the Maturity Stage

Blockage in the maturity phase of growth can lead to regression. A classic example is an alcoholic who, after 20 years of sobriety, begins to neglect the basic principles of recovery and falls into relapse. Another example is a pastor who becomes so involved in his congregation's needs that he neglects his own needs and becomes enmeshed in sinful behavior. Possible obstructions to growth in the maturity stage include a real or perceived sense of loss, burnout, severe or repeated adversity, deep hurt, and loneliness.

✎ The following list contains symptoms of difficulties arising in the maturity stage of development. Place a check mark beside each issue with which you have struggled at some time in your adult life.

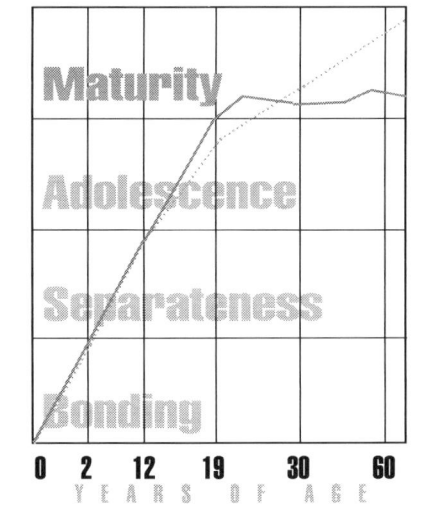

❑ Increasing anxiety about the future, resulting in sleeplessness, gastrointestinal disorders, chest pains, muscular tension, twitching, or profuse sweating
❑ Increasing depression along with lethargy, irregular eating and sleeping habits, boredom, and/or an inability to concentrate
❑ Being hurt and becoming preoccupied with revenge
❑ Becoming increasingly isolated and withdrawn by refusing to acknowledge and/or discuss negative feelings with others
❑ Becoming isolated by developing an attitude of pride. This attitude may be manifested by underlying beliefs such as: "I don't really need to (pray, confess my sins, read my Bible, attend church, repent, become involved in caring relationships) because I basically have things together" or "People need me; I just don't have time to (pray, study my Bible, attend church, develop mutually caring relationships, take a vacation, spend time with my family)."

✎ Review the list. Underline specific matters with which you presently struggle.

You may have checked any broad areas on the list, and you may have underlined any specific issues. Remember that honest struggle is not bad. The real danger comes when we cease to struggle and become stagnant. Stagnation in the maturity stage may bring with it an inability to continue growing in Christian virtues such as love, joy, wisdom, strength, faithfulness, gentleness, and self-control (Galatians 5:22-23). Or, as we mentioned previously, stagnation may lead a person to regress to a previous stage of development.

In some cases a person may appear to be progressing well until a tragic or painful event exposes hidden flaws in the developmental process. Diagraming an experience like this is more difficult because the appearance of progress hides one's underlying weakness. From a distance the person's life might resemble the graph in the margin, illustrating tragic consequences in a person's life. Unfortunately, such a pattern occurs frequently.

Jill seemed emotionally stable when she married. However, her husband's tendency to alcoholism became apparent when his business went bankrupt. Unfortunately, Jill never had truly developed a healthy sense of separateness. If she had, she would have been able to be more honest with her husband in the early stages of his drinking. She might have told him that he had to take responsibility for his behavior and that his increased irresponsibility was adversely affecting the family. Instead, Jill developed a habit of rescuing her husband by telling others that he was sick when he was really drunk. She made excuses for him to their neighbors and friends, avoided the real problem, and talked to him only about superficial concerns. After a year of living these deceptions, Jill became unsure of herself. Her sense of stability and confidence collapsed. She no longer felt that she was special and lovable. Her husband's alcoholism revealed a flaw in her development; and her emotional, relational, and spiritual health declined from apparent maturity to the point that she experienced problems with bonding.

Mark's story

Mark was fairly confident and secure when he tried out for the soccer team in high school. He was a good athlete, but his coach got upset with Mark on the first day of practice because he was not paying attention. Somebody else was talking to him, and he did not hear the coach's instructions. From that day on, the coach carried out a personal vendetta against the boy. He criticized Mark, ridiculed him, did not let him play in games, and consistently tried to humiliate him. His tactics worked. Mark was deeply hurt and lost confidence in himself. He became easily manipulated and indecisive. Mark, who had seemed to be progressing confidently through adolescence, now struggled with problems in separateness and bonding.

Summary

Understanding our home environment and how it affects us can give us a lot of insight into our past and present thoughts, feelings, and behavior. It can also help us see how we have progressed through the stages of development. To summarize your work in this unit, can you identify the stages in which you seem to have grown significantly and those in which you have not? Map your development by drawing a graph of your life on the chart in the margin on the next page.

68   Unit 3

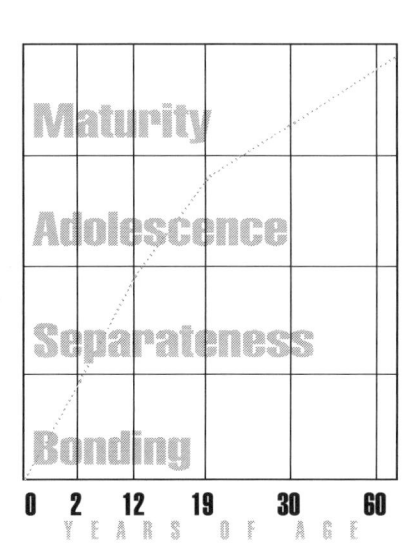

Understanding these stages of development has helped many people gain insights into why they think, feel, and act the way they do. Realizing the extent of one's hurt and its consequences often is very painful. The next several chapters describe some solutions to these problems.

Unit Review

✎ Review the five lessons in this unit. Find one statement in the text that helped you better understand the importance of relationships. Circle this statement in your text and rewrite it here in your own words.

_____
_____
_____

✎ Review your written work and prayer responses throughout the unit. What exercise was most meaningful to you during this week? Identify the exercise and explain your choice.

_____
_____
_____
_____

✎ Review the memory passage. Find it in your Bible and check your memory. Then close your Bible and write the passage in the left margin. How have you applied this passage during your study of this unit?

_____
_____
_____
_____

Notes
[1] Pat Springle, *Untangling Relationships: A Christian Perspective on Codependency* (Houston: Rapha Publishing, 1993), 156-57.

UNIT 4

Emotional Healing

Case in point

> THE COURAGE TO GROW
>
> Neglected by his workaholic father and manipulated and smothered by his insecure mother, Jeff grew up believing that nobody loved him and that nobody ever would. He learned to be socially skilled and professionally successful. For a long time his prowess in these areas masked his pain and insecurity.
>
> When he reached his mid-30s, however, Jeff started detecting problems in his relationships with God and with others. He realized that he performed for everyone yet felt accepted by no one. Over a couple of years Jeff began to identify the backlog of tremendous hurt and anger he had repressed. He also began to experience the emptiness and loneliness he had hidden for almost his entire life.
>
> As he gained awareness, Jeff realized that he had a choice: he could face the reality of his pain and work through it, or he could give up and deny it. The first route would lead to more pain but also to the possibility of fuller health. The other route would lead to immediate relief but long-term problems. Jeff determined to face and seek answers to his problems. (You will read more about Jeff on p. 71).

What you'll learn

This week you will
- examine four essential elements of healing and growth;
- describe specific steps to take if you are blocked in any of the four developmental stages;
- evaluate four essential characteristics of strong, healthy relationships;
- review key reasons we refuse to forgive;
- choose to begin to forgive those who have injured you.

What you'll study

Elements of Healing and Growth	The Steps to Take	The Role of Relationships	The Need to Forgive	The Reason to Forgive
DAY 1	DAY 2	DAY 3	DAY 4	DAY 5

Memory verse

This week's verse of Scripture to memorize
Everyone who hears these words of Mine, and acts upon them, may be compared to a wise man, who built his house upon the rock.
—Matthew 7:24

DAY 1

Elements of Healing and Growth

Where there is no guidance, the people fall, but in abundance of counselors there is victory.
—Proverbs 11:14

As you have worked through the first three units of this book, you may have gained insight into how you think, feel, and act. You may have read an illustration or a characteristic and thought: *That's me! I do that, too!*

Perhaps now you are wondering: *How does a person experience emotional healing and growth? What encourages that kind of development? What hinders it?* In today's lesson we will attempt to answer those questions by examining four important factors that result in healing and growth: courage, a deep understanding of why we are the way we are, appropriate steps toward change, and realistic expectations.

Practical application

> As you work through this unit, remember that this is only a book and that the actions discussed here will not produce life-changing results if you apply them only on an intellectual level. Rather, you need to experience them in the give-and-take of meaningful relationships, such as through participation in a discovery group or support group or through the direction of a Christian therapist or counselor. For instance, learning to deal with conflict requires both an understanding of the principles and the practical experience to go through the often difficult process of learning to apply those principles. As you complete this unit, also consider what environment and relationships will enable you to apply these principles at the very basic levels of your life.

Courage

The pain may be so overwhelming and threatening that facing it requires a great deal of fortitude.

Courage may seem a strange factor to consider in emotional health, but it is absolutely essential. The pain many people have repressed is so overwhelming and threatening that facing it requires a great deal of fortitude. Two stories illustrate the importance of courage.

Neglected by his workaholic father and manipulated and smothered by his insecure mother, Jeff grew up believing that nobody loved him and that nobody ever would. He learned to be socially skilled and professionally successful, and for a long time his prowess in these areas masked his pain and insecurity. When he reached his mid-30s, however, Jeff started detecting problems in his relationships with God and with others. He realized that he performed for everyone yet felt no one accepted him. Jeff began to identify the backlog of hurt and anger he had repressed. He also began to experience the emptiness and loneliness he had hidden for almost his entire life.

As he gained awareness, Jeff realized that he had a choice: he could face the reality of his pain and work through it, or he could give up and deny it. The first route would lead to more pain but also to the possibility of fuller health.

The other route would lead to immediate relief but long-term problems. Jeff determined to face and seek answers to his problems.

One day someone said to him: "Jeff, I admire you. You have tremendous courage. Many people would have quit if they had experienced the pain that you have, but you've kept going."

Russell's story

Russell was a different story. He grew up in a family filled with hurt and anger; but when someone asked probing questions, he responded: "They did the best they could. They were fine. They loved me." Russell signaled that he was not ready to talk about his problems. Even as time lapsed, Russell was still defensive and closed when anyone asked about him.

Russell is still not open to talking about the reality of his pain. What is the difference between Jeff and Russell? At least one factor is courage.

✎ What are your greatest fears as you consider applying what you are learning in *Breaking the Cycle?*

___

Many of us struggle with a variety of fears as we confront this growth process. We fear discovering something about ourselves we do not want to know. We fear being disloyal to our parents. We fear the work or the pain of change, and we fear the reactions of friends and family members if we change.

King David often experienced hopelessness, pain, and depression. In Psalm 27 he described his trust in the Lord, in spite of seemingly overwhelming military, political, and family problems. At the end of this psalm David expressed hope and courage:

✎ Read David's words that appear in the margin. Use his statement of faith to write your own statement of commitment or prayer to God.

___

> I would have despaired unless I had believed that I would see the goodness of the Lord in the land of the living. Wait for the Lord; Be strong, and let your heart take courage; Yes, wait for the Lord.
> –Psalm 27:13-14

Courage is essential in facing the reality of hurt and anger in our lives. One person wrote a prayer in which she said, "I will wait for the Lord as I walk through the painful process of breaking the cycle of hurt in my family."

Deep Understanding

Someone may ask: "Do I have to dredge up the negative events of my past and feel those awful feelings again? Can't I just pray for healing and then trust God to make me whole?" The answers are no, you do not have to examine your past and feel repressed emotions; and sure, you should pray that the

Lord will work in your life to bring emotional health. However, the more fully we understand the problem, the more likely we are to find the real cause and thereby to find a workable solution. Just as a doctor accurately diagnoses a disease; a mathematician understands a calculus problem; or a person understands the causes of his emotional, relational, and spiritual difficulties, the idea is to find the root of the problem.

In the same way, we cannot experience God's comfort and healing until we are aware that we need them. Such an awareness can enable us to apply His power to our lives deeply and specifically.

> An appalling and horrible thing has happened in the land: The prophets prophesy falsely, and the priests rule on their own authority; And My people love it so!
> –Jeremiah 5:30-31

The Book of Jeremiah describes the prophets and priests in Jeremiah's day who had become comfortable with easy answers. Read the prophets' words in the margin.

Did you catch the words " 'My people love it so!' "? The people loved the false leaders' message because it contained easy words that promised a quick and painless answer. The Bible passage was not talking about the same subjects we have been studying—but a parallel exists.

> They have healed the brokenness of My people superficially, saying, 'Peace, peace,' but there is no peace.
> –Jeremiah 6:14

✎ Read another passage from Jeremiah, which appears in the margin. Write your own moral to the phrase " 'They have healed the brokenness of My people superficially.' " Describe how the principle could apply to the need for deep understanding for healing.

_____

_____

Problems often seem to have obvious, simple answers. Unfortunately those solutions frequently are wrong. You may have said that genuine, deep healing occurs only when we face the pain. Beware of discount-house cures for deep-seated life problems.

The process of analyzing pain and defensive behaviors can be grueling—especially for those whose development was blocked in the bonding or separateness stages. These people usually are not objective about repressed pain and anger, their causes, or their behavioral consequences. In fact, all of us usually drift toward one of two extremes. Either we lean toward morbid introspection and self-condemnation because we see ourselves as bad people with bad problems, or we deny that we have any difficulties because we are afraid of facing pain. We may need to talk with an objective, affirming person who has experienced what we have experienced. Such a person can help us avoid these extremes and can move us along the right path.

An objective, affirming person can help us avoid extremes.

Appropriate Steps

Progressing toward emotional health requires that we focus on two fronts. The first is a deep level of growth, which includes understanding our concept of God and ourselves. The second focus is on a more immediate level in which, by our own choosing, we actively put ourselves in environments and situations where we can learn and grow daily. By focusing on both of these growth levels, we will gain more insight and make more concrete progress as we take appropriate steps toward continued emotional development.

Everyone who hears these words of Mine, and acts upon them, may be compared to a wise man, who built his house upon the rock.
—Matthew 7:24

✏️ Matthew 7:24, this week's Scripture-memory verse, appears in the margin. Jesus spoke these words at the conclusion of the Sermon on the Mount, His extended teaching about how to live effectively as a citizen of God's kingdom. Check the response that best expresses the verse's meaning.

❑ Pay attention! Learn the principles I am telling you.
❑ Apply and obey My words.

Write your own paraphrase of Matthew 7:24. Personalize and apply the verse to breaking the cycle of hurtful family experiences.

_____

_____

Doing what Jesus said is the key to effective living.

Jesus was saying that actually doing what He said—not just listening or learning—is the key to effective living (the second response). You may have written something like this: "All the understanding in the world will not change the cycle of hurtful experiences. I must act on my understanding and apply the principles to achieve genuine change."

Some steps are appropriate for all of us, regardless of our position in the developmental process. All of us can learn to be courageous as we discover how to apply the Scriptures deeply and specifically to our lives. All of us need to be involved in healthy relationships and in the study of God's Word. All of us can benefit from recognizing painful feelings, destructive behavior, and wrong thinking. All of us are affected to some degree by the tears of rejection, failure, punishment, and feelings of shame; but some have been more deeply affected than others. In the next lesson we will look at specific steps we can take in each stage of development.

Realistic Expectations

Many people with good intentions communicate that a quick fix is available for virtually any problem, no matter how big that problem may be. All things are possible with God, but expecting that a person will jump from deep bonding problems to maturity in an instant is unreasonable. Ultimately, expecting a quick fix can be very harmful. People looking for relatively instantaneous results often become disillusioned when the results do not happen overnight. They may give up the growth process entirely, perhaps condemning themselves because they believe that their inability to respond in the prescribed, rapid way proves that something is wrong with them.

Even worse, they may be condemned by the one who told them they could be healed so quickly. People who give simplistic answers, threatened by the failure of their theories or system, may express their fear and anger toward the ones who need their love and patient encouragement most.

A very few people experience almost miraculous healing; but for most of us, growth tends to come through spurts of insight, followed by long periods of consolidating and applying those insights in everyday life. Sometimes those insights cause rapid growth; sometimes months or years are necessary before we realize how those insights can affect our thoughts, emotions, and actions. One obvious principle is: The deeper the hurt, the longer it takes to heal.

The deeper the hurt, the longer it takes to heal.

Consider four persons involved in an auto accident, each of whom is in a different stage of development. The person in the maturity stage is alert and avoids the collision. He stops to help the others in the wreck. The person with problems in the adolescence stage has a cut on his arm. The others stop the bleeding and take him to the hospital for stitches. The person with boundary difficulties from the separateness stage has a broken arm, and the one with bonding problems has compound fractures in both legs.

The one with the broken arm will be in pain for a significant period of time and will need several months to build strength in that arm. The one with the broken legs will require surgery and will endure weeks of pain, several months in casts, and several more months of rehabilitation to regain her strength. Telling her that she will be able to run the next day would be senseless and cruel. If she tried, she could cause herself further damage. To avoid reinjury and promote healing, each needs to give his or her wounds time and attention, the amount and length depending on the degree of the wound(s). All of them however, can experience comfort, encouragement, and love from others in the weeks and months after the accident.

↪ Begin to memorize this unit's Scripture verse. Repeat the verse aloud; then spend time in prayer. Ask God to give you the courage and willingness to act on His truth.

Everyone who hears these words of Mine, and acts upon them, may be compared to a wise man, who built his house upon the rock.
–Matthew 7:24

SUMMARY STATEMENTS

- Four important factors that result in healing and growth are courage, a deep understanding of why we are the way we are, appropriate steps toward change, and realistic expectations.
- The more fully we understand the problem, the more likely we are to find the real cause and thereby to find a workable solution.
- The deeper the hurt, the longer it takes to heal.

The Steps to Take

DAY 2

Dill is not threshed with a threshing sledge, nor is the cartwheel driven over cummin; but dill is beaten out with a rod, and cummin with a club.
–Isaiah 28:27

This Scripture verse sounds rather odd until you learn to what it refers. The verse is part of a passage (Isaiah 28:23-29) that speaks of God's wisdom and care in His dealings with us. Just as a wise farmer knows how to harvest different crops differently—the tiny dill seed is not threshed in the same way as is wheat or corn. God knows that we each require individual care. One principle we might draw from the passage is this: deal with all situations, circumstances, and individuals appropriately.

The goal of the healing process is not self-improvement for selfish purposes but freedom and health to love and serve Christ without being encumbered by the hurts and distorted thinking of the past. Just as medical illness and treatment require time and care for physical healing, investing in our

The goal of the healing process is freedom and health to love and serve Christ.

Unit 4   75

emotional health enables us to experience healing and move on to focus on Christ and others instead of ourselves.

Emotional healing and growth are difficult but possible for all of us. A woman who was blocked in the bonding stage began to heal and grow in her 30s. Another person from an abusive home found people who loved him and bonded with him in high school. He then began to grow. A man who was stuck in the separateness stage began to grow in his 20s. A woman who experienced a reversal in development when the man she married became obsessed with professional success later began to experience hope and healing. In each of these cases the people were stuck in a developmental stage, but they recognized the problem, experienced love, and began to grow.

If You Are Blocked in the Bonding Stage

✎ Because we live in a world damaged by sin, everyone could identify to some degree with each level of blockage. Place an *X* on the scale to mark the degree that you have experienced healthy bonding.

| 0% | 50% | 100% |

Some people who have bonding difficulties have learned to be gregarious and socially adept to win the approval they so desperately want from others. Others, however, are more obviously insecure and withdrawn. Both types of individuals are very lonely and empty; some simply have done a better job of fooling others—and maybe themselves—about their pain. In whatever way you see yourself, consider the specific actions below.

Some have done a better job of fooling others—and maybe themselves—about their pain.

✎ In a context of love and honesty people whose growth has been blocked in the bonding stage need to work on the following actions. Check those you are willing to address as you continue studying **Breaking the Cycl**e.

❑ Understand why I feel, think, and act the way I do, accurately analyzing the causes and consequences of the lack of parental bonding and/or the severe emotional blows I experienced that triggered a later reversal in my life.
❑ Gain freedom and encouragement within a safe environment—where I can be genuinely honest and genuinely loved—to feel the hurt and anger of the past.
❑ Learn to forgive those who hurt me.
❑ Deal with any addictions (for example, alcohol, drugs, sex, food, and work) that I use to dull feelings of pain and emptiness.
❑ Take the risks necessary to get involved in relationships, to get close to people, to be known by them, to develop feelings of dependency as a transitional step toward independence and health, and again to face courageously the prospect of rejection.

What single, specific action will you take this week to grow in this area of your development?

_____

_____

You may have noted that since taking the risk of developing relationships is difficult, "This week I will take the initiative to meet someone new at work."

Or you might have written, "I will admit my addiction to _____ by attending a support-group meeting or by seeing a Christian counselor." Those who have problems with bonding generally have difficulties establishing limits and need to take steps in that stage after having developed some stability in the bonding stage. Many others have bonded fairly well. Their difficulties originate in the separateness stage.

If You Are Blocked in the Separateness Stage

Those of us with separation problems have not determined for what we are and are not responsible. We think, feel, and act the way we think others want us to, and we try to get others to respond the way we want them to. We act like puppets of others while also trying to get others to be our puppets.

We need to develop a mature, godly sense of independence through which we can appreciate and express our individuality while we give others the freedom to do the same with theirs. Paul wrote the Galatian believers, "Each one shall bear his own load" (Galatians 6:5); that is, each of us must make our own choices and bear the consequences of those choices.

Responsibility

✎ Place an *X* on the scale to mark the degree that you have experienced healthy separateness.

| 0% | 50% | 100% |

✎ Others who have learned—or are learning—to experience healthy independence can help us greatly as we take steps to work on the following actions. Check those you are willing to address.

❑ Understand why I am overly responsible or irresponsible.
❑ Learn to feel my own hurt, anger, and joy instead of feeling what others want me to feel.
❑ Learn to forgive those who have manipulated and hurt me.
❑ Think my own thoughts instead of adopting those of others.
❑ Do what I think is right instead of what others think I ought to do.
❑ Refuse to be manipulated and learn to say no.
❑ Let others be responsible for their lives and make their own choices without my interference.
❑ Avoid one-sided, black-or-white extremes in my analyses and conversations about people, events, or circumstances.
❑ Set limits about what I will be and do and what I will not be and do, so that I can respond to others calmly and confidently.

What single, specific action will you take this week to grow in this area of your development?

_____

_____

Each of us needs to learn to take care of his or her own ranch.

Each of us needs to learn to take care of his or her own ranch. We need to take responsibility for building strong fences and gates and for overseeing our own cattle, crops, home, and family. We can then invite others to join us for visits at our ranch, and we can visit theirs if we are invited. If they offend us, we can

Unit 4   77

be honest with them about the hurt and the consequences their behavior generates. If necessary, we can ask them to leave our ranch. With this kind of strength we can be calm, secure, and loving. We can then choose to give and serve rather than being compelled to do so in order to win someone else's approval.

A person with difficulties in the separateness stage almost certainly has difficulties with issues in the adolescence stage. Others, however, have bonded and separated quite well, yet they still have problems centered in the adolescence stage of development.

If You Are Blocked in the Adolescence Stage

In either physical or emotional adolescence, peer relationships seem to mean everything. If we find ourselves with people who are positive and encouraging, we tend to adopt their attitudes. In the same way, if we spend a lot of time with people who are negative, we usually become negative; if they are angry, we become angry; if they are violent, we tend toward violence. Adolescence is a very vulnerable stage of life; the strength that has been established in the bonding and separateness stages can be wasted by destructive peer relationships. The apostle Paul said it well: "Bad company corrupts good morals" (1 Corinthians 15:33).

✎ In adolescence we need to work on the following actions. Check those you are willing to address as you continue this study.

❑ Choose my friends wisely.
❑ Monitor my values, goals, and relationships to determine whether they are developing in the right direction.
❑ Develop good habits—personally, relationally, professionally, and so on.
❑ Identify my strengths and weaknesses and learn to accept myself.
❑ Learn to forgive others and myself.
❑ Learn that I cannot do everything and that I must pace myself.

Which of the issues in the list above causes you the greatest difficulty?

_____

✎ Place an *X* on the scale to mark the degree that you have experienced emotional and relational health in adolescence.

| 0% | 50% | 100% |

Someone who is learning and growing in these areas of life is well on the way toward maturity. However, we can be sidetracked in the maturation process.

If You Are Blocked in the Maturity Stage

Can we assume that someone who has reached the maturity stage is not vulnerable to blockages in development? On the contrary, stagnation and reversal also can occur in maturity if someone is not watchful and prepared. In fact, persons in this stage often experience extreme spiritual battles because the forces of darkness want to thwart their effectiveness (see Ephesians 6:10-

> Be of sober spirit, be on the alert. Your adversary, the devil, prowls about like a roaring lion, seeking someone to devour. But resist him, firm in your faith, knowing that the same experiences of suffering are being accomplished by your brethren who are in the world.
> –1 Peter 5:8-9

13; 1 Peter 5:8-9).

✎ Those of us in this stage who find ourselves stagnating, wandering, or becoming embittered need to to work on the following actions. Check those you recognize as ongoing needs in your life.

- ❑ Understand what is going on in my life. Are the worries of the world and the deceitfulness of riches beginning to choke out growth (Matthew 13:22)? Does my life show signs of spiritual conflict and oppression? Is the Lord pruning me (John 15:1-11), or am I experiencing consequences of a rebellious attitude?
- ❑ Seek the counsel of mature, godly persons.
- ❑ Be honest about unresolved hurt or anger in my life.
- ❑ Forgive those who have hurt me.
- ❑ Take time to replenish my emotional, relational, and spiritual reserves. Read, pray, relax, and laugh with friends.
- ❑ Determine the one thing to which I want to devote my life and accomplish instead of trying to do too many things well.

✎ What one concrete action from the list will you begin to practice in your life?

_____

✎ Place an *X* on the scale to mark the degree that you are experiencing the character, purpose and relational depth which characterize maturity.

| 0% | 50% | 100% |

✎ Repeat Matthew 7:24 aloud three times to help you memorize the verse. You will find the verse on page 70. Then copy the verse in the margin.

SUMMARY STATEMENTS

- The goal of the healing process is not self-improvement for selfish purposes but freedom and health to love and serve Christ without being encumbered by the hurts and distorted thinking of the past.
- We need to develop a mature, godly sense of independence through which we can appreciate and express our individuality, while giving others the freedom to do the same with theirs.

DAY 3

The Role of Relationships

Iron sharpens iron, so one man sharpens another.
–Proverbs 27:17

Must I participate in a group to experience growth? Why are reading and study not enough? In this lesson we will examine our need for healthy relationships to help us grow.

A blend of intimacy and separateness characterizes healthy relationships.

Unit 4   79

A blend of intimacy and separateness characterizes healthy relationships.

These qualities combine genuine love with a willingness to let others have their own identities and make their own decisions. Many of us have never experienced that kind of relationship. Some of us have known only surface relationships. Feeling isolated and lonely, we have covered up our hurts and fears with humor, success, withdrawal, or other defense mechanisms. Some of us have had relationships in which we have been smothered, condemned, manipulated, hurt, and angered. In turn, we have often treated others the same way, even though we have despised the way we have been treated.

✎ What defense mechanisms—those listed above or others—have you used or are you using to cope with loneliness, hurts, and fears?

_____

_____

You may have described any of a vast array of defense mechanisms we employ. Some of us become "heroes." We use achievement and success to avoid pain. Some of us withdraw by concentrating on pursuits as diverse as sex and romance, drugs, or religion. All of these coping mechanisms have one thing in common: they keep us from being vulnerable. They shield us from relationships.

We need a relationship with God and relationships with others.

The Lord created us as relational beings. He intends for us to find life's true meaning in the context of rich relationships. Our relational needs are genuine. We need a relationship with God and relationships with others if we are to become strong, healthy, loving persons. The following are some characteristics of healthy relationships, along with guidance for developing these kinds of relationships.

Love

"I really care about you." "You are special to me." "I love you." All of us want to hear genuine expressions of warmth and acceptance. We want to feel valued. We want to feel loved. Yet some of us have difficulty accepting expressions of care and affirmation because we feel unworthy of being loved.

✎ In the next two paragraphs circle words or phrases that describe feelings or actions you sometimes feel or do.

We remain in a shell, afraid that if people really knew us, they would not like us, much less love us. Pushing people away through sarcasm, busyness, or condemnation, we remain isolated and empty. On the other hand, we may be addicted to pleasing people. We try to say and do what makes others happy so that they will accept us. We may even seem to be very responsive to scriptural teaching—not because we are applying it deeply and experiencing the freedom and joy of being the independent, healthy persons Christ wants us to be—but because we are trying to earn approval by being "good Christians."

People who never have experienced genuine love have difficulty allowing the truth about God's love to take root in their lives. For some, the truth about God's love, forgiveness, and acceptance seems to bounce off their hearts like a seed bouncing off pavement. Many people, of course, are not in this extreme condition but are nonetheless hindered in experiencing life because of deficiencies in their relationships.

First Samuel 16 recounts the prophet Samuel's visit to Jesse's home to anoint one of his sons as the new king of Israel. When Samuel told Jesse to bring his sons to a sacrifice, Jesse brought all of his sons except David. Jesse did not value David enough to count him as one of his sons. David was a neglected child, yet God commanded Samuel to anoint him as Israel's new king.

The next chapter in 1 Samuel gives us another glimpse of David's relationships with his family members. David's father sent him to take food to his brothers, who had joined the army, and to their commanders. When David saw that the giant Goliath taunted the army of Israel, he asked some questions. His brother, Eliab, responded to David with bitterness and scorn.

✏️ In the margin read Eliab's words to his younger brother David. Describe how you would feel if you had been David in this situation.

> Eliab his oldest brother heard when he spoke to the men; and Eliab's anger burned against David and he said, "Why have you come down? And with whom have you left those few sheep in the wilderness? I know your insolence and the wickedness of your heart; for you have come down in order to see the battle." But David said, "What have I done now? Was it not just a question?"
> 1 Samuel 17: 28-29

_____

_____

You may have described how you would feel angry, saddened, embarrassed, or shamed. Certainly, Eliab's words were painful.

From these two snapshots of David's life, we can see that his father devalued and neglected David and his brother abused him. Later, when King Saul threatened to kill David because the people loved the strong young man, Saul's son, Jonathan, became David's friend.

> My father and my mother have forsaken me, But the Lord will take me up.
> –Psalm 27:10

The Book of 1 Samuel describes how Jonathan risked his life to encourage David and to help him escape his father's wrath. Though David's family had abandoned and abused him—in the margin see Psalm 27:10—Jonathan became a tangible example of God's love, acceptance, and strength. Many of us also need to be involved with a caregiver like Jonathan who is equipped in some way to communicate God's character to us. A counselor, mentor, or support group provides the opportunity to develop healing relationships.

Objectivity

One of the most common and pervasive defense mechanisms that block pain—and growth—in our lives is denial. Denial is the inability or the unwillingness to recognize truth or reality in one's life. Many of us from an early age have acted as though we do not feel hurt and anger. We may have learned denial because our parents did not acknowledge our feelings or because we experienced a severe emotional blow later in life. We may act like someone trying to walk on a broken leg who says: "I'm OK. It's not bad at all."

Few of us learn to be objective about ourselves without help.

Few of us learn to be objective about ourselves without help. Most of us learn to see reality more clearly only when someone loves us enough to speak the truth in love to us (Ephesians 4:15). Someone also can help by asking us questions and by affirming our fledgling feelings, especially when our emotions seem new to us.

Randal had just finished talking to his father on the phone. He was extremely

Unit 4 81

upset. During their conversation Randal had explained that he and his family would not be able to visit his parents at Christmas. His father had replied: "Then don't come! See if I care! Your mother and I have done so much for you, and you obviously don't appreciate us. Well, that's fine!" And he hung up.

Dan asked Randal, "How do you feel about your conversation with your father?"

"I'm hurt!" Randal snapped.

"I don't doubt that," replied Dan, "but you also seem to be angry."

Hurt and angry

"Angry," Randal repeated softly. "Yeah, I guess I am. I guess it seems more acceptable to be hurt than angry, but you're right. I'm angry with my Dad."

✎ What did Dan do to help Randal?

_____

_____

This short conversation shows how friends can help others be more objective about their thoughts and feelings. Dan helped Randal become more objective about his feelings. A friend can be instrumental in helping a person set boundaries in the separateness stage and develop adult goals and relationships in the adolescence stage. A friend can ask questions as well as give objective counsel and feedback. He or she can affirm one's progress and can correct errors in one's thinking and behavior.

As we develop objectivity, we become better able to come to terms with the depth of hurt that many of us have experienced. We can admit: *This is who I am. This is why I am the way I am. I'm not as healthy as I've tried to believe and portrayed myself to be, but in the long run it's better for me to be honest and feel pain than to deny it.* A doctor cannot treat a wound until the patient admits that he needs treatment. Similarly, people usually see little progress in their lives until they recognize their hurts and needs.

Hope

A relationship characterized by love and objectivity fosters hope. We often have superficial or false hopes. We hope that our pain will vanish magically. We hope that we can be successful enough for people to love us. We hope that we will find the "right" person—someone who will meet our needs and make us happy. These hopes stimulate us and give us confidence for a while, but they leave us shattered and confused when they do not materialize.

The only real hope we can rely on is found in a Person.

The only real hope we can rely on is found in a Person, rather than circumstances, and meets our most profound needs instead of superficial ones. Christ Himself is our hope. In Him we find enduring love, comfort, forgiveness, and strength. We hope that despite any sense of loneliness or isolation we feel, He will become real to us, even though we may never have experienced the reality of His love and strength before. We hope that He will comfort us and will give us wisdom and courage about what we need to do. Such hope does not just happen. Often it comes as a result of receiving His love through someone else consistently and tenaciously over a period of time. It may first appear as a faint glimpse that begins to grow only as our relationship with Christ grows, as our concept of Him becomes more accurate, and as we slowly learn that we can trust Him to meet all of our needs. Throughout this process we begin to learn that this kind of hope does not disappoint (Read about this in Romans 5:5, appearing in the margin).

> and hope does not disappoint, because the love of God has been poured out within our hearts through the Holy Spirit who was given to us.
> –Romans 5:5

Depth

As we grow and develop, our relationships will slowly acquire more depth. Whereas we may now work diligently to overcome the painful negatives in our lives and may deeply appreciate those who are loving and helping us through this process, we gradually will be able to move into more mature and healthy relationships with these persons and others. We then can experience the adventure of developing adult relationships in which we can be free to be ourselves. In the process we will learn to have a healthy give-and-take with others through which we can value their opinions even when we disagree. We can slowly replace our drive to succeed and to please people with the joy of loving and being loved. We can replace the shame and embarrassment that may have characterized previous relationships with honest interaction, openness, and affirmation.

We can experience the adventure of adult relationships.

Different people play different roles in our lives at different times. The Lord may use a caring and perceptive friend, pastor, or counselor to start us on the road to health. He may send others to help us take the next step and still others for another leg of our journey. In turn, He probably will use us in the lives of those who need to take steps we have already taken. Whether others are helping us or we are helping them, we must not allow our relationships to become ingrown so that we are absorbed in one another. Instead, we need to point one another to the Lord so that our human relationships and our relationship with Him can each enhance the other.

✎ Review this lesson. What are the four essential characteristics of the strong, healthy relationships we all need to grow?

1. _____ 2. _____

3. _____ 4. _____

Check your responses by referring to the four subheadings in this lesson.

✎ Attempt to write from memory Matthew 7:24 in the margin. You may look at page 70 to check your work.

SUMMARY STATEMENTS

- A blend of intimacy and separateness characterizes healthy relationships.
- We need a relationship with God and relationships with others if we are to become strong, healthy, loving persons.
- Christ Himself is our hope. In Him we find enduring love, comfort, forgiveness, and strength.

DAY 4

The Need to Forgive

I am writing to you, little children, because your sins are forgiven you for His name's sake.
—1 John 2:12

One of the most significant hindrances to our emotional, relational, and spiritual health is our failure to forgive others. Resentment and bitterness about another's offenses against us short-circuit our growth. Even though God has forgiven us, we seem to forget about this fact when we decide how we will treat others. We inflict punishment on those around us—and on ourselves—by refusing to forgive. We add up all the times someone has wronged us and all the things we do not like about the person.

Much of the material in this lesson comes from *Search for Significance* LIFE® Support Group Series Edition. When you have completed *Breaking the Cycle*, you may wish to participate in a *Search for Significance* group to develop a more Christ-centered sense of self-worth.

Reasons We Do Not Forgive

We often fail to forgive others (and ourselves) because we do not think we can forgive. Forgetting that God, through Christ's death, has graciously forgiven all of our sins, we devise reasons we cannot forgive.

✎ The following case studies represent many excuses we make for our unwillingness to forgive ourselves and others. Beside each case study write the letter of the matching reason in the left margin.

a. The person never asked for forgiveness.

b. The offense was too great.

c. The person does not accept responsibility.

d. I simply do not like the person.

e. The person committed the offense too many times.

f. The person is not truly sorry.

_____ 1. Grant's wife left him for another man, and Grant became bitter toward his wife. Her infidelity is too great a sin for him to forgive.

_____ 2. Janet's mother emotionally abused Janet as a child. Her mother never has admitted her harsh treatment of Janet. Janet refuses to forgive her mother.

_____ 3. John pulled a practical joke on you. His prank caused you to be late for class, and your professor refused to accept your paper because you did not submit it on time. John does not see anything wrong with a little joke. He made some rather insincere statements about being sorry, but he still thinks the incident was hilarious.

_____ 4. Darrell knows he made you angry when he deliberately did not invite you to his open house, but he never asked you for forgiveness. You decide to withhold forgiveness until he requests it.

_____ 5. Candy's husband stayed out late playing cards every Friday night for three years. Some nights he did not come home at all. "Forgive that jerk? Look how many times he's wronged me!" Candy exclaims.

_____ 6. Cindy does not like Martha, who constantly tries to make Cindy look bad at work. Every emotion in Cindy calls for getting back at her co-worker. She certainly does not want to forgive her.

✎ Which of the reasons in the margin has kept you from forgiving in the past? Describe how that reason has interfered with your ability to forgive.

_____
_____
_____
_____

Possible answers include 1. b, 2. c, 3. f, 4. a, 5. e, 6. d.

✎ Here are more excuses we make for our unwillingness to forgive ourselves and others. Again, write the letter of the matching reason in the margin beside each case study.

a. I have found an excuse for the offense.

b. Someone has to punish the person.

c. The person did it deliberately.

d. Something keeps me from forgiving.

e. If I forgive, I will have to treat the offender well.

f. I will forgive, but I will never forget.

_____1. George's best friend, Hal, swindled George out of $10,000 after careful planning. George's mind races through times he has been generous to Hal. George feels that he can never forgive the planned betrayal.

_____2. Ben excuses himself for slandering Steve by pointing out that Steve has offended him. He feels justified in lying to destroy Steve's reputation. Forgiving him might mean Ben would have to be nice to this scoundrel.

_____3. For two weeks Shirley has been cold to Greg, who has offended her. She will forgive him, all right—as soon as she finishes punishing him.

_____4. Steve knows that he should forgive Joe, but he tells others that the devil prevents his having a forgiving spirit toward Joe. Yet Steve shows no signs of trying to resist Satan, either.

_____5. Mary thinks she has forgiven her brother for his cruelty to her when they were children; but during arguments between the two, Mary repeatedly refers to past incidents. When Mary and her brother are together, she always seems to brood about these past misdeeds.

_____6. When Hank behaves irresponsibly, his wife, Sally, attempts to forgive him by placing the blame on his mother, who babied Hank even after he was grown. Sally thinks she has forgiven Hank when really she has just excused him.

✎ With which of the above case studies do you most readily identify? Describe a situation in which the excuse used in that case study kept you from forgiving.

_____
_____
_____
_____
_____

Possible answers include 1. c, 2. e, 3. b, 4. d, 5. f, 6. a.

When we fail to forgive others, our lives and our relationships suffer. We will

Unit 4   85

When we fail to forgive others, our lives and our relationships suffer.

look at some problems in our lives that stem directly from a lack of forgiveness.

• Stress. Sarah announced to the group that her husband did not deserve forgiveness. She vowed that she would not forgive him even if it meant her life. It turned out that it did. Sarah died of kidney failure, which physicians said was caused by the extreme stress under which she lived. She wanted to kill her husband, but in reality she caused her own death.

✎ Many people experience extreme stress because they hold inside bitterness and anger resulting from a refusal to forgive. Have you ever experienced physical illness because of the stress of unforgiveness? If so, describe this experience in the margin.

Describe a time when stress from a past wrong made you physically ill.

_____

_____

_____

_____

One way we deal with the pain of being offended is to withdraw. We refuse to love anymore.

• Self-inflicted reinjury. Robert recalled this incident: "As I drove home, the face of a guy I played basketball with in college flashed through my mind. He was a great enemy of mine. He was one of the few people I ever met whom I truly wanted to punch out. I began to remember the unkind things he did to me. Soon anger welled up inside me. I had not thought about this fellow for years, and I'm sure that he doesn't remember me at all. Yet my reliving this event caused me a lot of pain. Obviously, I had not properly dealt with it in the beginning."

• No more love. "I don't know if I can ever love someone again" is a frequent complaint of those offended by persons about whom they care deeply. Our deepest hurts occur at the hands of those we love. One way we deal with the pain of being offended is simply to withdraw. We refuse to love anymore. We often make this unconscious decision when we have not dealt adequately with an offense. We desperately may want to love again but feel that we cannot do so. Refusing to experience love and feeling unable to love can be devastating.

✎ Which of these three problems stemming from a lack of forgiveness do you most readily see in your life? Describe it here.

_____

_____

• Bitterness. Emotions trace their lines on our faces. We think that others do not notice what is going on inside us, but even a casual observer can usually detect our anger. Kristin recalled seeing a neighbor experience difficulties in her marriage. Hatred was so much a part of the neighbor's life that her face became permanently snarled. Kristin described the neighbor as having that ugly look on her face. Unforgiveness produces ugliness of all sorts.

• Perpetual conflict. A husband and a wife, both of whom had been married previously, received counseling several years ago. Having been hurt in their first marriages, each anticipated hurt from the present spouse. At the smallest offense each reacted as if the spouse were about to deliver the final blow. This husband and wife were constantly on the defensive, protecting themselves from the attacks they imagined their mate would deliver. Having been offended in the past, they anticipated more hurt in the present and the future. Then they reacted in a way that perpetuated the conflict.

• Walls that keep others out. Many of us refuse to experience love from those

Many of us refuse to experience love from those who love us.

who love us. We may often become anxious and threatened when personal intimacy becomes possible. Jane hoped and prayed that her husband, Frank, would come to know the Lord. She thought that if he were a Christian, he would be more loving toward her and toward their children. One day Frank accepted Christ, and his life began to change. He paid more attention to Jane and started spending time with her and the children. He became sensitive and loving. Was it a dream come true? Instead of rejoicing, Jane deeply resented Frank for not changing sooner! *If Frank is able to love us like this now, then he's always had the ability*, she thought. She also felt confused and guilty about her anger.

Jane used anger as a defense mechanism to keep distance between Frank and herself. She thought that the closer they might get, the more pain she might experience if he reverted to his old ways. She never really had forgiven Frank, so the bricks of unforgiveness formed a wall that kept him from getting too close. Hiding behind a wall of unforgiveness is a lonely experience.

✎ Do you see any of these results of unforgiveness in your life? Review the previous three results of unforgiveness; think about them for a few moments. Describe a time one of these problems affected you.

_____

_____

_____

Refusing to forgive keeps the cycle of hurtful relationships operative.

We have looked at what happens to us when we do not forgive. God loves us and expects us to care about ourselves because we are His creation. When we abuse our bodies and our emotions by not forgiving, we are not living the way God wants us to live. Refusing to forgive also keeps the cycle of hurtful relationships operative. Unforgiveness is the fuel for the cycle.

↪ Stop and pray, asking God to help you forgive others and to help you remember that forgiving others is a part of His plan.

✎ Below write from memory Matthew 7:24. Look on page 70 to check your memory work.

_____

_____

_____

SUMMARY STATEMENTS

- One of the most significant hindrances to our emotional, relational, and spiritual health is our failure to forgive others.
- We inflict punishment on those around us—and on ourselves—by refusing to forgive.
- When we fail to forgive others, our lives and our relationships suffer.

DAY 5

The Reason to Forgive

Whenever you stand praying, forgive, if you have anything against anyone; so that your Father also who is in heaven may forgive you your transgressions.
—Mark 11:25

Sometimes we think that forgiveness resembles a large eraser that wipes our offenses off the books. God never has forgiven like this. For each offense He demands full payment. This is the reason for the cross. Christ paid for our sins in full.

Christians can forgive as God does.

Christians have a special ability to forgive because we can forgive as God does. God has forgiven us fully and completely. We, of all people, know the experience of unconditional forgiveness. As a result, we in turn can forgive those around us. Think of it this way: we will not have to forgive anyone for anything that can compare with what Christ has already forgiven us for.

We can look at others' offenses in a different light when we compare them to our sin of rebellion, which Christ has forgiven completely. Read the verse appearing in the left margin about this kind of forgiveness.

Be kind to one another, tender-hearted, forgiving each other, just as God in Christ has forgiven you.
—Ephesians 4:32

✏ List 10 things for which you are glad God in Christ has forgiven you.

1. _____   6. _____
2. _____   7. _____
3. _____   8. _____
4. _____   9. _____
5. _____   10. _____

How does God's forgiveness prompt you to be willing to forgive those who have wronged you?

_____
_____

↪ Stop and pray, thanking God for forgiving you for the matters you mentioned above and asking Him to help you forgive others.

Your Forgiveness Guide

The following exercise will help you recognize any lack of forgiveness in your life and will help you move toward a lifestyle of forgiving others as God in Christ has forgiven you. It is not a mechanical formula but a living opportunity to exercise a life-changing power. Forgiving is one of the many awesome responsibilities God has given His children.

Forgiving is an awesome responsibility God has given His children.

On a separate sheet of paper write the headings listed below and complete the information requested.

- Offense. Describe in detail an event that caused you pain.
- Date. When did the offense take place?
- Persons to be forgiven. List everyone who participated in the offense.
- Reasons for not forgiving. Review the reasons for not forgiving that you studied in day 4. Which ones apply?

As an act of your will, and with God's help, choose to forgive. Remember the complete forgiveness you have in Christ. At the conclusion of the exercise, use the prayer provided at the end of this lesson (or use your own) as an exercise of faith for each offense. Add to this forgiveness guide when you need to and refer to it frequently. Focus on the forgiveness and not on the offenses.

Prayer of Forgiveness

Dear Lord,
I forgive _____ (name) for _____ (offense) because You have forgiven me freely and have commanded me to forgive others. I have the capacity to forgive this offense because Christ has completely forgiven me. I do not excuse this person's offense in any way, nor do I use any excuse for not forgiving. Thank You, Lord Jesus, for helping me forgive this person. I also confess that I have sinned by using the following excuses for not forgiving: _____ [name them specifically]. Thank You for forgiving me and for giving me victory in this important area of my life. Amen.

Unit Review

✎ Review the five lessons in this unit. Find one statement that helped you better understand the importance of relationships. Circle this statement in your text and rewrite it in your own words.

_____

_____

✎ Review your written work and prayer responses throughout the unit. What exercise was most meaningful to you during this week? Identify the exercise and explain your choice.

_____

_____

✎ Review the memory passage. Find it in your Bible and check your memory. Then close your Bible and write the passage in the left margin. How have you applied this passage during your study of this unit?

_____

_____

UNIT 5

Analyzing Your Family

Case in point

> HAUNTED BY THE PAST
>
> Sheila was only two years old when her mother abandoned her. She literally left Sheila alone in a house to die. Only the concern of neighbors and a lengthy hospital stay saved the little girl from death by malnutrition.
>
> The abandonment became the central shaping experience of Sheila's life. As a child she felt shame because she lived in foster homes. The cruelty of other children only served to make matters worse.
>
> As an adult Sheila continued to torture herself about the event. Even though she refused to talk about her past, she continually relived the circumstances. She thought, *If only I can understand why my mother abandoned me, that will make a difference.*
>
> Sheila's counselor urged her to complete a family-of-origin study. The counselor said that by facing and examining the pain and with Jesus' help, Sheila would be able to find the wisdom and strength she sought. (Your story may not seem as drastic as Sheila's, but in this unit you will learn more about the process that helped Sheila and may help you.)

What you'll learn

This week you will
- describe three misconceptions about and three benefits of family-of-origin work;
- complete an inventory describing your perceptions of and relationship with your father;
- complete an inventory describing your perceptions of and relationship with your mother;
- complete a family-of-origin study of your childhood home;
- analyze and evaluate the work you have done in the previous three lessons.

What you'll study

Family-of-Origin Work	Your Father and You	Your Mother and You	Your Family and You	Observations and Analyses
DAY 1	DAY 2	DAY 3	DAY 4	DAY 5

Memory verse

This week's verse of Scripture to memorize
Call upon Me in the day of trouble; I shall rescue you, and you will honor Me.
—Psalm 50:15

DAY 1

Family-of-Origin Work

Who can say, "I have cleansed my heart, I am pure from my sin"?
—Proverbs 20:9

Probably no part of the Christian recovery process has benefited more people—or generated more controversy—than family-of-origin work. This week you will take steps toward a better understanding of yourself by carefully studying your relationships with your parents or adult caretakers.

What Is Family-of-Origin Work?

Family-of-origin work means *a careful, structured study of childhood perceptions, experiences, and relationships for the purposes of understanding ourselves and dealing appropriately with grief, forgiveness, and needed change.* As you begin this process, you need to understand clearly what family-of-origin work does and does not mean.

✎ In the following three paragraphs circle three misconceptions—things the term does ***not*** mean—about family-of-origin work. Then describe these misconceptions in your own words.

Blaming others for our behavior is not the purpose of family-of-origin work. The purpose is to assign appropriate responsibility so that we can grieve, forgive, and make good choices. The Bible leaves no room for blaming. We are to blame neither others nor ourselves. Romans 7:6 reminds us that the old nature deals with blame but that God forgives our sins so that we may serve from grace and joy. We do not study our past to cast blame.

We should not study our past simply to experience feelings. Feelings are important. God created us so that emotions provide energy and drive for life. But simply feeling emotions will not make the positive change we seek.

We also should not study the past to stay there. Some people live their lives stuck in cycles of blame and reexperienced emotions from the past. They live with the illusion that if only they can figure out the past, this somehow will correct the present. Many people remain stuck in the past because they do not objectively study their families of origin. Because they never objectively examine their feelings and reactions, they remain stuck in blame and past emotions.

✎ Describe in your own words the three misconceptions about a family-of-origin study. You may add other concepts to the three discussed.

_____

_____

_____

We hope your response included these key elements: We do not do family-of-origin work to blame, simply to experience feelings, or to stay stuck in the past.

> Now we have been released from the Law, having died to that by which we were bound, so that we serve in newness of the Spirit and not in oldness of the letter.
> –Romans 7:6

What are the legitimate values of studying our family of origin? The process can be healing in the following ways. Understanding the influences that made us as we are can help us see ourselves objectively. This work can aid in the process of genuinely forgiving others. Finally, it can help us appropriately grieve our losses.

✎ In the next three paragraphs underline each word or phrase that describes a benefit of effective family-of-origin work.

Denial is basic to the human condition. In Matthew 7:3 Jesus spoke about our tendency to see faults in others' lives while we are blind to the truth about ourselves. We experience great difficulty becoming objective about ourselves without falling into one of the twin traps of pride or pity. The basic premise of *Breaking the Cycle* is that sin, in the form of learned behaviors, continues to devastate our families. This devastation will continue until someone becomes brave enough to look within and confront his or her own behaviors.

> Why do you look at the speck in your brother's eye, but do not notice the log that is in your own eye?
> —Matthew 7:3

Since we find objectivity so difficult, by studying our family of origin, we often can see truth about ourselves that we otherwise never would admit. When Charles studied his family of origin, he identified several destructive patterns in the way his parents had related to him. Then he began, for the first time, to see these same patterns at work in his relationships with his children.

Genuine understanding greatly aids authentic forgiveness.

Genuine understanding greatly aids authentic forgiveness. When Karen began to understand how the cycle of hurtful experiences had worked in her family, she began to identify with her mother as a hurting human being. For the first time she was able to see that her mother was a victim, too. The phrase "I hate the sin and love the sinner" became meaningful. She explained: "I have been angry at my mother instead of being angry at the Satan-inspired sickness that has haunted our family for generations. As I have been able to forgive her, I have also begun to forgive myself."

We all need the basic life skill of grieving over our losses. Everyone's life is filled with losses. We lose our youth. We lose relationships. Eventually, we lose our health and our physical lives. If we grieve over our losses appropriately, we grow through each experience. If we deny or stuff the loss inside—like stuffing leaves in a trash bag—we fail to grow and therefore increase our burden. For many people the burden becomes so heavy that they break down trying to carry it. Doing an effective family-of-origin study helps us grieve our losses so that we can leave the burdens behind.

✎ In the margin describe in your own words at least three values of doing a family-of-origin study.

How do you feel as you contemplate doing a serious study of your family of origin?

❏ Hopeful—maybe this could make a real difference in my life.
❏ Like a traitor—I'm not supposed to talk about family secrets.
❏ Scared—what will I find? Can I deal with this?
❏ Excited—I've needed to face this for a long time.
❏ Overwhelmed—it's just too much to face.
❏ Sad—I've given up so much already.
❏ Angry—I don't want to think about it, and I don't want to forgive.
❏ Other: _____

By studying my family of origin, I will gain—

1. _____

2. _____

3. _____

Studying our family of origin helps us see our own behaviors objectively.

Studying our family of origin helps us see our own behaviors objectively. It aids us in practicing genuine forgiveness. And it helps us grieve over and recover from our losses. You may be experiencing any of the feelings listed about the demanding work in this unit. Because doing family-of-origin work can be of such great value, we are devoting this entire first lesson to understanding what it is and what it is not.

Sheila continued to torture herself about events in her childhood. Sheila's mother had abandoned her when Sheila was only two years old. Sheila continually relived the circumstances. She thought, *If only I can understand why my mother abandoned me, that will make a difference.*

Sheila's counselor explained that the purpose of family-of-origin work was for Sheila to understand *her own* responses in life. "What decisions did you make because your mother abandoned you? What practices did you adopt because of your hurt and shame?" her counselor asked.

"What am I still doing in reaction to the past?"

Slowly Sheila began to see a different side of her past. The issue became not "What happened?" but rather "How did what happened shape me?" "What am I still doing in reaction to the past?"

✎ Can you identify one thing you are still doing in reaction to a past hurt that causes you difficulty in your relationships today?

_____

_____

You may have identified something very significant. One man said, "I still refuse to trust women because of what happened in my relationship with my mother." A woman said, "I'm still continually trying to please my dad." Sometimes we cannot determine what really happened, so we must deal with our perceptions of what happened. Gail said, "If I misunderstood what was going on because I saw the events through a child's eyes, that perception shaped my life nonetheless."

➥ Take a prayer break. Talk with the Lord about how you feel toward your family-of-origin study. Ask Him to guide you; to calm any fears; and to give you the insight, wisdom, and strength you need.

✎ Begin to memorize Psalm 50:15 by writing the verse in the margin. You will find the verse on page 90.

SUMMARY STATEMENTS

- We do not do family-of-origin work to blame, simply to experience feelings, or to stay stuck in the past.
- Studying our family of origin can help us see ourselves objectively, aid in the process of genuinely forgiving others, and appropriately grieve our losses.
- By studying our family of origin, we can often see truth about ourselves that we would otherwise never admit.

DAY 2

Your Father and You

When I was a son to my father, Tender and the only son in the sight of my mother, Then he taught me and said to me, . . .
—Proverbs 4:3-4

On Father's Day a caller to a radio talk show described her dad. She said that he was special and that she loved him dearly. Then she made a telltale statement: "My dad used to coach me in softball. No matter what I did, it was never good enough." Our relationships with—and our perceptions of—our fathers have an impact that lasts a lifetime.

Check the Blame at the Door

Remember that family-of-origin study is about us, our perceptions, and our decisions. Many times parents do things with good intentions but with devastating results for the child.

✏ Review the story above about the softball-coach dad. What do you suppose the father intended by his criticism?

_____

What do you suppose the daughter felt, heard, or concluded as a result of the criticism?

_____

Probably, the father intended the criticism purely to make the daughter a better ball player. Unfortunately, such "constructive criticism" frequently hurts very deeply. The daughter may have felt that she never could please her dad and that she somehow was defective as a person. She may have experienced shame, and that shame may still affect her life.

As you complete the exercises in this lesson, remember that blame is not the purpose of these tasks. The purpose is objectivity. We need to see reality clearly to practice healthy, Christ-honoring behavior in the present. These exercises will help you remember what your family relationships were like when you were growing up and will help you determine how they affected you. Attempt to complete the exercises as objectively as possible. Describe your relationship with your father as it was, not as you wish it had been or as you think you should say it was.

✏ Check the boxes beside the words that describe your father.

❏ Passive ❏ Outgoing ❏ Angry ❏ Sad ❏ Manipulative
❏ Strong ❏ Gentle ❏ Harsh ❏ Loving ❏ Other: _____

If you used words like *outgoing, strong, gentle,* and *loving,* you probably feel very close to your dad. If you used words like *passive, angry, sad, manipulative,*

> *The material and activities you are reading may or may not apply to your particular family. If you have experienced the painful family situations described, apply the learning activities to your situation. If you have not experienced the situations, the activities will help you to understand and minister to others.*

To practice healthy, Christ-honoring behavior we need to see reality clearly.

or *harsh*, you probably feel some degree of estrangement, anger, and grief when you think about your father. Some people can use only positive words to describe their fathers, although they feel alienation and pain. They may deeply deny the true nature of the relationship.

✎ Did your father take time to play with you and your brothers and/or sisters? ❑ Yes ❑ No

How do you *feel* about the time or the lack of time spent with your father when you were a child?

_____

_____

Many people do not experience intimacy because they cannot identify or talk about their emotions.

Many people deal with issues only on an intellectual level. They do not experience intimacy because they cannot identify or talk about their emotions. In the previous exercise did you use feeling words, or did you respond with factual and intellectual terms? *Angry, sad, joy, fear,* and *lonely* are feeling words.

Fred's story

Fred refused to recognize or deal with emotions. He frequently said: "You gain nothing by worrying about the past. You must pick up and go on." Fred came from an extremely painful past. His alcoholic father killed his mother. Fred's way of dealing with the pain was to ignore and bury it. When a member of a group began to describe a painful event from his past, Fred said: "You shouldn't worry about that. Forget about the past."

✎ Check the response that you think describes what having Fred for a father would be like.

   ❑ Wonderful. He would be able to identify with my hurts.
   ❑ Dreadful. When I hurt and needed sympathy or encouragement, he would be about as affirming as a jab in the eye with a sharp stick.

Fred's daughter became an addict. She gave the second answer. She said she now realizes that her father was incapable of giving her the support and love she needed. Fred's family is a perfect example of a cycle of hurtful family experiences. Because Fred refused to deal with the pain in his family, he passed on the addiction he hated most—even though he never used alcohol or drugs himself.

✎ Check the words that describe your father.

   ❑ Dictatorial   ❑ Indifferent   ❑ Interested in you
   ❑ Open   ❑ Tender   ❑ Protective

How important was TV to your father when you were growing up?
❑ Addicted to it
❑ Occasional viewer
❑ Seldom/never watched

Did your father have any hobbies that took him away from you and the family? ❑ Yes ❑ No If so, what were they?

_____

Unit 5 95

Did your father demonstrate affection toward your mother? ❑ Yes ❑ No
If so, how? If not, can you identify a reason he did not?

_____

_____

Are you afraid of becoming like your father? ❑ Yes ❑ No Why?

_____

_____

Describe your relationship with your father when you were a child.

_____

_____

_____

Describe your relationship with your father today.

_____

_____

_____

What is your greatest regret when you think of your father?

_____

_____

_____

... casting all your anxiety upon Him, because He cares for you.
—1 Peter 5:7

➦ Thank you for the courage and honesty to answer the questions in today's lesson. Some of them may have been difficult or painful for you. Spend a few minutes praying and reviewing your work in this lesson. Express your feelings to God. Cast your cares on Him.

✎ Write Psalm 50:15 in the margin to help you memorize the verse.

SUMMARY STATEMENTS

- Our relationships with—and our perceptions of—our fathers have an impact that lasts a lifetime.
- Family-of-origin study is about us, our perceptions, and our decisions. Many times parents do things with good intentions but with devastating results to the child.
- We need to see reality clearly so we can practice healthy, Christ-honoring behavior in the present.

DAY 3

Your Mother and You

Charm is deceitful and beauty is vain, But a woman who fears the Lord, she shall be praised.

–Proverbs 31:30

The verse above comes from Proverbs 31, a passage about a virtuous woman. The chapter is an idealized description of a perfect wife and mother. Jill Briscoe wrote a book called *The Proverbs 31 Woman*, in which she stated that this idealized, perfect woman had haunted her. Jill said that no matter how diligently she tried, she could never live up to the Proverbs 31 woman.

We all must come to recognize the gulf between the perfect ideal and reality. None of us are the Proverbs 31 woman, and none of our mothers were, either. As you complete the exercises in this lesson, remember that the purpose is to examine our experiences for our own reactions. We are not seeking to bash our mothers, but we never will be able to live in reality until we see them objectively.

Gina grew up in a family with an angry, domineering, abusive father. She married when she was 15 to get away from home. According to Gina's description, her mother was one of the greatest saints who ever lived. Her mother loved Gina, spent time with her, supported her, and affirmed her. This mother exactly embodied the Proverbs 31 woman. Gina became angry at the suggestion that she should do family-of-origin work about her mother.

✎ From the little information you know about Gina, what questions do you have about her idealistic picture of her mother? In the margin box write one or more questions that you would like to ask Gina about the situation.

I would like to ask—
_____
_____
_____
_____
_____

You may have suggested questions like these: If her mother was perfect, where was she when Gina's father was abusing Gina? If things were so wonderful, why did Gina leave home at 15? If she has nothing to fear, why does Gina become angry about examining her relationship with her mother?

When we are children, our security comes from our parents. We depend on them for our physical and emotional needs. When parents do not meet those needs—and they can never perfectly meet the needs because we all are sinners—we sometimes flee to a fantasy world. We pretend that things are the way we want them to be. Many people become like Gina. They live with illusions about their childhoods.

✎ The Bible teaches us to honor our parents. Which of the following responses best reflects genuine honor for our parents?

❑ To continue the cycle of hurtful experiences by refusing to evaluate my childhood experiences objectively
❑ Never to forgive childhood injuries and offenses because I maintain a false, idealized picture of my parents
❑ To evaluate objectively both the good and the bad in my relationships with my parents so that I can forgive, live in reality, and break the cycle of family dysfunction

Honoring our parents is not an optional commandment. We best honor our

Honor your father and your mother, as the Lord your God has commanded you, that your days may be prolonged, and that it may go well with you on the land which the Lord your God gives you.

–Deuteronomy 5:16

Unit 5   97

Honoring our parents is not an optional commandment.

parents by viewing them as genuine persons, objectively seeing our relationships, forgiving them when necessary, and breaking the cycles that have damaged both them and us. The last answer best reflects such honor.

As you complete the following inventory, try to be objective. Remember that we do not seek to blame but to learn and grow.

✎ Check the boxes beside the words that describe your mother.

❑ Passive ❑ Outgoing ❑ Angry ❑ Sad ❑ Manipulative
❑ Strong ❑ Gentle ❑ Harsh ❑ Loving ❑ Other: _____

Did your mother take time to play with you and your brothers and/or sisters? ❑ Yes ❑ No

How do you *feel* about the time or the lack of time spent with your mother when you were a child?

_____
_____

Patti responded that because her mother had eight children, she did not have time or energy to spend time with Patti. But Patti had evaded the question. The question was not about her mother. The question was how she *felt* about the time and attention she did or did not receive.

✎ Your answer to the previous learning activity was an intellectual response if you explained why your mother could not spend more time with you or if you expressed what you think instead of what you feel. If that was the case, circle the one feeling word from the margin that describes how you *feel* about your mother's spending or not spending time with you when you were a child.

Check the words that describe your mother.
❑ Dictatorial ❑ Indifferent ❑ Interested in you ❑ Open
❑ Tender ❑ Protective

How important was TV to your mother when you were growing up?
❑ Addicted to it
❑ Occasional viewer
❑ Seldom/never watched

Did your mother have any hobbies that took her away from you and the family? ❑ Yes ❑ No If so, what were they?

_____

Did your mother demonstrate affection toward your father?
❑ Yes ❑ No If so, how? If not, can you identify a reason she did not?

_____
_____

Are you afraid of becoming like your mother? ❑ Yes ❑ No Why?

I feel ...

**anger
fear
joy
guilt
loneliness
sadness
shame**
other: _____

Describe your relationship with your mother when you were a child.

Describe your relationship with your mother today.

What is your greatest regret when you think of your mother?

➥ To help you pray, below write two brief lists. In the first, list some things about your mother for which you are grateful. In the second, list some aspects of your relationship with your mother that you regret or that you wish could have been different. Thank God for the things in the first list. Honestly share your feelings with Him about the second list.

✎ Work on memorizing Psalm 50:15.

SUMMARY STATEMENTS

- We all must come to recognize the gulf between the perfect ideal and reality.
- We will never be able to live in reality until we look at our parents objectively.
- Honoring our parents is not an optional commandment.

DAY 4

Your Family and You

Better is open rebuke than love that is concealed.

—Proverbs 27:5

In the two previous lessons you examined your relationships with your father and mother. In this lesson you will turn your attention to your family unit. Attempt to answer the questions and respond to the activities as completely and as objectively as possible. You are doing detective work not to escape responsibility but to understand your development.

A child needs love and affirmation.

The proverb above says that open rebuke is better than concealed love. A child needs love and affirmation. Some of us came from cultures in which people showed very little emotion. Perhaps you have heard the story about the man who loved his wife so much that he almost told her. If you came from a family in which affection was not demonstrated appropriately, you can evaluate how that fact has affected your life.

✎ Check which of the following best describes your parents' marriage.

❏ Excellent ❏ Good ❏ Tolerable ❏ Poor

Would you describe your childhood home life as
❏ Excellent? ❏ Good? ❏ Tolerable? ❏ Poor?

As a child what did you most enjoy doing in a family setting?

_____

_____

Did your father and mother argue
❏ Frequently? ❏ Seldom? ❏ Never?

Would you classify your parents' economic status as
❏ Upper-class? ❏ Middle-class? ❏ Lower-class?

What impact did your parents' economic status have on you?

_____

_____

Are your parents living now?
Mother: ❏ Yes ❏ No   Father: ❏ Yes ❏ No

Are you close to your brothers and sisters?
❏ Yes ❏ No

Explain: _____

_____

Unit 5

Were you teased as a child? ❏ Yes ❏ No

If so, about what?

_____
_____

Who teased you the most? _____
_____

What was your emotional response? _____
_____

Did anyone in your family ever sexually abuse you when you were a child? Did anyone in your family look at you lustfully, tease you, touch you, or involve you in any type of behavior that exposed you to his or her sexuality? ❏ Yes ❏ No

Did anyone else abuse you by exposing you to adult sexual behavior during your childhood? ❏ Yes ❏ No

Distorted feelings

Notice carefully the description of sexual abuse in the question above. Sexual abuse can take many forms. The real issue becomes this: did age-inappropriate sexual behavior distort your feelings about yourself, your thinking about human sexuality, or your decision-making processes? As with other family-of-origin issues, the point here is not to determine what a perpetrator did but rather to identify how this incident affected your life.

✎ If you answered yes to either question above, how has childhood sexual abuse affected you and your relationships with others, including God?

_____
_____

To your knowledge, was either of your parents sexually abused as a child? ❏ Yes ❏ No

If so, how has the damage done to them affected you and your relationships with them and with others, including God?

_____
_____

Jean's story

Jean was sexually abused by several family members. At the first opportunity Jean married to escape the home situation. Her distorted feelings about sexual intimacy poisoned her relationship with her husband. He responded by

Unit 5   101

demanding sexual behavior, which further repulsed Jean, and by seeking extramarital affairs. Jean taught her children that sex is dirty and wrong. Thus, the sexual abuse Jean suffered damaged her children in several ways.

- They received a warped concept of sex and intimacy.
- Their parents were unable to love each other and their children appropriately.
- Their home became a virtual armed camp.

Eventually, Jean's children married. Each child formed another dysfunctional family situation.

✎ Did you ever try to manipulate your parents to get attention or special treatment? ❏ Yes ❏ No

If so, how? _____

_____

Did your parents agree with each other on how to discipline you?
❏ Yes ❏ No

Describe how your parents disciplined you when you were a child.

_____

Did you ever have any serious illness as a child? ❏ Yes ❏ No

If so, how did this affect you and your relationships with your parents and siblings?

_____

_____

Did your parents consistently disapprove of anything about you?
❏ Yes ❏ No If so, what? Why?

_____

_____

How did you feel when you were unable to gain your parents' approval or when they consistently criticized you?

_____

_____

Do you have difficulty remembering certain periods of your life?
❏ Yes ❏ No

If so, can you identify those periods and any significant events that occurred immediately before or after them?

_____

Which parent did you most enjoy being with as a child?
❏ Father   ❏ Mother

Why? _____

_____

Has this exercise prompted any personal feelings about your home life? If so, describe them.

_____

_____

_____

↪ Thank you for your willingness to answer these difficult questions. Understanding your family of origin will help you make the positive life changes necessary to break the cycle of hurtful family experiences. In prayer express to God how you feel about His promise to rescue you and to honor you.

✎ Attempt to write in the margin this unit's Scripture-memory verse.

SUMMARY STATEMENTS

- A child needs love and affirmation.
- If you came from a family in which affection was not demonstrated appropriately, you can evaluate how that fact has affected your life.

DAY 5

Observations and Analyses

If any of you lacks wisdom, let him ask of God, who gives to all men generously and without reproach, and it will be given to him.
—James 1:5

You have done some difficult but important work in this unit. Now the time has come to glean the practical benefits from your family-of-origin work. Imagine that you are a consultant in family relationships. Since you have reviewed the answers you wrote in lessons 2, 3, and 4, we have asked you to give an impartial analysis to your professional colleagues about this family. Write your conclusions. Use separate paper if necessary.

✎ Describe the strengths of this family.

_____

_____

Unit 5   103

What are some of the difficulties of this family?

Describe the relationship between the husband and the wife.

Describe the father's relationship with each child.

Describe the mother's relationship with each child.

How did these parents model God's character?

How did these parents distort God's character?

The Course Map

The course map on the inside back cover provides an overview of *Breaking the Cycle*. You are completing the first major portion of both the course map and of the study. Your study to this point has primarily been to understand the problem. During the rest of this study you will focus on the solution.

Chain margin text (circling the chain): *Distorted concept of God, bitterness, blocked human development, broken relationships, legacy of dysfunction, poor parental modeling, denial, chasing empty solutions, stuffing*

✏️ In the margin we have reproduced the left side of the course map. Notice that the words circling the chain represent the major factors that keep the cycle of family dysfunction in operation. As you consider what you have learned about your family, on the partial course map circle the words that you see have contributed to the cycle in your family.

Unit Review

✏️ Review the five lessons in this unit. Find one statement that helped you better understand the importance of relationships. Circle this statement and rewrite it in your own words.

_____
_____
_____

✏️ Review your written work and prayer responses throughout the unit. What exercise was most meaningful to you during this week? Identify the exercise and explain your choice.

_____
_____
_____

✏️ Review the Scripture-memory passage. Find it in your Bible and check your memory. Then close your Bible and below write the passage.

_____
_____
_____

How have you applied this passage during your study of this unit?

_____
_____
_____

Unit 5   105

UNIT 6

Bonding with God

Case in point

> **TERRY'S DILEMMA**
>
> Terry stated that for years he felt torn apart from the inside. His problem centered on his attempts to pray and to worship God. "No matter what I do, I never feel close to God. In fact, I never feel much of anything," Terry said.
>
> A friend suggested to Terry that he attend a group meeting at their church. When Terry attended for the first time, something amazing happened. People in the group told about feeling guilty for years because they could not pray as they thought they should or because they did not feel accepted by God.
>
> When the leader explained that our feelings for God are often formed by our life experiences—especially our experiences with our parents—the lights came on for Terry. He thought: *That's it! I feel exactly the same about God that I do about my parents. I know I'm supposed to love them, but I can hardly make myself call or visit.*
>
> Terry learned that he could begin to change his old feelings and could begin to bond with God. (Read this unit to learn the practical actions Terry took to build a loving relationship with God.)

What you'll learn

This week you will
- identify a major roadblock to believing and trusting;
- explain the biblical concept of adoption;
- explore the issue of an intimate love relationship with God;
- describe five characteristics of God's children.

What you'll study

God Is a Good Father	Received Through Adoption	Intimacy with God	Our Refuge and Supply	The Object of Our Worship
DAY 1	DAY 2	DAY 3	DAY 4	DAY 5

Memory verse

This week's verse of Scripture to memorize
"I know the plans that I have for you," declares the Lord, "plans for welfare and not for calamity to give you a future and a hope."

–Jeremiah 29:11

DAY 1

God Is a Good Father

He said to them, "When you pray, say, Father...."

–Luke 11:2

Mike, a leader in support-group ministry, says that his purpose is very simple: to help people believe that God is a good Father.

✎ Read Hebrews 11:6, which appears in the margin. The verse says that we cannot please God without faith. It also says that faith has two parts. Faith means believing that God is—that He lives, that He exists. What is the second part?

Believing that God is a _____

> Without faith it is impossible to please Him [God], for he who comes to God must believe that He is, and that He is a rewarder of those who seek Him.
> –Hebrews 11:6

The second part of faith matches Mike's stated purpose. We need to believe that God is a rewarder of those who seek Him. In other words, we need to believe that God is a good Father who wants us around, who loves us, who always has our best interest at heart.

A Major Roadblock

At the point of believing in and trusting God, many of us encounter a major roadblock. Our life experience has taught us to be skeptical rather than to trust. God intends for us to recognize and believe that He is a good Father. But our emotional experience with our earthly parents, authority figures, or the teachings we have received about God may be decidedly negative. We therefore expect God to be the opposite of "a rewarder of those who seek Him." We expect Him to be distant, critical, angry, hurtful, and mean. Most of us never would consciously state that we believe God has any of those characteristics, but those may be our *feelings* about God. Sometimes the language we use betrays our deepest feelings about God.

✎ Have you ever heard or said, "God won't lay more on you than you can bear"? ❏ Yes ❏ No

For some people, the often-repeated statement may reflect a concept of God as a taskmaster or possibly a sadist. They see God as stacking burdens and problems on people but always stopping just short of "the straw that broke the camel's back." What a different picture the Bible paints! Instead of stacking burdens on your back, God promised that your strength will be equal to your days. Someone said it this way: "God is not in the burden-stacking business. He is in the strength-supplying business."

> The bolts of your gates will be iron and bronze, and your strength will equal your days.
> –Deuteronomy 33:25, NIV

> "I know the plans that I have for you," declares the Lord, "plans for welfare and not for calamity to give you a future and a hope."
> –Jeremiah 29:11

Deuteronomy 33:25, in the margin, is part of the blessing Moses left to the children of Israel. Compare Moses' words to the promise God gave in Jeremiah 29:11, which also appears in the margin.

In the New Testament Jesus told us about the Comforter—the Holy Spirit. In John 14:16 Jesus said the Holy Spirit would come to be our Comforter, Counselor, or Helper.

Unit 6 107

> I will pray the Father, and he shall give you another Comforter, that he may abide with you for ever.
> –John 14:16, KJV

✎ Below you will find W. E. Vine's explanation of **Comforter,** the word Jesus used for the Holy Spirit. Circle each word or phrase in the definition that encourages you. Underline each part of the definition that discourages you.

> *Parakletos*, lit., called to one's side, i.e., to one's aid . . . suggests the capability or adaptability for giving aid. It was used in a court of justice to denote a legal assistant, counsel for the defence [sic], an advocate; then, generally, one who pleads another's cause, an intercessor, advocate. . . . In the widest sense, it signifies a succourer, comforter.[1]

You may have circled almost every word of the definition. You probably had great difficulty finding discouraging words to underline.

✎ Describe the difference between the concept of a god who heaps burdens on you and the God the Scriptures depict and that you have been studying.

_____

_____

_____

One person said: "These two descriptions don't sound like the same God at all. One God is loving and just. He wants to strengthen us so that we may honor Him. The other 'God' is distant and aloof. He makes life miserable just to see if we can take it." You may have observed that many of us seem to have two different, almost opposite, concepts of God at work in our lives.

> When tempted, no one should say, "God is tempting me." For God cannot be tempted by evil, nor does he tempt anyone.
> –James 1:13 NIV

The Holy Spirit that Jesus described in the New Testament is the same Creator God of the Old Testament. This same God "cannot be tempted by evil, nor does he tempt anyone." The statement "God won't lay more on you than you can bear" implies that God is the one who "lays" all of your woes on you. James tells us that God gives good and perfect gifts, not torture and burdens.

> Don't be deceived, dear brothers. Every good and perfect gift is from above, coming down from the Father of the heavenly lights, who does not change like shifting shadows.
> –James 1:16-17 NIV

Not Indulgent of Sin

The Bible presents God as both loving and strong. Many people attempt to resolve the conflict between the angry "God" in their minds and the loving God in Scripture by imagining God as a kindly, indulgent grandfather. They conjure up a God who, no matter what we do, pats us on the head and says, "That's OK." Such people need to examine 1 Corinthians 10:13. Incidentally, this verse apparently is the source of the misquotation "God won't put more on you than you can bear."

> No temptation has overtaken you but such as is common to man; and God is faithful, who will not allow you to be tempted beyond what you are able, but with the temptation will provide the way of escape also, that you may be able to endure it.
> –1 Corinthians 10:13

✎ Read 1 Corinthians 10:13, which appears in the margin. Check all of the answers that accurately reflect the teaching of the verse.

❏ 1. Grace means that God overlooks our sin.
❏ 2. God loves us even when we sin, but He has no intention of allowing us to continue our sinful behavior.
❏ 3. God will not allow us to suffer more than we can bear.
❏ 4. God will not allow us to be tempted more than we can bear.

Answer 1 reflects the "God as a kindly grandfather" thinking. Answer 3 mentions suffering, but the Scripture speaks of temptation not suffering. Answers 2 and 4 are both correct. They reflect the intent of the verse. God is vitally concerned that we become free from the chains of sin. He will not allow us to be tempted without supplying a means of escape.

The Nature of the Problem

God's intention for humanity is pictured in the following graphic.

God intended that you have godly, emotionally healthy, loving, and strong parents—parents whose character resembled God's. Those parents would point you to God so that you could come to know Him and then be like Him.

Tragically, sin reverses the process. Instead of our becoming like God, we remake God in our own image. The process looks like this:

If we have parents who are inadequate models of God's character, we remake God in the image of our parents and other authority figures.

He is a double-minded man, unstable in all he does.
—James 1:8

The result of this process is a double-minded person. We have two concepts of God at war within us. One is the living God. The other is the god of our life experience—the god of our own making.

God Wants Us to Know Him as Father

You have studied your family of origin. You have identified the deficiencies in your childhood experiences that have influenced your present perceptions and behaviors. Now what do you do? God wants you to know Him as the ideal Father. He wants you to replace the deficiencies in your experience with accurate perceptions of Him and with loving obedience to Him.

We need to rework our experience and the perceptions and habits that have resulted from our experience.

Some people use the term *reparenting*. A more appropriate term is *rechildhooding*. We need to rework our experience and the perceptions and habits that have resulted from our experience. This time we can allow God to be the good Father we need. The rechildhooding process requires work. We must specifically and intentionally replace false perceptions and wrong behaviors with the truth. We apply God's love and holy character to every area of our lives. Rechildhooding is practical discipleship.

Mike is right. Much of effective living is seeing God as our good Father. In the next lesson you will explore God's attitude toward us as His adopted children.

✎ Begin to memorize Jeremiah 29:11. Copy the verse three times in the margin.

Unit 6   109

> **SUMMARY STATEMENTS**
>
> - God intends for us to recognize and believe that He is a good Father.
> - God desires that we become free from the chains of sin. He will not allow us to be tempted without supplying a means of escape.
> - God wants you to replace the deficiencies in your experience with accurate perceptions of Him and with loving obedience to Him.

DAY 2

Received Through Adoption

You have not received a spirit of slavery leading to fear again, but you have received a spirit of adoption as sons by which we cry out, "Abba! Father!"
–Romans 8:15

In yesterday's lesson you began to identify the need to replace thoughts, feelings, and habits built on an inaccurate concept of God with godly and true beliefs, feelings, and actions. Today you will explore more specifically the nature of God's relationship with and attitude toward His children. That attitude appears in the subject of adoption.

✎ Read the following stories of two adoptions. In the margin box describe the difference between the stories.

Some friends recently adopted a child after trying for years to have a baby. The little boy was only three days old when they took him home from the hospital, and though this couple was given only a few days' notice from the adoption agency, they were thrilled beyond words! Their love for this infant could not have been stronger if he had been of their own flesh and blood.

An illustration that better describes our situation as God's adopted children is the story of a couple in Iowa who has adopted a houseful of children between the ages of 5 and 12. Each of these children was deeply hurt by neglect, abuse, or the sudden loss of both parents. Nobody else wanted these "misfits"—these "problem children"—but the Iowa couple gave them a home and a name. Some of the children were more emotionally stable than were the others, and they responded relatively quickly to the couple's love and care. Most of them, however, did not respond well when they first entered the family because they did not trust their new parents.

Only after months of consistent, patient affirmation and correction, after months of wiping up spills without condemning words, after months of reading to them and playing with them did the message start to sink into these children's hearts and minds one by one. They could trust their new parents. Each child could have a new identity.

You may have noted that the key difference was the children's experience before the adoption. The baby had not learned to distrust or to hide his feelings. The children in the second story had to "unlearn" the dysfunctional teachings from their pasts before they could learn to accept love and to respond accordingly.

> **The difference between the two adoption stories is—**
>
> _____
> _____
> _____
> _____
> _____

110   Unit 6

As Christians, we also have been adopted. The Scriptures teach us that God has adopted us into His family, but our adoption is not quite like the one in the first story. We did not come to God like infants with virtually blank slates. Much of our emotional and behavioral grid was firmly in place when we became Christians. We are like the children in the second story.

How we think about God and about ourselves determines virtually every attitude and action in our lives.

Some of us can respond to our adopted Father fairly easily. Some of us need a little more time to understand His love and care so that we can trust Him, feel close to Him, and obey Him. How we think about God and about ourselves determines virtually every attitude and action in our lives. Until we are convinced that our new Father is loving and strong, we will continue to be bitter and self-reliant or fearful and withdrawn. We desperately need to comprehend the meaning of our new identities as God's adopted children.

But—Aren't We New Creatures?

If any man is in Christ, he is a new creature; the old things passed away; behold, new things have come.
–2 Corinthians 5:17

Many people respond with the Scripture verse in the margin. *Since we are new creatures in Christ*, they reason, *why worry about the past?* The apostle Paul, who wrote the verse in the margin, later wrote the Book of Romans. In Romans 8 he further explained the nature of the new life God gives His children. The following drawing illustrates his teaching.

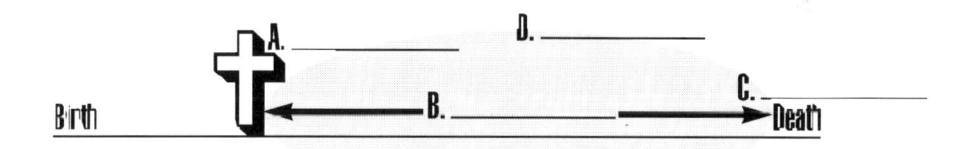

The drawing represents your life. The cross (point A) represents the time when you received Christ as Savior and Lord. The Bible calls that event regeneration (being born again), or justification. Your life from the time you became a Christian until your death or until the second coming of Christ (point B) is called sanctification. The event when you die or when Christ returns (point C) is called glorification. The following may help you remember the three parts of a Christian's experience.

- Justification is deliverance from the *penalty* of sin.
- Sanctification is deliverance from the *power* of sin.
- Glorification is deliverance from the *presence* of sin.

✎ In the appropriate points on the drawing write the words ***justification, sanctification,*** and ***glorification.***

For a Christian, justification is an accomplished fact; sanctification is a daily process; and glorification is our sure and certain future hope. On the drawing the shaded area represents the entire process of justification through glorification. The biblical term *adoption* applies to that entire process. Please write *adoption* beside point D on the illustration.

You have not received a spirit of slavery leading to fear again, but you have received a spirit of adoption as sons by which we cry out, "Abba! Father!"
–Romans 8:15

Today's Scripture verse, Romans 8:15, appears in the margin. Notice that the verse does not say we have received adoption—the whole thing. The verse says we have received the spirit of adoption—the awareness of God's presence as our loving Father.

Unit 6   111

> Not only this, but also we ourselves, having the first fruits of the Spirit, even we ourselves groan within ourselves, waiting eagerly for our adoption as sons, the redemption of the body.
> –Romans 8:23

In the margin read Paul's further explanation in verse 23. The adoption process will continue until we are removed from the presence of sin. Therefore, all believers can say: I have been adopted—justification. I am being adopted—sanctification. I will be adopted—glorification.

Paul clearly stated that "when we are in Christ, we are new creatures." He explained, however, that not all of that newness occurs at the same time. We have been adopted as God's beloved children, but He does not immediately remove us from our difficulties. Those difficulties include the effects of the wrong perceptions and behaviors we have learned from growing up in a world and a family damaged by sin.

Do Only Persons from Dysfunctional Homes Have This Problem?

Sometimes even persons who are deeply loved and thoroughly cared for have poor perceptions of God. The story of the prodigal son in Luke 15 illustrates this dilemma. The younger of two sons asked for his share of an inheritance and, after receiving it, wasted it in an immoral lifestyle. When he found himself destitute, he realized that he could ask his father to let him be a lowly hired hand. Instead, when he went home, his father lovingly forgave him and reinstated him to the full privileges of sonship. End of story? Not quite.

The older son was in the field when he heard the sound of music and dancing. A celebration was taking place. When a servant reported that the festivities honored his wayward younger brother, who had selfishly wasted part of the family fortune and whom his father had forgiven and received back into the family, the older brother was furious!

> Look! For so many years I have been serving you, and I have never neglected a command of yours; and yet you have never given me a kid, that I might be merry with my friends; but when this son of yours came, who has devoured your wealth with harlots, you killed the fattened calf for him.
> –Luke 15:29-30

The father begged him to join the party, but the older brother refused. In the margin read the older brother's response.

Although he had worked hard all his life, he never had been given a party like his repentant brother received. He was bitter and jealous. The father gently responded: "My child, you have always been with me, and all that is mine is yours. But we had to be merry and rejoice, for this brother of yours was dead and has begun to live, and was lost and has been found" (Luke 15:31-32).

The father had been kind and generous to both sons, but the older one never had noticed. His younger brother, who had come home expecting to be a field hand, was experiencing the blessings of a beloved son. In contrast, the older brother, who had been around his loving father all his life, saw himself as only a field hand. His false perception of his father cost him dearly!

✎ Check which of the following you consider to be the best moral to the story of the older brother, or write your own moral to the story.

☐ Having good parents does not guarantee a positive perception of myself or of the relationship with my parents.
☐ What really happened in my childhood is not as important as is my perceptions of events and relationships.
☐ Few things in life are as important as how I see myself.
☐ The way I am is my parents' fault.
☐ Other: _____

When I think of the verse, I feel—

_____
_____
_____
_____
_____

You may have chosen any but the last statement, or you may have written your own.

☞ Spend a few minutes in prayer. You may want to thank God for freely and lovingly adopting you into His family. Praise Him for all He still has in store for you when your adoption becomes complete.

✏ Work on memorizing this unit's Scripture verse, Jeremiah 29:11. In the margin describe how the message of the verse makes you feel about God and His attitude toward you.

SUMMARY STATEMENTS

- We desperately need to comprehend the meaning of our new identities as God's adopted children.
- For a Christian, justification is an accomplished fact; sanctification is a daily process; and glorification is our sure and certain future hope.
- Sometimes even persons who are deeply loved and thoroughly cared for have poor perceptions of God.

DAY 3

Intimacy with God

Let us therefore draw near with confidence to the throne of grace, that we may receive mercy and may find grace to help in time of need.
—Hebrews 4:16

intimate—adj. marked by very close association, contact, or familiarity, marked by a warm friendship developing through long association (Webster's)

✏ Read the definition of the word **intimate**, which appears in the margin. Describe the degree to which you feel that you have an intimate relationship with God—a relationship marked by warm friendship developed through long association.

_____
_____

To what degree do you feel that you have intimate relationships with your parents?

_____
_____

To what degree do you feel that you have intimate relationships with your spouse, family members, or others?

_____
_____

Unit 6　113

Most of us feel dissatisfied with our answers to questions like those above. We have difficulty forming the intimate relationships that make life worthwhile. We may feel especially unfulfilled in our relationships with our parents, spouses, and God.

A Love Relationship with God

We often use the term *child of God*, but what does it mean? What difference does it make? How can a person experience the intimacy and blessing of being God's child?

We probably never will be able to feel intimately related to God until we become convinced of some basic issues. We can believe that He really wants to have a love relationship with us—that He is not merely tolerating our presence as a preoccupied parent might. We need to know that we are secure in His love—that He will not abandon us. We need to know that His acceptance does not depend on our performance—that He will love us no matter what.

✎ The three thermometers pictured in the margin represent how you feel about the three basic issues above. For each issue, draw in the temperature to represent how you feel about the matter. The issues are: 1. He wants me with Him. 2. He will not abandon me. 3. He accepts me as I am—not based on my performance.

✎ In the following two paragraphs look for evidences that God wants a relationship with you, that you are secure in Him, and that He will love you no matter what. Circle the words or phrases that give evidence of those truths. Write in the margin your paraphrase of each word or phrase.

God Himself initiated our adoption as His sons and daughters; therefore, we are secure in our relationship with Him (Galatians 4:4-6). We are the recipients of the spirit of adoption, which overcomes and casts out the fearful spirit of slavery (Romans 8:15). Our status as God's children is made possible entirely by His grace, so that our security is based on His strong love and power, not on our self-righteous efforts and fickle emotions (Titus 3:3-7).

We have more than legal standing with God (as wonderful as that is!). We have intimacy with Him. In the Old Testament God's mighty character produced a sense of fear and dread in people. The New Testament also portrays the awesomeness of God, but it adds the truth that this mighty God is the Father of believers. Instead of shrinking back in terror or dread, we are encouraged to "draw near with confidence to the throne of grace so that we may receive mercy and may find grace to help us in time of need" (Hebrews 4:16). Although God is the majestic, sovereign, omnipotent Creator, we can actually have an intimate relationship with Him. We are assured of this by the inner witness of the Spirit (Romans 8:16) as He communicates His love and His direction to us (Romans 8:14). Paul gives us the overwhelming reason God wants us to experience this intimacy with Him: "the kind intention of His will, to the praise of the glory of His grace, which He freely bestowed on us in the Beloved" (Ephesians 1:5-6). What a statement of the Lord's strong affection toward us!

You may have circled numerous statements in the passage. One person circled

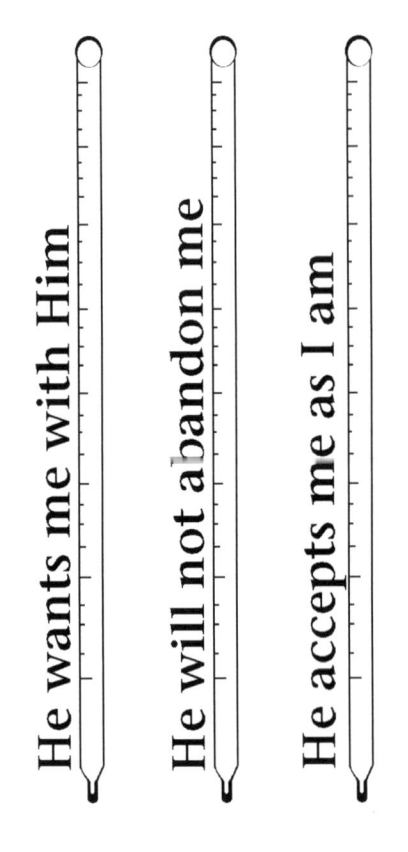

114   *Unit 6*

the words *God initiated our adoption*. She wrote, "Since God cared enough to die for me, it is unlikely that He will throw me out over some trivial matter." Another person circled *we are encouraged to draw near*. He wrote, "The God of the universe would not have wasted His time sending an invitation if He did not mean for me to accept it."

Parents Provide for Children

Part of God's design involves provision for children. God intends for parents to take care of children. Unfortunately, we often see young children taking care of parents. When the Lord adopted us as His children, He pledged Himself to provide for us. Jesus assured us of the Father's generous response to our needs.

✎ Read Matthew 7:7-11, which appears in the margin. Do you feel more like the first part of the passage—that if you ask, God will answer—or do you feel that if you ask for a fish, you may get a snake instead?

_____

> Ask, and it shall be given to you; seek, and you shall find; knock, and it shall be opened to you. For everyone who asks receives, and he who seeks finds, and to him who knocks it shall be opened. Or what man is there among you, when his son shall ask him for a loaf, will give him a stone? Or if he shall ask for a fish, he will not give him a snake, will he? If you then, being evil, know how to give good gifts to your children, how much more shall your Father who is in heaven give what is good to those who ask Him!
> –Matthew 7:7-11

Dan said: "I always heard, 'Be careful what you pray for, because you might get it.' I only recently identified the concept of God that statement implied. I don't believe that the God I have come to know and love is waiting for me to ask for the wrong thing just so He can zap me."

↪ Spend some time in prayer. Tell God how you honestly feel about Matthew 7:7-11. Ask Him to help you learn to trust Him. Ask Him to help you believe what James 1:17 says about Him.

> Every good thing bestowed and every perfect gift is from above, coming down from the Father of lights, with whom there is no variation, or shifting shadow.
> –James 1:17

God has granted to His children the status of being heirs of His promises, purposes, and provisions. Our response to this kind of relationship is fairly predictable. As we begin to understand the fatherhood of God and our identities as His sons and daughters, we respond in affection by calling Him Abba, Father (Romans 8:15; Galatians 4:4-7). This is not an arms-length relationship; rather, it is one of depth, honest expression, and intimacy. We respond to His love by taking steps to purify our motives and actions (2 Corinthians 6:14—7:1; 1 John 3:3). We want to honor the One who is our Father. The intensity of our desire to honor Him enables us to suffer rejection and deprivation for His sake (Romans 8:17) and to love other members of His family even if they are radically different from us (Ephesians 2:11-22).

✎ Describe as many results as you can that occur when we genuinely believe that God wants us, loves us, and will not abandon us.

_____

_____

_____

Your list could have included responding in affection, developing honest expression and intimacy, purifying our motives and actions, desiring to honor Him, suffering rejection, and loving others in spite of differences.

The more we understand our identities as God's sons and daughters, the more

Unit 6   115

The more we understand our identities, the more we will sense the privilege of being His children.

we will sense the tremendous privilege of being His children. We will begin wanting to honor Him. Instead of having a foot-dragging, "have-to" attitude about obeying and serving God, we will begin to develop a "want-to" attitude.

Making the Change

How can we change our sense of identity to reflect what Scripture says is true of us? Our identity changes as our perception of God and of ourselves changes. This change usually requires a blend of three elements: cognitive, volitional, and relational.

✏ The three words ***cognitive, volitional,*** and ***relational*** are important. Write your own personal definitions of the words. You may base them on the definitions in the margin.

Cognitive: _____

_____

Volitional: _____

_____

Relational: _____

_____

cognitive–adj. based on or capable of being reduced to empirical factual knowledge (Webster's)

volition–n. an act of making a choice or decision (Webster's)

relation–n. a narrating, recounting, or telling; the connections between or among persons in business or private affairs (Webster's Unabridged)

Explain in your own words why lasting life change—like the change necessary to break the cycle of hurt—occurs only when we combine the three areas.

_____

_____

_____

Your definitions could have included these words:

- Cognitive: understanding, facts, knowledge
- Volitional: choices, decisions, will
- Relational: sharing with people, mutual support, friends

Explaining why the three areas are necessary for life change was a difficult assignment. The combined wisdom of Scripture and human experience demonstrates that real, lasting change does not happen easily. Simply knowing the facts does not change lives. First Corinthians 8:1 says that knowledge alone makes us arrogant, but loving relationships build us up. In addition, no amount of knowledge, even with all of the loving relationships in the world, will bring change unless we make some decisions. Thus, all three parts of growth are essential.

Knowledge puffs up, but love builds up.
–1 Corinthians 8:1, NIV

✏️ The following paragraph describes how we can experience deep, lasting change. Write a *C* in the margin beside the actions that are cognitive, a *V* beside the volitional actions, and an *R* beside the relational actions.

Some people had parents who did a good job of modeling God's character. Thus, they were able to assume identities as God's loved and accepted children fairly easily. But those of us whose earthly parents neglected, abused, or manipulated us began forming our true identities by contrasting God the Father with our earthly parents instead of equating Him with them. We can change, however, by taking several steps. First, we can say: "Even though my parents neglected me, the Lord never does. He cares for me and provides for me. Even though my parents didn't give me much attention, the Lord is always thinking about me. He knows my every thought, feeling, and need." Studying God's Word gives us basic truths we need for meditation and incorporation into our lives. Second, specific instances each day require that we make choices: *Will I respond like an unloved, cast-off orphan or like a loved and accepted child of Almighty God?* Third, the modeling and affirmation of other members of God's family help us understand and grow in our new identities.

You may have written a *C* beside the statements of facts we can say and beside studying God's Word. You could have written a *V* beside the words about making choices. The *R* goes with the last sentence in the paragraph.

Asking for help

A child's identity grows and develops if these three elements are present. But another element is needed to help a child assume a healthy identity. The child needs parents' active and specific involvement. If the child is struggling with his or her identity and asks the loving parents, "Will you help me?" they must respond with compassion and strong action. If the child is unable to recognize the need and to ask for help, the parent needs to be able to recognize the need and then respond.

Our adopted Father will respond the same way. If we are struggling to understand and apply our new identities as His children, we can ask Him for help. The Holy Spirit is our Helper, and He will give us the wisdom and courage we need to live according to our new identities.

✏️ Below write this week's Scripture-memory verse. Practice repeating the verse until you can say it from memory.

SUMMARY STATEMENTS

- God Himself initiated our adoption as His sons and daughters; therefore, we are secure in our relationship with Him.
- When the Lord adopted us as His children, He pledged Himself to provide for us.
- No amount of knowledge, even with all of the loving relationships in the world, will bring change unless we make some decisions.

DAY 4

Our Refuge and Supply

God is our refuge and strength, A very present help in trouble. Therefore we will not fear, though the earth should change, And though the mountains slip into the heart of the sea; Though its waters roar and foam, Though the mountains quake at its swelling pride.

–Psalm 46:1-3

Our heartfelt response to God grows from a deep awareness of His attitudes and actions on our behalf. In the remaining lessons of this unit we will look at five characteristics we share as God's children.

God Is Our Refuge

Are you fearful? Does an unexplainable dread occupy your thinking, or do you experience a peace that surpasses your normal response to stress?

When we experience difficulties, we quickly look for solutions. Usually, we try to solve our problems by using our own wisdom and strength or by using the resources of another person or organization, but the Lord's abilities far exceed those of the world combined. He may use the resources He has given to us or others to meet our needs; but God Himself is our refuge, the source of all wisdom, strength, and peace. Three classic passages communicate this truth: Psalm 46:1-3; Proverbs 3:5-6; and John 14:27.

✎ Read Psalm 46:1-3 above and the two Scripture passages in the margin. Think of one of the most difficult times of trouble in your life. Describe how it felt or would have felt to run to God and have Him shelter and protect you.

_____

_____

Our dependence on the physical world can mislead us. God, our loving and powerful Father, lives. He is greater than any problem we could encounter. Because He sees the big picture, He will not always protect us in the specific ways we ask. Sometimes He allows us to experience rather than to avoid difficulty, but in any and all circumstances remember that God is our refuge.

John Rippon's great hymn "How Firm a Foundation" expresses the promise that God is our refuge.

> *Fear not, I am with thee; O be not dismayed*
> *For I am thy God, and will still give thee aid;*
> *I'll strengthen thee, help thee, and cause thee to stand,*
> *Upheld by my righteous, omnipotent hand.*
>
> *When thro' fiery trials thy pathway shall lie,*
> *My grace, all-sufficient, shall be thy supply;*
> *The flame shall not hurt thee; I only design*
> *Thy dross to consume and thy gold to refine.*

Trust in the Lord with all your heart, And do not lean on your own understanding. In all your ways acknowledge Him, And He will make your paths straight.

–Proverbs 3:5-6

Peace I leave with you; My peace I give to you: not as the world gives, do I give to you. Let not your heart be troubled, nor let it be fearful.

–John 14:27

↪ The words of the song were written as if God were speaking to you. Although the song is not directly from Scripture, it clearly expresses biblical truth. Take a few minutes to read or sing the words as if God were speaking to you. Then express to Him your feelings about the words—including your hope, joy, doubt, fear, or anger.

God Is Our Source of Supply

Often in our daydreams we wish we had someone who would supply all of our needs. We do! Our Heavenly Father can—and will—supply them. Because we do not understand His character, we may have developed alternative supply lines. We may fail to believe that God will meet our needs.

We have developed alternative supply lines.

Here is a painful test. Think about all the things you own. Who supplied them? If we think of our possessions as being supplied without God's intervention, we reveal a faulty belief system.

✎ For each of the following possessions, write who or what you usually think of as your source of supply.

1. Car: _____
2. House: _____
3. Clothing: _____
4. Food: _____
5. Furniture: _____
6. Personal possessions: _____

One Christian honestly confessed: "When I think about my house and car, I believe they resulted from my job. Actually, when I look around my house, I think of each piece of furniture as being supplied by a source other than God. My parents gave me the living-room furniture for a wedding present. My wife bought me my favorite chair. I bought many other items on an installment plan with my bank's help. In all honesty I don't really think much at all about God's being my Provider."

Serious thinking makes us recognize that we can and must look to our Father as our Provider. In fact, our jobs and possessions are really not ours. Provided by God, they belong to Him at all times.

We Are Precious to God

The very hairs of your head are all numbered.
—Matthew 10:30

Our Father is so concerned about us that He knows when we lose a hair from our heads. He never ceases to love, to nurture, to care for, and to protect us. We are very special to Him!

Coming to Him as to a living stone, rejected by men, but choice and precious in the sight of God, you also, as living stones, are being built up as a spiritual house for a holy priesthood, to offer up spiritual sacrifices acceptable to God through Jesus Christ.
—1 Peter 2:4-5

The apostle Peter wrote to comfort and encourage the Christian Jews who had been scattered because of persecution. In the passage printed in the margin Peter explained that Christ is a living stone, who, though rejected by people, is choice and precious in God's sight. Then Peter identified us with Christ. He said that we too are living stones—choice and precious in God's sight. Peter did not stop there but described the results of understanding this wonderful identity. Those who realize that they are precious to God learn to hate sin the way God does. Their passion in life is to honor the Lord through love, obedience, and service.

✎ The previous paragraph contains an overview, based on 1 Peter 2:4-5, of the complete Christian life. Number from 1 to 5 in the correct order the following parts of that overview.

___ a. We develop the same values that God expresses.
___ b. Christ is the unique, only-begotten Son of God.
___ c. We are identified with Christ through the new birth.
___ e. Humanity rejected Jesus, and He died for our sin.
___ f. Since we are identified with Christ, we are precious to God.

Our status before God is one of great security and significance. In verse 9, appearing in the margin, Peter went on to capsulize our position in Christ and our subsequent response. We have great worth because of our relationship with God. As we are increasingly convinced of our new worth and identity, we will want to honor God more and more. The answers are 1. b, 2. e, 3. c, 4. f, 5. a.

✎ The transformation described above does not occur automatically. List actions in the following areas to describe the steps we need to take to cooperate with God.

Cognitively: _____

_____

Volitionally: _____

_____

Relationally: _____

_____

Your response could have included many actions. Cognitively, we can learn the facts about ourselves, about God, about the gospel message, and about God's attitude toward and plans for us. We can meditate on the great love God demonstrates for us. This study contains much cognitive material to help you grow. Volitionally, we need to choose to commit our lives to God through Jesus Christ. Then we need to make godly choices in all areas of our lives. Relationally, we need to spend time building relationships with God and with His people, the church. If we consistently take these actions, we will grow in our relationship with and obedience to Christ. We will grow in our positive attitude toward ourselves as God's valued children. And we will grow in our relationships with others.

↪ Repeat this week's Scripture-memory verse three times. You may check the verse on page 106.

> You are a chosen race, a royal priesthood, a holy nation, a people for God's own possession, that you may proclaim the excellencies of Him who has called you out of darkness into His marvelous light.
> –1 Peter 2:9

SUMMARY STATEMENTS

- The Lord's abilities far exceed those of the world combined; He is our refuge, the source of all wisdom, strength, and peace.
- Serious thinking makes us recognize that we can and must look to our Father as our Provider.
- God never ceases to love, to nurture, to care for, and to protect us.

DAY 5

The Object of Our Worship

Ascribe to the Lord the glory due his name; worship the Lord in the splendor of his holiness.
—Psalm 29:2, NIV

Yesterday you examined three characteristics we share as believers: God is our refuge; God is our source; and God values us. Today you will consider the facts that as God's children, we worship Him, and He rules over us.

We Worship God

Consider the emotions of young people who have fallen in love. They experience tremendous joy and excitement when the loved one arrives. What about your emotions when you approach the time for your personal Bible study and devotions? Does worship bore you, or do you get excited when you prepare to meet with God?

You met Terry in the unit story on page 106. Terry says he now realizes that his life experience twisted the way he saw God. He worked to apply deeply the truth of Scripture to his life. Cognitively, he meditated on Scripture and completed studies like this one. Volitionally, he began deliberately to choose healthy and Christ-honoring actions. Relationally, he attended a support group and began to apply the principles he learned to all of his relationships.

"I've fallen in love with God."

Terry said an amazing thing has happened in his life. He explained: "I've fallen in love with God. I had no idea God really cared about me. Now I worship Him because I want to. His love motivates me more than all the guilt I once heaped on myself."

✎ Check the responses that reflect how you feel about Terry's story.

❑ 1. Hopeful: If it worked for Terry, maybe hope exists for me.
❑ 2. Confused: What's this stuff all about?
❑ 3. Skeptical: It won't work.
❑ 4. Tired: I don't have the energy to do this kind of work.
❑ 5. Excited: I'm seeing what I've dreamed about.
❑ 6. Relieved: I'm so glad I'm not the only one.
❑ 7. Other: _____

✎ In the paragraph below underline the actions we can take—as acts of our wills—to worship God. Then write in the margin one specific action, from the paragraph or from your own reflection, that you will take this week.

If we really see God as our Father, we will recognize that He is both loving and majestic. He delights in being worshiped! And He is worthy of our praise and obedience. As we get to know Him as He really is, worship becomes our natural response. At the same time, remember that worship is not based just on emotion; it is an act of the will. No matter what our emotions are like (happy or sad, glad or angry, thankful or sullen), we can choose to reflect on God's character. Perhaps thinking about His faithfulness will encourage us when we are depressed. Perhaps as we think about His love, we will realize that we have not acted lovingly toward someone in particular. If that is the case, we can confess our sin to God (and perhaps to that person) and then rejoice in His grace and faithfulness more fully.

Your responses may have included reflecting on God's character, thinking about His faithfulness or His love, confessing a sin to God and perhaps to the person.

God Reigns over Us

Our world mistakenly believes that people can dictate terms to God, determining for ourselves how we will relate to Him. Many of us have fallen into the trap of trying to make God our servant instead of allowing Him to be our Lord. When God does not respond as we want Him to, we often become angry with Him. But God relates to us on the basis of who He truly is, not as we think Him to be.

God relates to us on the basis of who He truly is.

At our conversion God rescues us from eternal condemnation, makes us His children, and gives us a sense of purpose. At that point we are to surrender our lives to Him. We are not to withhold any area of our lives from His right to reign over it. The Holy Spirit later will reveal areas in our lives that we have not placed under the total lordship of Christ. We then are to yield those areas to Him as He makes us aware of them.

If we clearly understand Christ's nature and character, we can yield to Him more easily.

If we clearly understand Christ's nature and character, we can yield to Him more easily. As our Savior, He rescues us from selfish and ultimately empty lifestyles. As our Lord, He is our acknowledged Owner and Master. We are His bond servants. We delight to do the will of the One who loved us enough to rescue us from hell and give us peace and purpose.

The Bible and Obedience

Our final authority

Scripture is our final authority. The Bible is the inspired Word of God. If we believe that the Bible is God's message to us, we will not use it as just an ornament to carry in and out of church services. Reading it will have a daily, vital priority in our lives because we will see our need to draw on its insight, wisdom, strength, and comfort.

If the Lord is to rule over us on a moment-by-moment basis, we must look toward Him and let His Word speak to us. Memorizing verses, "hiding them in our hearts," is an excellent way to remember His lordship over us. In reading the Gospels, note how many times the writers quoted Scriptures from the Old Testament. To do so, they had to know the Scriptures intimately.

Knowing God's Word is no less important for us. We cannot interpret life around us accurately unless we do so in light of the Scriptures. And we cannot know the Scriptures unless we spend time studying them.

God is our loving and powerful Father. The more accurately we perceive His character, the more we will believe that we can count on Him. We will learn to depend on His constancy even when our feelings and circumstances change. For instance, when a child goes through the "terrible twos," dependably loving parents do not react to the child's tantrums in anger and condemnation. The child's anger does not manipulate or control them. Instead, the parents maintain a calm, nurturing environment. The parents serve as containers for the child's anger while helping the child come to grips with the fact that the world is a hostile place where things will not always go his way. In the same way, we can learn that God provides a constant, loving environment for us as we learn to cope with the problems we face. Our emotions will change. Our circumstances may fall apart. But He remains loving and strong on our behalf. He is worthy of our affection, obedience, and service. By studying in the next unit about the names Scripture uses to describe Him, we will explore God's character.

God provides a constant, loving environment for us as we learn to cope with the problems we face.

Unit Review

✎ Review the five lessons in this unit. Find one statement that helped you better understand the importance of relationships. Circle this statement and rewrite it in your own words.

_____
_____
_____

✎ Review your written work and prayer responses throughout the unit. What exercise was most meaningful to you during this week? Identify the exercise and explain your choice.

_____
_____
_____

✎ Review the Scripture-memory passage. Find it in your Bible and check your memory. Then close your Bible and write the passage in the left margin. How have you applied this passage during your study of this unit?

_____
_____
_____

Notes
[1] W.E. Vine, *An Expository Dictionary of New Testament Words*, Vol.1 (Grand Rapids: Fleming H. Revell, Company, 1966), 208.

UNIT 7

Getting to Know God

Case in point

> TRUSTING GOD AS FATHER
>
> Although Sharon worked in a church office, her work was emotionally draining. She always seemed to have too many phone calls, too many deadlines, too many interruptions. She developed severe tension headaches.
>
> Sensing Sharon's unrest, the church pastor became concerned about her. He asked, "Sharon, are you allowing your circumstances to control your life, or are you allowing God to be in control?" She resented the question at first; but as they talked about her past, she began to realize that her relationship with her father was a great part of her difficulty. When she was growing up, her father was a drifter who frequently moved his family from town to town. By the time she entered the 10th grade, Sharon had attended 11 schools. She married when she was 17 to get away from home.
>
> Sharon continued to talk to her pastor during the next several weeks. Finally, she was able to say: "I've been controlled by my life circumstances for as long as I can remember. I've never been able to trust God as Father." (You will read more about Sharon on p. 138.)

What you'll learn

This week you will
- explore the significance of the Bible's use of different names for God and describe the term *Elohim*;
- consider the terms used to describe God as our Lord;
- learn to apply four special terms for God that describe aspects of His character;
- describe how five additional names for God affect your life;
- describe three more aspects of God's character that are portrayed by His names and summarize the study.

What you'll study

The Names of God	The Personal, Covenant Name	Compound Names, Part 1	Compound Names, Part 2	Compound Names, Part 3
DAY 1	DAY 2	DAY 3	DAY 4	DAY 5

Memory verses

This week's verses of Scripture to memorize

Bless the Lord, O my soul; And all that is within me, bless His holy name. Bless the Lord, O my soul, and forget none of His benefits.

–Psalm 103:1-2

DAY 1

The Names of God

O Lord, our Lord, how majestic is Thy name in all the earth, who hast displayed Thy splendor above the heavens!
—Psalm 8:1

In unit 6 you identified what is for many of us a major roadblock to a relationship with God. Our concept of *father* is a product of our life experiences and relationships. Therefore, when we hear that God is our *Father*, we automatically may race to the wrong conclusions. We may need to rework our experience to fit reality more closely.

As a part of that process, we can learn more about God's true nature and character. We can create a mental category for the Lord, based on the truth of Scripture. As we do, we will form a new foundation for our lives—a new source of love, faith, and obedience. By changing our understanding of who He is, we will draw closer to Him.

By changing our understanding of who God is, we will draw closer to Him.

In this unit you will study a distinct way to learn more about God. You will meet Him through the names He has chosen to reveal Himself to us.

What's in a Name?

In ancient times names did more than identify people and their family relationships. They were used to designate a particular characteristic of the person named. An example is the name Jacob, which means *supplanter—one who overthrows another by force or treachery*. He was a crafty, self-seeking person until he met God. After his encounter with the angel of the Lord, his name was changed to Israel, meaning *prince of God* or *one who rules with God*. In Scripture a person's name often reflects the person's character.

Scripture gives many descriptive names for God. Most of them today are translated as *God, Lord,* or *Lord God,* but in the original Hebrew text every name for God revealed something special about His character. Humans have not given Him these names. His names are His own selection—used to reveal Himself in all His fullness. By examining His names, you can better appreciate God and His character.

By examining His names, you can better appreciate God and His character.

Elohim: God

The Hebrew word *Elohim* is the nearest equivalent to our term *God*. The term *Elohim* appears in the English translations as the word *God*. The term is the most general of the Old Testament words for God, but we still can gain insight from the word.

✏ As you read the next two paragraphs, circle the characteristics of God that are part of the word **Elohim.**

The Hebrew word *Elohim* is the plural form of *'eloah,* which is an assumed root of *'el,* a term associated with strength, power, angels, men of might, gods, and God. Both terms, *'el* and *'eloah,* present the idea that God is full of

Unit 7   125

strength and power. The name first appears in Genesis 1:1 and subsequently through the remaining verses of that chapter, which reports God's great power and masterful creativity.

Elohim is a plural term, but it is used most of the time with a singular verb. Hebrew scholars call this the plural of majesty, since by definition it describes divine majesty and power. Both the unity and the unique nature of God are often presented by attaching the definite article (the Hebrew *ha*). The resulting form, *ha'Elohim*, designates the one true God. This is the form used in the example appearing in the margin, Deuteronomy 4:35.

> You were shown these things so that you might know that the Lord is God [*ha'Elohim*—the one true God]; besides him there is no other.
> –Deuteronomy 4:35, NIV

✎ Write the words you would use to explain to another person the meaning of the name ***Elohim***.

_____

_____

How does reflecting on the words *full of strength, power, masterful creativity,* and *divine majesty* make you feel about God?

_____

_____

Some of us thrill to the awareness that God is the God of glory and might. Others of us feel fearful, doubtful, or confused. You even may feel anger because of a time when God chose not to intervene in your life circumstances. We can choose to follow the example of those gathered before the throne of God in Revelation 4. Read their hymn of praise which appears in the margin. Their words are directed to the majestic and powerful One who created the universe.

> Worthy art Thou, our Lord and our God, to receive glory and honor and power; for Thou didst create all things, and because of Thy will they existed, and were created.
> –Revelation 4:11

✎ Take your cue from the praise in Revelation. Write a prayer of praise to God for the attributes related to His name ***Elohim***, the God of might, creativity, and majesty. If praise proves too difficult, simply describe to God how you feel about His creative power.

_____

_____

The First Hint

> God [*Elohim*] said, "Let Us make man in Our image, according to Our likeness."
> –Genesis 1:26

Genesis 1:26 presents the concept of plurality within the Godhead. After using the singular through the chapter, the writer used the plural form of the verb in the verse appearing in the margin. Although we cannot say that the Hebrews who first read this understood the concept of the Trinity—the triune nature of God, this is the first hint to appear in Scripture of the fact that God is the Father, Son, and Holy Spirit. The Trinity is central to the Scripture because Jesus Christ is fully God yet became a human being in order to pay for our sins.

He is the image of the invisible God, the firstborn of all creation.

–Colossians 1:15

In Him all the fulness of Deity dwells in bodily form.

–Colossians 2:9

God never becomes too busy to keep His promises.

The two verses appearing in the margin make an unmistakable connection between *Elohim*—the God of the Hebrews, the one true God—and Jesus. These two verses are Colossians 1:15; 2:9.

✎ What difference does it make in your feelings about God the Father to realize that the "fulness of Deity" dwells bodily in Jesus, which means that Jesus is God truly, genuinely, in every way? Check one.

❏ No difference. I already had emotionally connected Jesus and God.
❏ Wow! I'll have to think about this one. I've always seen Jesus very differently than I've seen God.
❏ I think I could love a God like that.
❏ Other: _____

Some people struggle because of an inaccurate or inadequate concept of God. A well-known entertainer said he believes in a limited God because he could not believe that God would allow suffering. If he understood the meaning of *Elohim*, he would know that God is limited only by His self-imposed limits. Another woman said she could not believe in a God who abused His Son by sending Him to the cross. If she understood the Bible's teaching about *Elohim*, she would know that God did not abuse Jesus. Jesus is God. God took our sins on Himself.

Jesus Christ revealed to us the One who always keeps His covenant with people. He will do what He has sworn to do. His power is constant, never wavering. We can know and depend on God's covenant promises, and we can be sure that He will not change His mind. He has sufficient power to create all things and to sustain them. He never becomes too busy to keep His promises. He is totally dependable.

Perhaps your father often promised to do things for you or with you and then did not follow through. If your father category has been shaped by an undependable parent and if you now find trusting God to be difficult, then this name for God will be important to you. *Elohim* means that by His very nature, God cannot break His covenant promises with us!

✎ Reflect for a few moments on the name **Elohim**. In the margin write some practical ways you can incorporate God's name into your life.

Elohim is a name for God that will enrich your prayer life. It will continually remind you that His power is limitless and that He always, always keeps His promises. Think about this name when you are claiming His promises to you as recorded in His Word. Meditate on the verses that speak of *Elohim*, God of creation and majesty.

✎ Begin learning Psalm 103:1-2, this week's memory verses.

SUMMARY STATEMENTS

- In the original Hebrew text every name for God reveals something special about His character.
- The use of the plural form of God, *Elohim*, is the first hint to appear in Scripture of the fact that God is Father, Son, and Holy Spirit.

DAY 2

The Personal, Covenant Name

Worship the Lord with reverence, And rejoice with trembling.
—Psalm 2:11

God first revealed Himself by His personal, covenant name to Moses. In Exodus 3 God commissioned Moses to free the Israelites from Egyptian bondage. Moses asked, "What will I say when they ask me Your name?"

✎ In the margin verse read God's strange-sounding reply to Moses. What did God say His name was?

_____

> God said to Moses, "I AM WHO I AM"; and He said, "Thus you shall say to the sons of Israel, 'I AM has sent me to you.'"
> —Exodus 3:14

God revealed Himself to Moses as I AM. The Hebrew verb *hayah*, meaning *to be*, formed the basis of God's personal, covenant name.

Yahweh or Jehovah?

People often have been confused by the terms *Yahweh* and *Jehovah*. The terms are different pronunciations of the same word; they refer to the same name of God, the name revealed to Moses and used throughout the Old Testament. Hebrew originally was written with consonants only. No vowels were used. The name for God was written *YHWH*—called the tetragrammaton. The Old Testament Jews considered the name so sacred that they never spoke it audibly. When readers came to it in the text, they vocalized the word *Adonai*, the Hebrew word for Lord or Master. No one is certain how the name *YHWH* was pronounced. The usual vocalization of the name is *Yahweh*. The word first began to be pronounced in English as *Jehovah*. Thus the pronunciation *Jehovah* is more familiar to many people, but *Yahweh* is more accurate. In this study, we will use *Yahweh*. As you study this material, you may use the Jewish term *Adonai*, the English word *Lord*, or you may pronounce the name as either *Yahweh*, or *Jehovah*.

Yahweh is the most sacred name for God to the Old Testament reader. It has practical importance because it means that God is eternal and self-existing. The name *Yahweh* presents the faithfulness of God "to be" whatever He needs to be in relation to His people. It portrays Him as faithful to keep all of the promises He has made. He will continue "to be" what He has always been: *Yahweh*, the God who makes and keeps promises. His Word is a testimony to His faithful character.

The name Yahweh *portrays God as faithful to keep all of the promises He has made.*

✎ ***Self-existing*** may not immediately sound like an exciting concept, but think of this: everything that exists depends for its being on **Yahweh**. He is the one and only—the only object, being, person, creature—that is self-existing. That means nothing, ***nothing*** can shake Him. In the margin draw a picture of an object that is sturdy or reliable. Let the picture remind you of the absolute dependability of **Yahweh**.

128   Unit 7

↪ Take a few moments to pray. Simply tell *Yahweh* what His absolute dependability means to you.

A pastor drew a picture of an anchor to represent the unshakable self-existence of *Yahweh*. You may have drawn any object that reminds you of strength and dependability.

Yahweh is and eternally will always be the self-existing God. Every moment the universe exists, every atom and every subatomic particle depends for its existence on *Yahweh*.

Majestic and Personal

Yahweh also is the personal name for God. While *Elohim* refers to His power, *Yahweh* refers to His intimate relationship with us. God took the initiative with Moses and the Israelites and deliberately intervened in the lives of slaves (Exodus 3:7).

When you feel that God is not really interested in you and your problems, remember the meaning of God's name, *Yahweh!* This name is connected with His mighty acts of setting people free, of redeeming them from slavery. It assures you that God is personally and vitally interested in every single point about you and that He is committed to leading you to a solution for your difficulties. As a Father who cares, He is not bored by your difficulties, even when they are repetitious.

✎ In the paragraph you just read, underline the statement describing the extent of *Yahweh's* concern for you.

> Did the portion you underlined include the words "every single point"? Think of two events. First think about one of the most painful events in your life. Then think about one of the most trivial events you can remember. Below write just enough to remind yourself of those events.
>
> Most painful event: _____
>
> Most trivial event: _____

Yahweh is intimately concerned about you. He loves you. He cares about both of the events you have described. In the margin describe your feelings about His desire to be included in the great and small things of your life.

Jesus and *Yahweh*

Jesus referred to Himself in John 8:58 by saying, " 'I tell you the truth, before Abraham was born, I AM.' " He did not say, "I was" but "I am," which was an obvious reference to God's self-disclosure to Moses at the burning bush. Once again, the Bible reminds us that Christ has fully revealed the Father to us.

By studying passages in which the term *Yahweh* is used, we learn that God existed before anything had been created, that He is holy, that He hates and judges sin, and that He loves and saves sinners. In all cases when the name is used, it focuses on His deeply personal relationship with us.

Margin notes:

The Lord said, I have surely seen the affliction of My people who are in Egypt, and have given heed to their cry because of their taskmasters, for I am aware of their sufferings.
–Exodus 3:7

When I think of God's care for me, I feel—

_____
_____
_____
_____
_____

Adonai: Lord

In Joshua 3:11 God is called Lord (*Adonai*) of all the earth. As with *Elohim*, this word for God is plural and may hint at another reference to the Trinity. It refers to God as One high and above all things, the Ruler of all that exists.

The name *Adonai* often is coupled with *Yahweh* to remind us that although we have an intimate relationship with God, we are not to view Him as a human counterpart. The name *Adonai* emphasizes that God is Lord and Master, one who exercises rule and authority. The emphasis is on a relationship between a master and a servant. Our Master has the right to expect absolute obedience from us. In return, we have the right to expect provision and direction from our benevolent Master.

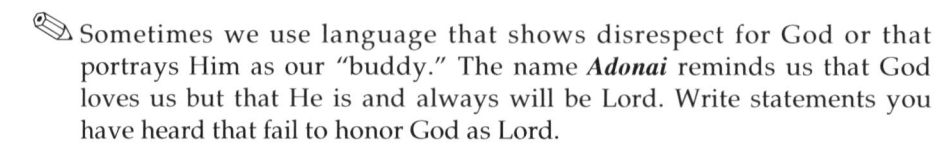

The name Adonai *emphasizes that God is Lord and Master, one who exercises rule and authority.*

✎ Sometimes we use language that shows disrespect for God or that portrays Him as our "buddy." The name **Adonai** reminds us that God loves us but that He is and always will be Lord. Write statements you have heard that fail to honor God as Lord.

_____

_____

You may have written any of a range of common statements that reflect a lack of respect for God. In our opinion one of the worst, at least bordering on blasphemy, is "the man upstairs." Sometimes people make remarks like, "God and I have it all worked out," as if they have domesticated God. The name *Adonai* reminds us that God will not be tamed. He remains Lord.

We have the privilege of representing the God of the universe.

Being a servant to *Adonai* is a fantastic arrangement! We have the privilege of representing the God of the universe. What could bring greater meaning to our activities? In return, He provides all of the resources we need to do His will.

When you see yourself as a servant of *Adonai*, you will be thankful that He will provide for all of your needs. You also will recognize the necessity of being obedient to His guidance, because He knows best and has your welfare in mind. If you sometimes use *Master* or *Lord* in your prayers, remember the One who exercises all rule and authority. Then respond in faith, obedience, and glad service to Him.

✎ In the margin write Psalm 103:1-2, this week's Scripture-memory passage. You may check your work on page 124.

SUMMARY STATEMENTS

- The name *Yahweh* presents the faithfulness of God "to be" whatever He needs to be in relation to His people.
- Every moment the universe exists, every atom and every subatomic particle depends for its existence on *Yahweh*.
- The name *Adonai* emphasizes that God is Lord and Master, one who exercises rule and authority.

DAY 3

Compound Names, Part 1

He who dwells in the shelter of the Most High will abide in the shadow of the Almighty.

–Psalm 91:1

In addition to the three primary names for God, four names combine with the word *El* to describe His character. Today you will study the terms *God Almighty, most high God, the everlasting God,* and *the God who sees.*

El Shaddai: God Almighty

The Scriptures emphasize the Lord's nature as *El Shaddai*, meaning *God Almighty, who is the Giver and Sustainer of life*. While the meaning of the term *Shaddai* is uncertain, it may be associated with the mountains, which were places of worship. These high places suggested God's position as the Lord of the mountains and thus the Ruler of all. Psalm 121:1-2 may reflect this idea:

> I lift up my eyes to the mountains—
> from whence shall my help come?
> My help comes from the Lord,
> who made heaven and earth.

The term El Shaddai *is used in intimate and personal circumstances in the Old Testament.*

The term *El Shaddai* is used in Genesis 17:1; 28:1-4; Psalm 91:1, as well as in other intimate and personal circumstances in the Old Testament. For example, God was called by this name in reference to the birth of Isaac—the miracle child born to a man and a woman too old to expect a baby. The name was used again when circumcision was instituted as a covenant sign between God and Israel. This rite, performed on every Israelite male, symbolized the special covenant relationship between God and His people.

✎ The name **El Shaddai** reminds us of God's tender care. Name three times in your life when you particularly needed to recognize His presence and to draw strength from **El Shaddai**. You may want to describe general and recurring times, like being afraid, or you may want to describe specific times.

1. _____
2. _____
3. _____

Use the name El Shaddai *when you need God's care and provision.*

One friend with a chronic illness depends on the care and nurture of *El Shaddai* every morning when she seeks to get an uncooperative body out of bed. You can use this name when you need God's care and provision.

El Elyon: Most High God

This name reminds us that the Father is the Possessor of heaven and earth. He is the omnipotent, almighty God. This description is found in Genesis 14:18-23; Daniel 5:18; and Psalm 83:18.

Unit 7 131

El Elyon (el-ee-OWN) demonstrates God's supremacy over all pagan deities. The name *Elyon* comes from a root word meaning *to go up* or *to ascend* and, when used with *El*, has the meaning of most high God. When the Scripture emphasizes that God is supreme over all pagan gods, this does not suggest that other gods in the universe exist who are less powerful than *El Elyon*. The pagan notion that He is the highest among a huge community of gods is absurd, because only one God exists. All others are myths or demons. Nevertheless, people in our world today still worship tens of thousands of so-called gods. In reality, the power usually attributed to them is the activity of Satan, who attempts to counterfeit the acts of God.

> Daniel answered and said before the king, "Keep your gifts for yourself, or give your rewards to someone else; however, I will read the inscription to the king and make the interpretation known to him. O king, the Most High God [*El Elyon*] granted sovereignty, grandeur, glory, and majesty to Nebuchadnezzar your father."
> –Daniel 5:17-18

✎ In the Scripture appearing in the margin, the prophet Daniel spoke to Belteshazzar, an ungodly, pagan king. God had written a message of judgment on the wall at one of Belteshazzar's feasts because the king dared to mock God. No one in the kingdom but Daniel could read the words God had written, so the king sent for Daniel. Below describe why you think Daniel answered in the way he did. Why did Daniel tell the king to keep his promised gifts? Why did Daniel use the name **El Elyon** when he spoke of God?

_____

_____

_____

> *When we encounter resistance in following God's will, we can call on* El Elyon.

Daniel apparently wanted Belteshazzar to know in no uncertain terms that his gifts were worthless and his false gods were nothing compared to the most high God. When we encounter resistance in following God's will, either within ourselves or from outside influences, we can call on *El Elyon*.

In Abidjan, the capital of the Ivory Coast in West Africa, the Christians fervently sing: "Jesus is higher! Satan is lower! Jesus is higher! Satan is erased!" Like the Christians in Abidjan, we can trust and triumphantly announce that our God is most high—*El Elyon*.

El Olam: The Everlasting God

Olam (oh-LAM) means *long duration, antiquity, everlasting*. This name directs our attention to God's timelessness, His vast knowledge, and His constancy. The term is used, among other references, in Genesis 21:33; Deuteronomy 33:27; and Psalm 90:1-2.

> Abraham planted a tamarisk tree at Beersheba, and there he called on the name of the Lord, the Everlasting God.
> –Genesis 21:33

In Genesis 21:22-31 the patriarch Abraham had a confrontation with King Abimelech and Phicol, commander of the Philistine forces. When a treaty between them had been completed, Abraham planted a tree as a monument and called on the name of *El Olam*. He knew that these two men were as changeable as the weather and that the treaty would be worthless apart from God's unchanging nature. In verse 34 we are told that Abraham stayed in the land of the Philistines for a long time. *El Olam* was his security!

> Lord, you have been our dwelling place throughout all generations. Before the mountains were born or you brought forth the earth and the world, from everlasting to everlasting you are God [*El Olam*].
> –Psalm 90:1-2, NIV

In Psalm 90 Moses, the author, meditated on God's eternal presence. Referring to *El Olam*, verses 1-2 transcend time and space and cause us to recall that our Heavenly Father is unlimited by conditions that restrict and inhibit us.

Moses again used this word for God in his final address to his people: " 'The eternal God [*El Olam*] is your refuge, and underneath are the everlasting arms' " *(Deuteronomy 33:27, NIV).* Moses must have felt comforted to entrust his beloved Israel to such a God!

✎ Name one situation, person, or need in your life that, like Moses in his final address, you cannot control, fix, or solve.

Could you, like Moses, commit that situation to the hands of *El Olam*, the everlasting God? ❏ Yes, I think I can ❏ No, I do not believe so

You can trust El Olam with situations in which His stability is all you have to depend on.

God's nature, as revealed in the name *El Olam*, will be very important to you when you must trust God and God alone with situations in which His stability is all you have to depend on. One couple found themselves in such a situation when their teenage son ran away from home. For several days they suffered the agony of not knowing if he was alive or dead or if they would ever see him again. As they prayed, they called on *El Olam*, who gave them His peace that surpasses understanding. He will do the same for you. When conditions get stormy, speak His name. *El Olam* ever stands ready to support you.

El Roi: The God Who Sees

This Hebrew name means *the One who sees*. Our God is revealed as One who watches over us, concerning Himself with our needs. He sees that our needs are met. He also knows our every thought, word, and deed.

She gave this name to the Lord who spoke to her; "You are the God who sees me [El Roi]." That is why the well was called Beer Lahai Roi [well of the Living One who sees me].
    –Genesis 16:13-14, NIV

Other passages in Scripture speak of this aspect of God's character, but the name appears only in Genesis 16:13-14. Hagar's condition was miserable. Hagar was the maid-servant of Sarah, the wife of Abram (later known as Abraham). Sarah could bear no children. In a selfish attempt to start a family—and without consulting God—she called on Hagar to become pregnant by Abram. Then, in a fit of jealousy Sarah threw her out of the house while she was carrying the unborn child. Without a destination Hagar found herself alone beside a spring in the desert. Her loneliness and feelings of rejection were intense. God appeared to her in Genesis 16:7-12 and advised her to return to Sarah. He then told her he would increase her descendants through Ishmael. In the margin read the words of Hagar.

God is with you constantly, understanding your circumstances and able to meet your needs.

Does God know your condition? Of course He does! He is *El Roi*. Again we see the common theme in all of these names for God: His awareness of everything about us. If your earthly father failed to mirror this understanding and awareness of your needs, reflect on the truth that God is with you constantly, understanding all of your circumstances and able to meet all of your needs.

✎ Review the four compound names you have studied by matching the names with their meanings.

    ___1. *El Elyon*   a. God Almighty
    ___2. *El Roi*   b. most high God
    ___3. *El Olam*   c. the everlasting God
    ___4. *El Shaddai*   d. the God who sees

The answers are: 1. b, 2. d, 3. c, 4. a.

✎ Seek to repeat from memory Psalm 103:1-2. You may check the verses on page 124. Below list several of the "many benefits" He has provided in your life.

_____

_____

_____

_____

> ### SUMMARY STATEMENTS
>
> - The Scriptures emphasize the Lord's nature as *El Shaddai*, meaning *God Almighty*, who is the Giver and Sustainer of life.
> - When we encounter resistance in following God's will, either within ourselves or from outside influences, we can call on *El Elyon*.
> - God's nature, as revealed in the name *El Olam*, will be very important to you when you must trust God and God alone with situations in which His stability is all you have to depend on.

DAY 4

Compound Names, Part 2

Abraham called that place The Lord Will Provide. And to this day it is said, "On the mountain of the Lord it will be provided."
—Genesis 22:14, NIV

In yesterday's lesson you examined the compound names of God that come from the general name God (*El* or *Elohim*). These marvelous names represent only the beginning of God's revelation about Himself. We now shall consider eight compound names related to the name *Yahweh*.

Yahweh-Jireh: The Lord Will Provide

The name *Jireh* means *to be seen* or *to provide*. The name is connected in Scripture to a decision we all must face. We all must determine what we value most. When we determine that we will value God above all else, He proves to be our Provider. In the margin read Jesus' promise of provision.

Seek first His kingdom and His righteousness; and all these things shall be added to you.
—Matthew 6:33

In Genesis 22:1-19 Abraham's relationship with God and with his son, Isaac, was severely tested. Abraham faced the ultimate question. He had to discover what was more important to him: obedience to God or his most prized possession—his son, Isaac. God gave the unimaginable command. He told Abraham to offer his son as a sacrifice. Obeying God completely, Abraham took his son to the mountain and prepared to obey God. He prepared to do the unthinkable—to sacrifice his son as requested. As they climbed together to the altar site, Isaac asked, "Where is the lamb for the burnt offering?" Abraham responded, "God Himself [*Yahweh-Jireh*] will provide the lamb."

This story is the best imaginable way to illustrate the significance of this name. God never intended for Abraham to kill Isaac. He wanted Abraham to demonstrate that his love for God was greater than was his love for his son. Abraham prepared to follow through with God's demand, but the Lord stopped him. His provision was a ram, a substitute sacrifice for Isaac.

> Jesus felt a love for him, and said to him, "One thing you lack: go and sell all you possess and give it to the poor, and you shall have treasure in heaven; and come, follow me." But at these words his face fell, and he went away grieved, for he was one who owned much property.
> –Mark 10:21-22

✎ The story above contains a truth we all must face. We come to times when we face a crisis of belief. We must choose to obey God—often when obedience seems impossible and the results catastrophic—and depend on Him to be our **Yahweh-Jireh**, our Provider, or to rely on ourselves. The Scripture in the margin contains the story of a rich young man's crisis of belief. He wanted to inherit eternal life, so Jesus told him what he must do. Describe the difference between Abraham's response to his crisis of faith and the young man's response in Mark 10.

_____

_____

_____

Abraham obeyed, and the rich young man disobeyed. That was the initial difference. Think beyond the story. For Abraham God provided blessings for time and eternity. God became his *Yahweh-Jireh*. As far as we know, the young man missed all blessings. He was left with nothing but his money.

✎ Describe a time when you faced a crisis of belief and had to depend on yourself or on God to provide. What was the outcome?

_____

_____

_____

Yahweh-Jireh presented a substitute for us, too. The Lamb of God was Jesus Christ. He came to provide for our sin problem by offering us the only possible solution to our separation from God. If He cared enough to die on the cross to provide for our most fundamental spiritual need, then we may be certain that He will not stop there. He provided a dry path through the Red Sea for Israel. He provided release from a prison cell for Peter. He still provides all we need to walk with Him. In the margin read the words of Paul the apostle.

> He who did not spare His own Son, but delivered Him up for us all—how will He not also, along with Him, graciously give us all things?
> –Romans 8:32, NIV

The Lord is gracious and generous, but do not use this name to manipulate Him for your selfish wants. Those who have tried to manipulate God have been disillusioned by His lack of cooperation. As a perfect Father, He knows what we need, and He knows when we need it. Understanding His will and His purpose will save us a lot of frustration in expecting His provisions to be what we want when we want them.

Yahweh-Nissi: The Lord My Banner

The word *nissi* (knee-SEE) refers to a banner, an emblem, a war flag. This description of God's character refers to an army going to war. Flying as a banner before them is *Yahweh-Nissi*. This wonderful name reminds us that all power is with Him and all strength for battle comes from Him. He will lead us to victory. In Exodus 17:15, after God won the victory over Amalek, Moses built a memorial altar and called it *The Lord is My Banner*.

> Moses built an altar, and named it The Lord is My Banner.
> –Exodus 17:15

Sometimes we too find ourselves seemingly helpless before circumstances. In those cases we can raise our banner high and remember that *Yahweh-Nissi* is our strength and shield for our every battle.

> *Yahweh-Nissi is our strength and shield for our every battle.*

Yahweh-Tsidkenu: The Lord Our Righteousness

Tsidkenu (seed-HAY-noo "h" as <u>h</u>anukkah) means *righteousness*. Added to *Yahweh*, the name reminds us that God is the only truly righteous One. Just as *Yahweh*—I Am—reminds us that only God is self-existing and thus all other existence flows from Him, He is also the only source of righteousness. He Himself is the absolute, impeccable standard. Perfect righteousness is the natural attribute of God; we cannot find it elsewhere. This name is a reminder that the only righteousness we will ever have is His righteousness.

✎ In Jeremiah 23 the Lord spoke of the promised Messiah. Read the passage that appears in the margin. Who is this person referred to as the Branch and the Lord Our Righteousness?

_____

> "The days are coming," declares the Lord, "when I will raise up to David a righteous Branch, a King who will reign wisely and do what is just and right in the land. In his days Judah will be saved and Israel will live in safety. This is the name by which he will be called: The Lord Our Righteousness [*Yahweh-Tsidkenu*]."
> –Jeremiah 23:5-6, NIV

Our right standing before God is not based on how good we are. (If it were, we would be in big trouble!) It is based on the greatest swap in history: the Lord's exchange of His righteousness for our sin. Paul describes this exchange in his second letter to the believers in Corinth: "He [God] made Him [Christ] who knew no sin to be sin on our behalf, that we might become the righteousness of God in Him" (2 Corinthians 5:21). The very core of the biblical message—what the Bible calls the gospel—is this: God has freely given His righteousness to believers, and He has taken their sins on Himself. Thus, when God the Father looks at a believer, He sees not our sin but the righteousness of God the Son. Jesus is the Branch. He is our Righteousness.

✎ Take a few moments to review the two previous names of God. Consider that the Lord of glory is your Banner and your Righteousness. On the blank banner in the margin draw or write something to depict His Righteousness as your Banner. Make a mental note that this standard flies over your life—your *Yahweh-Nissi* and *Yahweh-Tsidkenu*.

Yahweh-Raah: The Lord My Shepherd

The phrase *the Lord is my Shepherd* begins the best-known psalm in the Bible, Psalm 23. The term nowhere appears specifically as a name of God as do the other names, but the concept of the Lord my Shepherd is so prominent in Scripture that it merits a place in this lesson.

136   Unit 7

> Never again will they hunger; never again will they thirst. The sun will not beat upon them, nor any scorching heat. For the Lamb at the center of the throne will be their shepherd; he will lead them to springs of living water. And God will wipe away every tear from their eyes.
> –Revelation 7:16-17, NIV

> The Lord is my shepherd, I shall not be in want. He makes me lie down in green pastures, he leads me beside quiet waters, he restores my soul. He guides me in paths of righteousness for his name's sake. Even though I walk through the valley of the shadow of death, I will fear no evil, for you are with me; your rod and your staff, they comfort me. You prepare a table before me in the presence of my enemies. You anoint my head with oil; my cup overflows. Surely goodness and love will follow me all the days of my life, and I will dwell in the house of the Lord forever.
> –Psalm 23, NIV

> He said, "If you listen carefully to the voice of the Lord your God and do what is right in his eyes, if you pay attention to his commands and keep all his decrees, I will not bring on you any of the diseases I brought on the Egyptians, for I am the Lord [*Yahweh-Rapha*], who heals you."
> –Exodus 15:26, NIV

As our Shepherd, God tends, pastures, leads, feeds, and protects His flock. As His sheep, we depend completely on our Good Shepherd. His compassion for us is so complete that He laid down His life for us, and He will gather us as a flock when He returns to earth. We find examples of this concept in Numbers 27:16-17; Psalm 23; Ezekiel 34:23; Matthew 9:36; and Revelation 7:16-17.

Interestingly, this name for God communicates our status as sheep. Of all God's creatures none has a poorer sense of direction. Sheep are also among the few animals that have no means of protecting themselves. When wolves attack them, they simply panic and run around until they are killed. They must be watched and protected constantly and found when they have strayed.

✎ Revelation 7:16-17 and Psalm 23, two of the many wonderful passages about *Yahweh-Raah*, appear in the margin. As you read them, carefully circle all of the promises God made to those who are His sheep.

Reflect on this name for God the next time you face a decision and do not know what choice to make. Think about it when you are under attack and cannot defend yourself. Remember it when you feel that your life has just fallen off a cliff and you are clinging, helpless and frightened, to the last limb you can reach. He is *Yahweh-Raah* at such times for you.

Yahweh-Rapha: The Lord Who Heals

The Hebrew word *rapha* means *to cure, to heal, to restore*. The Bible describes our Lord as the One who heals the physical, moral, and spiritual illnesses of His children. Although in His sovereignty He does not always choose to heal our physical ailments, He has the power to do so. This lovely name is found in Exodus 15:26, which appears in the margin.

In Matthew 9:12 Jesus spoke of spiritual healing when He said, "It is not the healthy who need a doctor, but the sick" (NIV). Peter reminds us that Jesus "bore our sins in his body on the tree . . . ; by his wounds you have been healed" (1 Peter 2:24, NIV).

Call on God by this name when you need healing. His power can heal shattered marriages and ugly memories of past events. He can restore children who have become rebellious. He can touch physical illnesses and change destructive habits. And He can break the cycle of hurtful family experiences.

↪ Review this week's Scripture-memory verses and the names of God you have studied in this lesson. Spend time thanking God for the benefits His mighty presence provides.

SUMMARY STATEMENTS

- As a perfect Father, God knows what we need, and He knows when we need it.
- When God the Father looks at a believer, He sees not our sin but the righteousness of God the Son. He is our Righteousness.
- His compassion for us is so complete that He laid down His life for us, and He will gather us as a flock when He returns to the earth.
- His power can break the cycle of hurtful family experiences.

DAY 5

Compound Names, Part 3

Gideon built an altar there to the Lord and named it The Lord is Peace.
—Judges 6:24

✎ Review the compound names of God you studied yesterday. Match the following names with their meanings.

    ___ 1. *Yahweh-Jireh*   a. the Lord our Righteousness
    ___ 2. *Yahweh-Nissi*   b. the Lord my Banner
    ___ 3. *Yahweh-Tsidkenu*   c. the Lord my Shepherd
    ___ 4. *Yahweh-Raah*   d. the Lord will heal
    ___ 5. *Yahweh-Rapha*   e. the Lord will provide

The names of God reveal Him as our Provider, our Righteousness, our Banner, our healer, and our Shepherd. The answers are: 1. e, 2. b, 3. a, 4. c, 5. d.

Today you will learn the meanings of three additional names of God.

Yahweh-Shalom: The Lord My Peace

Most of us are familiar with the Hebrew word *shalom*, meaning *peace*. This term describes the end of all strife and conflict, the removal of everything that causes division or destroys harmony. Other concepts that describe its meaning include wholeness, completeness, being well or perfect, harmony of relationships with God, and reconciliation based on a completed transaction. In the New Testament you will find this concept used as the basis for Ephesians 2:14-17 and Colossians 1:20.

> You will keep in perfect peace him whose mind is steadfast because he trusts in you . . . Lord, you establish peace for us; all that we have accomplished you have done for us.
> —Isaiah 26:3, 12

> *We find peace in a Person, not in a condition.*

Do not miss the important fact that we find peace in a Person, not in a condition. Jesus said that He brings a special kind of peace that the world cannot give or take away. He is our Peace.

✎ If you depend on the Lord your Peace, how might that action change your life? Describe at least one area in which you need peace.

_____

_____

Sharon's story

Sharon's story illustrates the difference the peace of *Yahweh-Shalom* can make in a person's life. Although Sharon worked in a church office, her work was emotionally draining. She always seemed to have too many phone calls, too many deadlines, too many interruptions. She developed severe tension headaches.

Sensing Sharon's unrest, the church pastor became concerned about her. He asked, "Sharon, are you allowing your circumstances to control your life, or are you allowing God to be in control?" She resented the question at first; but as they talked about her past, she began to realize that her relationship with her father was a great part of her difficulty. When she was growing up, her father was a drifter who frequently moved his family from town to town. By the time she entered the 10th grade, Sharon had attended 11 schools. She married when she was 17 to get away from home. During the next several weeks Sharon continued to talk to her pastor. Finally, she was able to say, "I have been controlled by my life circumstances for as long as I can remember. I've never been able to trust God as Father."

Like others, Sharon had used her father category, based on her experiences, to define God's character. As *Yahweh-Shalom* slowly became more real to her, she developed a new lifestyle. Even in the midst of phone calls, deadlines, and interruptions, Sharon began to experience God's peace. As time passed, Sharon began to influence all who related to her. The attitudes resulting from her previous circumstances slowly were replaced by a new perspective and understanding of God's character. Her tranquility resulted from her newfound relationship with her Heavenly Father.

Yahweh-Sabaoth: The Lord of Hosts

Sabaoth (sev-ah-OATH), meaning *lord of armies*, is from a root word that means *to wage war* or *to serve*. This is God's fighting name as the Lord of hosts. He is the Leader, the all-conquering Savior, the Guide, and the Guardian of His people. He is the Commander of invisible armies.

> He answered and said to me, "This is the word of the Lord to Zerubbabel saying, 'Not by might nor by power, but by my Spirit,' says the Lord of hosts [*Yahweh-Sabaoth*]."
> –Zechariah 4:6

Jerusalem had been reduced to a pile of rubble, and the temple was totally demolished. The people of Judah lived as prisoners in Babylonia for many years. When Zechariah and Zerubbabel returned to Jerusalem, God told them to rebuild the temple, an overwhelming request! How could these powerless people accomplish so great a task? The answer is recorded in Zechariah 4:6, appearing in the margin. If ever a group of people needed the strength and protection of the Lord of hosts, surely this was the group. By themselves they could do nothing, but with *Yahweh-Sabaoth*'s help they rebuilt the temple, a base that sustained the nation through the next five centuries.

Yahweh-Shammah: The Lord Is Present

Shammah means *is present*. With this beautiful term God pledges to us His presence. Further, the name reminds us that we cannot escape His presence. We find the term in Ezekiel 48:35. Passages such as Matthew 28:19-20 communicate this idea in the New Testament.

> The name of the city from that day shall be, "The Lord is there [*Yahweh-Shammah*]."
> –Ezekiel 48:35

Corrie ten Boom, the author of *The Hiding Place*, had a habit some people found irritating. As she visited with someone, her lips often shaped words that could not be heard. On one occasion a person talking to her stopped in the middle of a sentence and asked: "Miss ten Boom, are you saying something to me? I didn't catch it." She replied: "You must excuse an old woman. I was just talking to our Lord about what we are saying to each other." For her, *Yahweh-Shammah* was a participant in her every conversation. His presence was her joy, His companionship as real as the presence of the people around her.

You too can delight in His constant presence. One man decided to turn off the radio in his car and to use his commute to work each morning to communicate with the Lord. A mother chose to arise each morning one hour before the family to enjoy her morning coffee with *Yahweh-Shammah*.

Generations ago Brother Lawrence wrote a book on this subject—a classic of Christian literature called *Practicing the Presence of God*. You can know that the Lord is never absent from you.

In a very real sense, the name *Yahweh-Shammah* summarizes all of the other names of God. Whether your condition requires Him to provide, protect, defend, comfort, or guide, He is present with you and will be what you need. Meditate on these names of God. You will profit greatly by committing them to memory. Deliberately use them in the place of *Father* or *Lord* when you pray. Find peace, strength, and wisdom in your new knowledge of His character.

He is present with you and will be what you need.

➥ Take a few minutes off for a prayer break. Go for a walk or sit in your favorite spot. Tell God about your feelings. Do you live with an awareness of **Yahweh-Sabaoth**—that He is Lord of Hosts, able to defeat any enemy? Does the reality of **Yahweh-Shammah** make an impact on your loneliness and fear? Ask God to make you more aware of His power, presence, and care.

A Life-Changing Project

To help you remember and meditate on the names of God, make a memory card. Write on one or more three-by-five-inch cards the names of God and the meanings of the names you have studied in this unit. Carry the card with you and refer to it any time you have a moment to memorize and meditate on these names of God.

Elohim—God, emphasizing creation, majesty, and strength
Yahweh—Lord, the covenant, personal, most sacred name of God
Adonai—Lord, emphasizing respect, the Lord our Master
El Shaddai—God Almighty, associated with mountains, Ruler of all, God of might but also God of tender care
El Elyon—God most high, supreme over all pagan deities, Possessor of heaven and earth
El Olam—The everlasting God, the unchanging God
El Roi—The God who sees, the One who watches over me and meets my needs
Yahweh-Jireh—The Lord will provide. I choose obedience in my crisis of belief, and God provides for me.
Yahweh-Nissi—The Lord my Banner, who goes before me
Yahweh-Tsidkenu—The Lord my Righteousness, who grants me His perfect righteousness
Yahweh-Raah—The Lord my Shepherd, who tends, pastures, feeds, and protects me
Yahweh-Rapha—The Lord my Healer, who cures, heals, and restores me
Yahweh-Shalom—The Lord my Peace, who gives me peace
Yahweh-Sabaoth—The Lord of hosts, who fights my battles
Yahweh-Shammah—The Lord is present, who will never leave me or forsake me

---

The Names of God in the English Bible

The English translations of the Bible do not use the names of God that you have been studying this week. The majority of readers would not understand if the translations used these words. Bible translators, however, have given

> This is the account of the heavens and the earth when they were created, in the day that the L*ORD* God made earth and heaven.
>
> –Genesis 2:4

you a key to identify the primary names. You may look in the preface of your particular translation to find that system explained. Generally, all of the translators have used the following plan. The references to *Elohim* in the Old Testament are rendered simply *God*. In the Old Testament the references to *Yahweh* are written with all capital letters like this: L*ORD*. The references to *Adonai* appear as *Lord* with only the first letter capitalized. You can identify many of the compound forms for God, such as L*ORD* *God* in Genesis 2:4. Since books other than the Bible usually do not make the distinctions in type between Lord and L*ORD* when they reproduce a Scripture passage, you have one more reason to use your copy of the Bible itself regularly.

The Names of God in the New Testament

You may have noted that this unit was based almost exclusively on the Old Testament. The names you have been studying are Hebrew names for God. You can relate the New Testament references to God to the Hebrew references, primarily by context.

The basic term for God in the New Testament is the Greek word *Theos*. *Theos* is basically the equivalent to the Hebrew *Elohim*, the generic term meaning *God*. The early Christians also frequently used the term *Kurios*—meaning *Lord*. *Kurios* is the spoken equivalent of *Adonai*, which you recall the Hebrew believers would vocalize for either the term *Adonai* or the term *Yahweh*. Thus, the Greek language does not have the richness of the Hebrew terms used to refer to God. Instead, the New Testament talks about God in ways that obviously reflect the early Christians' Old Testament heritage.

✎ You may end this week's study of the names of God by supplying the appropriate name of God for each of the following New Testament verses that describe Him.

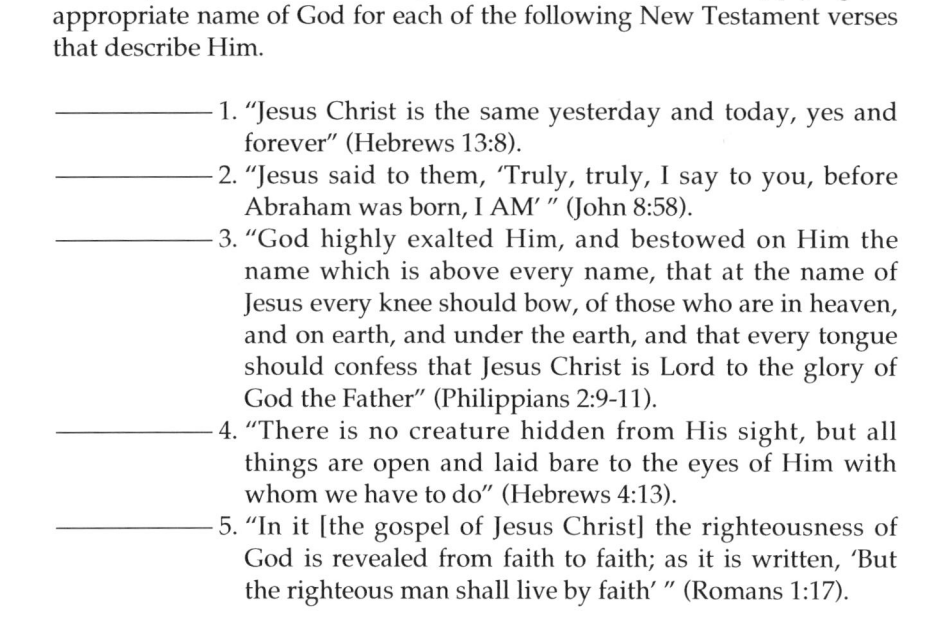

_____ 1. "Jesus Christ is the same yesterday and today, yes and forever" (Hebrews 13:8).

_____ 2. "Jesus said to them, 'Truly, truly, I say to you, before Abraham was born, I AM' " (John 8:58).

_____ 3. "God highly exalted Him, and bestowed on Him the name which is above every name, that at the name of Jesus every knee should bow, of those who are in heaven, and on earth, and under the earth, and that every tongue should confess that Jesus Christ is Lord to the glory of God the Father" (Philippians 2:9-11).

_____ 4. "There is no creature hidden from His sight, but all things are open and laid bare to the eyes of Him with whom we have to do" (Hebrews 4:13).

_____ 5. "In it [the gospel of Jesus Christ] the righteousness of God is revealed from faith to faith; as it is written, 'But the righteous man shall live by faith' " (Romans 1:17).

You may have noticed a bonus truth in the activity. Each New Testament allusion to the name of God also refers to Jesus. The New Testament writers made a very deliberate point that their readers, most of whom were acquainted with the Old Testament, would not fail to understand. In speaking of Jesus, they used the language of the names of God, saying clearly that Jesus Christ is the God of the Old Testament.

Jesus Christ is the God of the Old Testament.

You may have answered as follows: 1. *El Olam,* 2. *Yahweh,* 3. *Adonai,* 4. *El Roi,* 5. *Yahweh-Tsidkenu.*

Unit Review

✎ Review the five lessons in this unit. Find one statement that helped you better understand the importance of relationships. Circle this statement and rewrite it in your own words.

_____

_____

_____

✎ Review your written work and prayer responses throughout the unit. What exercise was most meaningful to you during this week? Identify the exercise and explain your choice.

_____

_____

_____

✎ Review the Scripture-memory passage. Find it in your Bible and check your memory. Then close your Bible and write the passage in the margin. How have you applied this passage during your study of this unit?

_____

_____

_____

UNIT 8

Metamorphosis

Case in point

> ### YEARS OF CONDITIONING
>
> Sam grew up in a home in which his performance was highly scrutinized, but he rarely was affirmed. He always was pressured to do better. His father was too involved with his business to spend time with Sam. His mother was a perfectionist; nothing Sam did was ever quite enough to please her. More than anything Sam wanted to make his parents happy so that he could win their love. But they used this eagerness to manipulate him to do what they wanted him to do. They seldom gave him the reward of their praise and approval.
>
> Sam was a highly successful young man, but he also was driven—driven to perform to earn the approval of others. No matter how well he did, he felt a nagging sense of condemnation.
>
> Sam's parents had withheld their love and affirmation so that he would do what they wanted him to. The need for approval drove him, and he thought his situation was normal. He never understood that the way his parents had been treated him was not God's design for families. After years of conditioning, he thought manipulation was normal. (You will read more about Sam on p. 144.)

What you'll learn

This week you will
- describe the first two actions in a four-part plan to achieve deep, lasting life change;
- describe the third and fourth actions in the four-part plan to achieve life change;
- identify a five-part method for changing incorrect perceptions of God;
- explore five common distortions about God's care for us;
- identify the painful results of four basic false beliefs and a plan for replacing the false beliefs.

What you'll study

How to Achieve Change, Part 1	How to Achieve Change, Part 2	Perceptions at Work	Five Common Distortions	Results of False Beliefs
DAY 1	DAY 2	DAY 3	DAY 4	DAY 5

Memory verses

This week's verses of Scripture to memorize

The angel of the Lord encamps around those who fear Him, And rescues them. O taste and see that the Lord is good; How blessed is the man who takes refuge in him!
–Psalm 34:7-8

143

DAY 1

How to Achieve Change, Part 1

The wisdom of the prudent is to give thought to their ways, but the folly of fools is deception.

–Proverbs 14:8, NIV

We might paraphrase and apply Proverbs 14:8 this way: "Those who are wise carefully evaluate their thoughts, feelings, and behaviors; but foolish people deceive themselves." This unit deals with the practical question "How can I cooperate with God to achieve genuine, lasting change in my life?" Genuine, lasting change does not occur easily. It requires giving thought to our ways, but authentic change is possible.

✎ Imagine that you are the counselor in the following story. As you read the story, underline clues that tell you why Sam is having difficulty.

Sam's story

You met Sam in the unit story. Sam grew up in a home in which his performance was highly scrutinized, but he was rarely affirmed. He was always pressured to do better. His father was too involved with his business to spend time with Sam. His mother was a perfectionist; nothing Sam did was ever quite enough to please her. More than anything Sam wanted to make his parents happy so that he could win their love. But they used this eagerness to manipulate him to do what they wanted him to do. They seldom gave him the reward of their praise and approval.

Sam was a highly successful young man, but he also was driven—driven to perform to earn others' approval. No matter how well he did, he felt a nagging sense of condemnation. He casually visited a few times with a counselor. Through these visits he began to understand more about his family. Then one day he asked his counselor how he could cope with his parents.

The need for approval is compelling!

As they talked, he realized that his parents had manipulated him all his life. They had withheld their love and affirmation so that he would feel compelled to do what they wanted him to. The need for approval is compelling! But this realization was a new revelation to Sam. He never had understood that the way his parents had treated him was not God's design for families. After years of conditioning, he thought manipulation was normal.

✎ Describe what you consider to be the basis of Sam's difficulty. Include what you think Sam needs to do about the problem.

_____

_____

_____

You may have underlined many elements of Sam's story. He was scrutinized but not affirmed. He could not gain the affirmation he needed. His parents manipulated him. Sam's view of God was based on his relationships with his parents. Seeing God as aloof and demanding, Sam tried to win His approval by performing for Him just as he had for his parents; but the results were the same. He felt that he could never do enough for God. In fact, Sam's erroneous perceptions of God led him to believe that God condemned and criticized him. Years of parental modeling having strongly influenced Sam's view of God, Sam needed to change his underlying view of God.

Four Key Actions to Achieve Change

At least four principles are central to deep, lasting change in our perception of God. These principles define and describe a process of change and give us hope for progress when quick fixes do not provide the help we need. In today's and tomorrow's lessons you will study these four principles:

1. Recognize the contrast between God's character and that of your parents.
2. Choose God as your source of security and significance.
3. Dwell on God's love, forgiveness, and power at any and every given moment.
4. Be patient; develop a "siege" mentality.

The course map on the inside back cover is a way to envision the entire process of understanding and *Breaking the Cycle*. The arrow from the course map appears in the margin.

✎ Pretend that you are explaining the course map, and the process of ***Breaking the Cycle***, to a friend. Below write what you would say about the four statements in the center of the arrow.

_____

_____

You could explain to your friend that the four statements describe the four key actions necessary to break the cycle. You might go on to explain the purpose for a discovery or support group. These principles are very difficult to apply by ourselves. Most of us need the encouragement, accountability, insight, and honesty that a friend or a group of friends can give us. Even in the context of affirming relationships, growth is not easy, but it can be an adventure. Let us examine each of these principles.

Action 1: Contrast God's Character

You did some difficult and extensive work in unit 5 to evaluate your relationships with your parents. In unit 7 you studied the names of God to get to know His character. Now you need to contrast God's character with that of your parents. By realizing the stark contrast between the character of the living God and that of the *god* you have constructed in your head—modeled after your parents—you can begin to break the bondage of parental modeling.

✎ A list of descriptive terms appears in the margin. Write the letter **F** beside at least six terms that most remind you of your father or the male parent figure who influenced you most when you were a child.

Write the letter **M** beside at least six terms that most remind you of your mother or the female parent figure who influenced you most when you were a child.

- Contrast God and Parents
- Choose God
- Dwell on God's Love
- Develop a "Siege" Mentality

Gentle
Stern
Loving
Disapproving
Distant
Close, intimate
Kind
Angry
Caring
Demanding
Harsh
Trustworthy
Joyful
Forgiving
Good
Cherishing
Impatient
Unreasonable
Strong
Protective
Passive
Encouraging
Sensitive
Unpredictable

Now circle at least six terms on the list that describe your personal concept of God. Do not answer as you think someone would want you to answer. No correct answers exist. Describe as objectively as possible your perception of God. Your feelings may differ greatly from what you know intellectually to be true. Seek to describe your perception as it was before you began this study.

✎ Compare the words you selected. Write a paragraph describing what you have discovered about each of the following aspects of your concept of God.

How are your feelings about God and your feelings about your father similar?

_____
_____
_____

How are your feelings about God and your feelings about your mother similar?

_____
_____
_____

How do your feelings about God differ from your feelings about your father and mother?

_____
_____
_____

A great similarity exists between your feelings about your parents and your feelings about God.

You may have discovered, as many of us do, either through this activity or earlier, that a great similarity exists between your feelings about your parents and your feelings about God. No parent is perfect; none perfectly communicates the loving and powerful character of God. But some do a good job. Some parents give love unconditionally. They protect and provide for their children. They correct poor behavior with loving discipline.

Some parents, on the other hand, are guilty of neglect, condemnation, manipulation, and other forms of abuse. They effectively destroy their children, who, apart from God's grace and power, will reproduce the same patterns for generations to come.

The vast majority of parents fall between these extremes. We may think that Christian parents always are good models, while unbelievers always are poor models; but that is not the case. Some parents who are unbelievers model God's love, protection, and provision, while some Christian parents do not. Both Christian and non-Christian parents are likely to model some aspects of

Parents are probably doing the best they know how, based on the imperfect modeling they received.

God's character well at some points in their lives and poorly at others. In these cases they give mixed signals; but remember, they are probably doing the best they know how, based on the imperfect modeling they received.

As we begin to recognize the contrast between God's character and that of our parents, we may respond in any number of ways. If the contrast is not too great, we may better understand God's love and rejoice in that new understanding. But if the contrast is great, we may experience an initial stage of anger and resentment. Feelings like these are not wrong and should not be repressed. Identifying and facing your emotions are part of the healing process. In unit 9 you will do more work on dealing with emotions.

Action 2: Choose God

As you deliberately contrast God's character with the concept you acquired from your parents, you can choose God as your source of security and significance. The process of correcting our misperceptions of God involves making some monumental decisions: to recognize the difference between our parents and God, to feel the pain of our losses and enter the process of healing, and to study God's Word and pray.

My father and my mother have forsaken me, But the Lord will take me up.
–Psalm 27:10

Can a woman forget her nursing child, And have no compassion on the son of her womb? Even these may forget, but I will not forget you.
–Isaiah 49:15

Our conceptual metamorphosis also involves a multitude of daily decisions to choose God as our source of security and significance. The shift from getting our sense of self-worth from our parents to getting it from the Lord is difficult but necessary. The Lord is loving and faithful. Read in the margin the words of David and of Isaiah about God's faithfulness.

When a farmer's well runs dry, he digs a new one to meet the needs of his family and farm. When an army runs out of supplies, it does whatever is required to provide for the soldiers' needs. When we realize that no human being can meet our needs for security and significance, we must go to the source of abundant affirmation and purpose: Jesus Christ. We can (we must!) cling to Him. He is worthy of our affection and obedience.

The angel of the Lord encamps around those who fear Him, and rescues them. O taste and see that the Lord is good; How blessed is the man who takes refuge in him!
–Psalm 34:7-8

✏ Begin to work on memorizing Psalm 34:7-8, this week's Scripture-memory verses, which appear in the margin. Write your own paraphrase of the verses.

_____

_____

SUMMARY STATEMENTS

- Genuine, lasting change does not occur easily. It requires giving thought to our ways, but authentic change is possible.
- By realizing the stark contrast between the character of the living God and that of the god you have constructed in your head—modeled after your parents—you can begin to break the bondage of parental modeling.
- When we realize that no human being can meet our needs for security and significance, we must go to the source of abundant affirmation and purpose: Jesus Christ.

DAY 2

How to Achieve Change, Part 2

I will put My law within them, and on their heart I will write it; and I will be their God, and they shall be My people.

–Jeremiah 31:33

Yesterday you examined the first two core steps to change: (1) to contrast God's character with that of your parents and (2) to choose God as your source of security and significance. Today you will consider these actions: (3) dwell on God's love, forgiveness, and power and (4) develop a "siege" mentality.

Action 3: Dwell on God's Love

After you recognize the contrast between God's character and that of your parents, spend time studying God's love, forgiveness, and power portrayed in Scripture. He is the source of our security and significance. Only He loves us perfectly. The famous French philosopher and physicist Blaise Pascal said of Christ's exclusive ability to meet our needs: "There is a God-shaped vacuum in the heart of every human which cannot be filled by any created thing, but by God the Creator, made known through Jesus Christ."

Only God loves us perfectly.

Even if no one else loves you, Christ loves you deeply. Even if no one else accepts you, the Lord accepts you unconditionally. Even if no one else forgives you, Christ's death is the payment and the proof of His complete forgiveness. We need to dwell on these powerful and transforming truths every day.

✎ In unit 6 you considered three elements necessary to create change: the cognitive, volitional, and relational areas. In the margin write as many specific actions as you can to change in these areas. Try to include at least one action in each area.

"A chapter a day keeps the devil away" may be a cute saying for Vacation Bible School, but to transform our minds and to change our perspective of God requires concerted effort, study, and focused prayer. The modeling of a lifetime does not change easily. We would do well to plan regular times to study, think, pray, and memorize God's Word so that His truth can fill our minds and change our hearts (cognitive actions). We can consciously choose to apply the cognitive facts we learn to specific situations (volitional actions). We can enlist the aid of others and share with others to reinforce the change in our lives (relational actions).

Choose to give thanks for God's love, purpose, and power.

A commitment to radical thankfulness helps us make these daily choices. When someone's disapproval threatens to crush you, when you fail in an important task, when you do not feel that you look your best, when you are feeling introspective and depressed, or when you are angry, be honest about how you feel and choose to give thanks for God's love, purpose, and power.

Notice that I did not say that you need to *feel* thankful. You cannot control your feelings, but you can choose—as an act of your will—to dwell on God's character. You can thank Him for His compassion and His direction for your life, knowing that He can use any situation for good.

➥ As an act of radical thankfulness, stop and pray. Think of the three areas of your life that give you the greatest difficulty. Thank God for His love, purpose, and power in the midst of your most trying struggles.

Radical thankfulness rivets our attention on the Lord, not on the fickle approval of others or on the often distressing circumstances of life. Having the encouragement of a support group is often helpful as you learn to make these choices. Most people learn best with a combination of cognitive teaching and relational reinforcement. If you are not already participating in a group, you may want to find a friend or a small group to study this workbook with you. A group can aid you greatly in the process of change.

Action 4: Develop a "Siege" Mentality

Deep change takes time.

Be patient; develop a "siege" mentality. Quick fixes sound great, but they seldom work. For most of us, deep change takes time. Avoid looking for an instant way to transform your misperceptions of God. Developing these distorted concepts took time; changing them also will take time. Change is a process.

When a Roman army attacked a fortified city, the commander did not shoot a few arrows and expect the city to fall. The army spent months and sometimes years in siege warfare. It was slow and tedious, but it was usually successful. Our warfare against our inaccurate perceptions of God is like siege warfare. It is slow and tedious, but if we persevere, we have great hope for success. In the margin read what Paul wrote about warfare to the believers in Corinth.

> Though we walk in the flesh, we do not war according to the flesh, for the weapons of our warfare are not of the flesh, but divinely powerful for the destruction of fortresses. We are destroying speculations and every lofty thing raised up against the knowledge of God, and we are taking every thought captive to the obedience of Christ.
> –2 Corinthians 10:3-5

✎ Against what kinds of fortresses do the verses say we need to wage siege warfare?

_____

_____

You may have noted that we need to war against thoughts, speculations, and things raised up against the knowledge of God. Our misconceptions about God are speculations. Our wrong perceptions are lofty things raised up against the knowledge of God. These fortresses require a siege mentality, patience, and endurance. In the end the walls will fall, and the captives will be released.

✎ As a reminder to yourself that you often can change lifelong habits only through a deliberate effort of siege warfare, practice something distinctly childlike. In the margin draw a picture of a fort or a castle. Draw a moat and a drawbridge or high, difficult-to-scale walls. Throw in a few moat-monsters if you like. Then draw an attacking army. Do not worry about the quality of the artwork. This bit of play will imprint the concepts in your mind. Finally, label your artwork with a name like "The Siege of Fortress Headbackward."

You may gain a flash of insight and experience a surge of freshness at the beginning of your metamorphosis, but do not be discouraged if you do not experience deep emotional healing and transformation overnight. Realize that changing fundamental perceptions about God and ourselves takes time.

Realize that the Word of God and the power of His Spirit are a powerful combination. The process may be slow and painful, but it is worth it.

As you work through the principles outlined in this lesson and in the previous lesson, remember to be kind to your parents. No, they were not perfect; and yes, they may have harmed you terribly. But they probably did the best they knew how to do. Even if they did not, you can extend God's love and forgiveness to them as you learn to experience it yourself. These two lessons have explained the process of change. The next one identifies what we need for effective change to occur.

✎ Write this week's Scripture-memory verses in the margin. Spend a few minutes memorizing the passage.

SUMMARY STATEMENTS

- To transform our minds and to change our perspective of God requires concerted effort, study, and focused prayer.
- Radical thankfulness rivets our attention on the Lord, not on the fickle approval of others or on the often distressing circumstances of life.
- Our warfare against our inaccurate perceptions of God is slow and tedious; but if we persevere, we have great hope for success.

DAY 3

Perceptions at Work

Do not conform any longer to the pattern of this world, but be transformed by the renewing of your mind. Then you will be able to test and approve what God's will is—his good, pleasing and perfect will.
—Romans 12:2, NIV

By now you probably have recognized how significantly your parents shaped your perception of God. You may have enjoyed reliving pleasant memories associated with a loving and protective family, or you may have discovered that your memories are quite painful. Hopefully you have realized that no one's parents are perfect; all fall short of God's grace. For that reason this lesson deals with the question, How can our perception of God more exactly represent who He truly is?

The Lord has reserved many blessings for us. We increasingly will recognize and experience these blessings as we gain a more accurate understanding of who He is. In the verse above Paul tells us that God intends for us to experience the transformation of our thinking processes. To change our relationship with God, we must replace our wrong perceptions with truth because the way we think usually affects the way we feel, and the way we feel often determines the way we act. Therefore, we must reject any lies that Satan has planted in our minds about God's nature and character.

We must reject any lies that Satan has planted in our minds about God's nature and character.

The following examples illustrate a five-part method that may help you understand the process for changing incorrect perceptions of God to true and accurate perceptions.

Example #1

The Way You May Have Perceived God

Situation: Your relationships with your parents
Category: Your beliefs about your parents
Thoughts: *God is like my parents; therefore, I will relate to Him in the same way I relate to my parents.*
Emotions: Depending on your relationship with your parents, emotions about God may be love or fear, dependence or distrust, affection or anger.
Actions: Depending on your relationship with your parents, either obedience, trust, and service or anger, rebellion, and withdrawal

Compare the previous example with the following accurate perception of God.

Example #2

An Accurate Perception of God

Situation: Truths and biblical accounts about God and His activities
Category: Beliefs about God
Thoughts: *God is loving, kind and powerful. I can relate to Him, knowing that He is glad I am His child.*
Emotions: Comfort, thankfulness, joy, security, significance, contrition, humility, freedom, zeal, and so on
Actions: Obedience, trust, seeking His will, service, loving others, evangelism, discipleship, and so on

Our distorted relationship with God comes from our false beliefs.

Our distorted relationship with God comes from our false beliefs. The poor relationship then affects our actions. For example, consider the following case study.

Example #3

Results of a False Belief

Situation: My employer has dismissed me.
False belief: God punishes people by making bad things happen to them.
Thoughts: *God has decided I need to be punished. No one can please or understand Him. He's just like my father. I could never please him either! I've got to have someone hold me and tell me I'm loved* or *I've got to prove myself in my next job* or *I need to escape this pain.*
Emotions: Fear associated with loss of income, anger and shame resulting from loss of job
Actions: Told no one, including my wife; cleaned out my desk; went to favorite bar and got drunk

Our beliefs are embedded in our thoughts and control our emotions.

Do you see how our beliefs are embedded in our thoughts and how they control our emotions? In turn, our emotions direct us to act in certain ways. If Satan has convinced us to believe his lies about God, we are imprisoned by them, acting as though they were true.

✎ In example #3, what false belief lies at the core of the man's response?

_____

_____

Unit 8   151

Why do we so easily believe lies about God? Why can we not recognize them for what they are? The reason may be that our beliefs combine both truth and deception; and until we see the contrast between them, we cannot separate the two. In the case study it is true that the man was fired, but to believe that God's cruelty caused the employer's decision is a wrong perception. Therefore, the man was believing both truth and deception at the same time.

Most of our painful emotions are actually signals that help us uncover deceptions in our belief system.

Most of our painful emotions actually are signals that help us uncover deceptions in our belief system. Fear, anger, depression, and stress are some results of believing Satan's lies. When we begin to feel these emotions, we must learn to ask ourselves, *What lie am I believing in this situation?*

Search for Significance LIFE® Support Group Series Edition explains that we can almost always trace painful emotions back to one of four false beliefs. These deceptions distort our perceptions of God's intimate love, forgiveness, and power, keeping us in a constant state of insecurity and turmoil. The following chart not only contains the four foundational lies (or false beliefs) but also gives the contrast to the lies: God's specific scriptural solutions to replace the false beliefs.[1]

propitiation–n. describes what happened when Christ, through His death, became the means by which God's wrath was satisfied and God's mercy was granted to the sinner who believes on Christ (Vine's)

	False Beliefs	**God's Truths**
THE PERFORMANCE TRAP	I must meet certain standards to feel good about myself.	Because of *justification* I am completely forgiven by and fully pleasing to God. I no longer have to fear failure.
APPROVAL ADDICT	I must have the approval of certain others to feel good about myself.	Because of *reconciliation* I am totally accepted by God. I no longer have to fear rejection.
THE BLAME GAME	Those who fail (including myself) are unworthy of love and deserve to be punished.	Because of *propitiation* I am deeply loved by God. I no longer have to fear punishment or punish others.
SHAME	I am what I am. I cannot change. I am hopeless.	Because of *regeneration* I have been made brand-new, complete in Christ. I no longer need to experience the pain of shame.

✎ Which of the false beliefs was most affecting the man who lost his job?

_____

Satan encourages us to question God's intentions for our lives.

False beliefs are not benign. They result in depression, fear, anger, or hopelessness. The man in the case study based his response on false belief 3: he believed that God was blaming and punishing him. As a corollary to presenting us with false beliefs, Satan also encourages us to question God's intentions for our lives. In the next lesson you will explore some of his distortions of God's desires for us.

✎ In the margin attempt to write this week's Scripture passage from memory. Then check your work on page 143.

SUMMARY STATEMENTS

- We will increasingly recognize and experience God's blessings as we gain a more accurate understanding of who He is.
- Our distorted relationship with God comes from our false beliefs.
- Satan's deceptions distort our perceptions of God's intimate love, forgiveness, and power, keeping us in a constant state of insecurity.

DAY 4

Five Common Distortions

When tempted, no one should say, "God is tempting me." For God cannot be tempted by evil, nor does he tempt anyone.
—James 1:13

Satan wants us to doubt the core truth you studied in unit 6, that God is a good Father. In this lesson you will examine five key distortions that Satan seeks to plant in our minds.

Distortion 1: Evil Comes from God

We hear that a child has been brutally murdered, and we ask, *God, why did You let this happen?* Does God care that this tragedy happened? Yes! But God did not cause the murder. Someone who was out of control caused it. In a fallen world many tragic and evil things happen. The nature of sin is that it always produces heartache and pain. God does not snatch people from the fallen world the moment they become Christians. He leaves us here in the midst of pain and suffering to be salt and light to the rest of the fallen race.

Does God know about such suffering? Does He care? We need only think of Jesus on the mount overlooking Jerusalem, weeping over the result of evil in that city. Or we may watch Him weeping at the tomb of His dear friend Lazarus. Our God is compassionate. His heart breaks when sin smashes lives.

How deceitful Satan is! First Peter 5:8 tells us that he goes about like a roaring lion, seeking someone to devour. At the very moment he infests people with murderous intent, he tries to make us think God is the cause! Satan wants us to blame God when we hear about a tragic accident or a serious illness. What does Scripture say about blaming God? Read the passage from James that appears in the margin.

✎ What would you say to a friend who has experienced a tragedy and who thinks that the evil has come from God?

_____

_____

Margin:

When tempted, no one should say, "God is tempting me." For God cannot be tempted by evil, nor does he tempt anyone; but each one is tempted when, by his own evil desire, he is dragged away and enticed. Then, after desire has conceived, it gives birth to sin; and sin, when it is full-grown, gives birth to death. Don't be deceived, my dear brothers. Every good and perfect gift is from above, coming down from the Father of the heavenly lights, who does not change like shifting shadows. He chose to give us birth through the word of truth, that we might be a kind of first fruits of all he created.
—James 1:13-18, NIV

God may test us to strengthen our faith; but He never tempts us, because the goal of temptation is to cause a person to sin. Your response may have included that God never is the source of evil. God gives good and perfect gifts. Those gifts include the strength and wisdom to endure difficulties and the promise that He will bring good in our lives as a result of the difficulties.

What will we believe, Satan's lie or the Bible's clear explanation? If we believe that God is responsible for evil, we distort the truth. Who could trust a God like that? The Scriptures teach us that God is sovereign. That does not mean He always intervenes in negative circumstances. It means that He has a purpose and that He will fulfill that purpose, despite the evil of our fallen world.

God does not always intervene; but He has a purpose and will fulfill it, despite the evil of our fallen world.

Distortion 2: God Does Not Care About Me

God rarely is praised for anything and often blamed for everything. We make prayerless choices, sometimes knowing they are not what He wants for us. Yet, when things turn out bad, we wonder, *God, if you really love me, why didn't You prevent my doing that?*

✎ At what time or times do you find yourself thinking that God does not care about you?

_____

_____

_____

You may have described a single time or a pattern of recurring times when this distortion affects your thinking. Perhaps a passive, absent, or insensitive parent modeled to you the idea that parents do not really care about their children and that children just need to do the best they can on their own. But our Heavenly Father is not like that! The Scriptures teach that He is loving, compassionate, and protective of His children.

God is loving, compassionate, and protective of His children.

The obvious solution is to recognize that God does not force us to follow Him. He has built natural consequences into the spiritual realm, even as He has built physical laws into the universe. With open arms He reaches out to us. He offers us full access to His wisdom and power if we will follow Him. At the same time, He is not a vending machine to supply all of our whims and wants. As a Father, He knows when it is best to say no to His children and when we need to wait. Regardless of His response, we can be assured that we will always receive His best when we leave those choices up to Him!

Distortion 3: My Trials Do Not Benefit Me

God causes all things to work together for good to those who love God, to those who are called according to His purpose.
–Romans 8:28

Romans 8:28 is familiar to many of us. We often misunderstand this promise to say that we will be perfectly happy with the outcome of our difficulties, but it does not say that. The verse talks about God's purpose, not ours. Often, our purposes are self-serving. God's design is to wean us from our self-centeredness to a life of devotion and service to Him. Our trials may not benefit us in the way we want but in the way He wants.

✎ As an exercise in faith, think of a major struggle or trial you have experienced. Briefly describe that trial. Then list some benefits that have resulted from the difficulty.

___

___

___

___

___

God can take the painful events of your life and make them work together to bring good.

Joni Erickson is a marvelous example of Romans 8:28 in action. As a teenager Joni broke her neck in a diving accident and since then has been a quadriplegic—confined to a wheelchair and without the use of her arms or legs. She says that the accident caused her to turn to Jesus Christ and that the accident, as terrible as it is, has benefited her more than any other element in her life. Your example probably was not as dramatic as Joni's, but you may be able to identify ways God has taken the painful events of your life and made them work together to bring good.

Distortion 4: God Will Not Meet Our Needs

"My thoughts are not your thoughts, Neither are your ways My ways," declares the Lord. "For as the heavens are higher than the earth, So are My ways higher than your ways, And My thoughts than your thoughts."
–Isaiah 55:8-9

Satan whispers in our ear, "No wonder God has so few friends; He treats the ones He has so shabbily." With His complete knowledge of the present and the future, the Lord often acts in ways we do not understand. Because our knowledge is limited, we often question God's care and provision. The Lord is powerful and compassionate. He can meet our needs, but sometimes His perception of our needs is different from ours. He may know that we need courage, wisdom, and faith more than we do money, praise, and health. He will provide what we need when we need it.

✎ In the margin describe a time when God met a need that you thought He would not care about.

☞ If you were able to write something in the margin, stop and pray. Thank Him for graciously meeting your needs. Make a note to yourself to remember His provision and to rejoice in His grace. If you had difficulty identifying a time when God met your need, stop and pray. Honestly tell God how you feel about the situation. Ask Him for the ability to see Him at work in your life.

Distortion 5: God Should Have Made Me More Attractive

We ask, *How can I trust God after He created me with this body and face?* The advertising industry wants us to believe that our appearance must be perfect if we are to experience true happiness and fulfillment. But comparison does not breed contentment, only pain and emptiness. When we compare our appearance to someone else's, we forget that our worth is based not on how we look but on God's love, forgiveness, and acceptance. We need to accept who we are as a gift from the Lord and let Him show us how our appearance

> We do not dare to classify or compare ourselves with some who commend themselves. When they measure themselves by themselves and compare themselves with themselves, they are not wise.
> –2 Corinthians 10:12, NIV

fits into His overall plan for our lives. In the margin read how Paul warned the Corinthians not to play the destructive game of comparison.

If we allow the Holy Spirit to replace lies and distortions with the truth about God's character and our new identity in Christ, we will discover that we no longer need to be controlled by circumstances. Further, these circumstances will have less influence on our emotions. Our emotions usually are based on our beliefs about a situation, not on the situation itself.

Jim, for example, broke his engagement with his fiancée, Susan. Susan became deeply depressed. Her emotions directly resulted from her beliefs about the situation, not from the situation itself. Let us consider two ways she might respond. In the scenario below you will see a pattern that is based on a distorted view of God and of herself.

Example #1

> Situation: Jim has broken our engagement.
> Belief: *God didn't create me as a beautiful woman; He created me to be ugly.*
> Thoughts: *I'm not capable of attracting a husband. My mother always made fun of the way I looked. Now I know she was right.*
> Emotions: *I'm angry with my mother when I remember the way she ridiculed me; I'm angry with Jim when I think that he has destroyed my dream of being loved and accepted; I'm angry with God because He made me with such an ugly appearance.*
> Actions: Repressed anger, depression, withdrawal, self-condemnation

✎ In the margin describe what you see as the root of Susan's difficulty.

Susan does not have to arrive at these conclusions! Because she has a distorted view of God, she blames Him for the breakup. In blaming Him, she isolates herself from the One who should be her greatest comfort and her closest companion. Her problem is not really the situation. Instead, it is the way she perceives it and responds to it. She believes that God deliberately chooses ugliness for some people and forces them to be unattractive. But she can respond with faith and hope if she believes the truth about God's character. Built on the truths of God's Word, her responses can resemble the scenario below.

Example #2

> Situation: Jim has broken our engagement.
> Belief: *Even though this hurts, I know that God loves me and gives His best to me.*
> Thoughts: *I can learn to be content in the Lord as a single adult* or *I'm being guided to the husband He has for me.*
> Emotions: *O God, this hurts so much! I really wanted to marry Jim and have a loving and affirming husband, but thank You, Lord, for keeping me from marrying the wrong person. Thank You for being my constant Companion.*
> Actions: Honest expression of emotions to the Lord. Appropriate expression of emotions to other people. Developing and enjoying other friendships. Behavior characterized by thankfulness.

Susan can be objective and honest, and she can experience inner peace by trusting in God's character instead of living in anxiety and nursing her hurt.

Satan's lies bring depression, but God's truths produce rest!

Satan's lies bring depression, but God's truths produce rest! She can experience what matters most in life: she is deeply loved by God, completely forgiven, fully pleasing, totally accepted, and complete in Christ. She can live a life of love and depth and meaning.

✎ Review the five distortions of the truth. Beside each of the five headings write a number from 1 to 10 describing the degree to which that distortion of the truth affects your life. The number 1 represents "Very little effect; I seldom believe this lie." The number 10 means "I struggle with this distortion a great deal."

As we learn to identify the deceptions in our belief system and discover in Scripture who God truly is, we can move into a totally new lifestyle. He has given us His Word; His Holy Spirit; and loving, mature believers to guide us on our journey. He provides all we need.

God provides all we need.

➥ Review this week's Scripture-memory passage, Psalm 34:7-8. Spend time in prayer. Ask God to help you genuinely "taste and see that He is good."

SUMMARY STATEMENTS

- God is never the source of evil.
- God's design is to wean us from our self-centeredness to a life of devotion and service to Him.
- If we allow the Holy Spirit to replace lies and distortions with the truth about God's character and our new identity in Christ, we will discover that we no longer need to be controlled by circumstances.
- Satan's lies bring depression, but God's truths produce rest!

Results of False Beliefs

DAY 5

As he thinks within himself, so he is.

–Proverbs 23:7

You studied the four basic false beliefs in day 3. In this lesson you will take another look at their consequences.

✎ In following descriptions of the four false beliefs, underline words or phrases that describe how you often feel.

The Fear of Failure
Are you overly sensitive to criticism? Are you compelled to justify and explain your mistakes? Do you become depressed when you fail? Do you get angry with people who interfere with your attempts to succeed and then make you feel incompetent? Traits like these characterize a fear of failure, which is rooted in the false belief *I must meet certain standards in order to feel good about myself.*
The Fear of Rejection

False Belief 1
I must meet certain standards in order to feel good about myself.

False Belief 2
I must be approved by certain others to feel good about myself.

Do you go out of your way to get people to like you, or do you compromise your convictions to earn their approval? Do you avoid certain people? Are you devastated when someone else gets more attention than you do? Do you daydream a lot about promotions or compliments? Do you compare your looks, possessions, status, prestige, or abilities with others? Actions like these typify those who fear rejection. A fear of rejection results from the false belief *I must be approved by certain others to feel good about myself.*

The Fear of Punishment
and the Propensity to Punish Others
Are you afraid to make a mistake because you fear that someone will criticize you? Do you fear what God might do to you? After you fail, do you feel that God is disgusted or angry with you? Do you condemn yourself when you fail as a type of self-punishment? How do you respond when others fail, especially when you are depending on them? Are you generally accepting or critical of others? Guilt and condemnation are consequences of the false belief *Those who fail (including me) are unworthy of love and deserve to be punished.*

False Belief 3
Those who fail (including me) are unworthy of love and deserve to be punished.

The Feeling of Shame
Do you dislike the way you look? Do you feel that past experiences have ruined your life? Do you see yourself as a loser and often feel inferior when you are with a group of friends? These feelings result from the false belief *I am what I am. I cannot change. I am hopeless.*

False Belief 4
I am what I am. I cannot change. I am hopeless.

You may have underlined many of the phrases or only a few. All of us have been affected to some degree by the four false beliefs. For some, these concepts are crippling.

A Formula for Change

Try using the plan below the next time you need to tackle negative feelings generated by people or circumstances. The six stages of the process are:

1. Realize that you are experiencing anger, fear, or anxiety.
2. Identify which of the basic lies you are believing.
3. Reject the lie because it distorts your perception of God and produces painful consequences in your life.
4. Replace the deception with the truths of God's Word.
5. Reflect on these truths to decide how they apply in your present situation.
6. Praise the Lord for His love, forgiveness, and power.

Using a plan like this can help you defeat the harmful effects of hurt, anger, and fear by confronting those emotions with the truth of God's Word. Over time you will discover that situations you normally might flee can be used as opportunities for reflection, growth, prayer, and praise.

You can defeat hurt, anger, and fear by confronting those emotions with the truth of God's Word.

✎ In the following story seek to identify the point when Robert applied each of the six stages in the formula. Write the number of the stage in the margin beside the sentences describing his action.

"I (Robert S. McGee) recently had an encounter with a longtime friend. Several years ago I helped him when he felt insecure about his job and some central relationships in his life. I had been vulnerable with him, hoping that some transparency on my part would help him be more honest about his fears and

Robert's story

hurts. Not long ago, however, I learned that he had told several persons some things about me that weren't true. In the past I would have felt angry, but I wouldn't have admitted that my anger was the result of feeling deeply hurt. I would have excused the offense by saying: 'That's OK. It doesn't matter. I don't really care.' But excusing someone isn't the same as forgiving him or her.

"This time I wanted to be more honest with myself, with the Lord, and with my friend. First, I realized that I had experienced not only a fear of rejection but also actual rejection. I admitted that my friend's offense both hurt and angered me. Then I reflected on the incident by asking myself a few questions, such as: What is true here? How would I usually respond? How does the Lord want me to respond this time? I read several Scripture passages about God's unconditional love and acceptance and the true nature of forgiveness.

"Then I went to see my friend. I told him what I had heard and that I was deeply hurt and angry with him. Although I had difficulty being so honest, I knew that I needed to be. The results were mixed. I felt that I had achieved my goal of being honest and knew that I had chosen to forgive him, but my friend didn't respond as I'd hoped he would. He apologized to me when we met, but I've since learned that he has told more untrue things about me.

"I may need to confront him again, but at least I'm being more honest about my emotions and learning to apply the Scriptures more deeply in my life."

You may have noted that Robert recognized what he was feeling when he said that in the past he would have felt angry but would not have admitted the source of the anger. He identified the lie he was believing when he spoke of a fear of rejection, which comes from the false belief that "I must be approved by certain others to feel good about myself." He worked to reject and replace the lie when he asked himself how he would usually respond and what the Lord would have him do.

Other people's offenses often play on our insecurities.

Other people's offenses often play on our insecurities: our fears of failure, rejection, and/or punishment, as well as our sense of shame. We need to learn how to detach from our hurt long enough to determine which fears someone else has triggered, the lie behind those fears, and the truth of God's Word.

The Need to Forgive

We also need to forgive anyone who has offended us—past or present. In the margin read the words of Jesus and of Paul the apostle.

"I say to you who hear, love your enemies, do good to those who hate you, bless those who curse you, pray for those who mistreat you."
–Luke 6:27-28

Forgiveness does not mean submitting to someone else's abuse, whether verbal or physical, nor does it mean that we are to rescue others from the consequences of their harmful behavior. It means that after being completely honest about the gravity of another's offense and the hurt it has caused us, we choose to release the offender from any debt we perceive he or she owes us as a result of the offense. Forgiveness replaces the motive for revenge with compassion.

Put on a heart of compassion, kindness, humility, gentleness and patience; bearing with one another, and forgiving each other, whoever has a complaint against anyone; just as the Lord forgave you, so also should you.
–Colossians 3:12-13

Forgiveness is not a feeling but a decision. In unit 9 we will explore ways to deal with our emotions surrounding this issue.

Unit 8   159

Unit Review

✎ Review the five lessons in this unit. Find one statement that helped you better understand the importance of relationships. Circle this statement and rewrite it in your own words.

_____

_____

_____

✎ Review your written work and prayer responses throughout the unit. What exercise was most meaningful to you during this week? Identify the exercise and explain your choice.

_____

_____

_____

✎ Review the Scripture-memory passage. Find it in your Bible and check your memory. Then close your Bible and write the passage in the left margin. How have you applied this passage during your study of this unit?

_____

_____

_____

Notes
[1] Robert S. McGee, *Search for Significance* LIFE® Support Group Series Edtion (Houston: Rapha Publishing, 1992), 39, 49.

UNIT 9

Grieving and Healing

Case in point

AN INADEQUATE SON

Chris was bright and athletic but also very shy. He seemed to feel ill at ease in social situations. One day a counselor friend asked him a few questions about his background. "Chris, what are your parents like?" the friend inquired. Chris responded: "They're OK. Dad's an engineer, and Mom's a high-school English teacher."

"How did you get along with your parents when you were growing up? How did they treat you? Did you feel loved and accepted?"

After a long pause Chris looked down and said: "I guess I was somewhat of the ugly duckling in the family. My brothers and my sister were smart and did well in sports; but I came along last and, well, I guess I didn't do as well as my parents wanted me to." "How do you know that, Chris?" his friend asked.

"No matter how hard I tried, they never seemed to be satisfied. They always said things implying that I should have done better." His voice got lower as he concluded, "I just wasn't the son I should have been." (You will read more about Chris on p. 162.)

What you'll learn

This week you will
- study three principles for dealing with your emotions;
- explore three causes for the evil and suffering in the world and in your experience;
- describe how God can turn problems into strengths;
- apply the stages of the grief process to your emotional healing;
- learn a model for moving from hurt and anger to acceptance.

What you'll study

What About My Emotions?	Why the Suffering?	Turning Problems into Strengths	Overcoming Roadblocks	Dealing with Hurt and Anger
DAY 1	DAY 2	DAY 3	DAY 4	DAY 5

Memory verse

This week's verse of Scripture to memorize
When the storm has swept by, the wicked are gone, but the righteous stand firm forever.

–Proverbs 10:25, NIV

DAY 1

What About My Emotions?

Trust in Him at all times, O people; Pour out your heart before Him; God is a refuge for us.

–Psalm 62:8

catharsis–n. the alleviation of fears, problems, and complexes by bringing them to consciousness and giving them expression (Webster's Unabridged)

When some people first analyze the difference between God's character and that of their parents, they experience immediate insight and relief: *Oh, so that's why I've felt distant from the Lord! Now I understand.* For them the transition to a deep, fresh experience with the Lord is fairly easy. But for others this catharsis occurs later. When they begin to recognize the contrast between God's unconditional love and their parents' neglect, abuse, or manipulation, they experience a period of great pain before they can experience relief. A person cannot brush aside or solve easily and quickly years of repressed emotions.

Chris' story

On the unit page you read about my friend Chris. I (Pat Springle) asked Chris, "Did you think you had the responsibility of making your parents happy?" Chris replied, "Of course! If I had been the kind of son I should have been—like my brothers were—my parents would have been happy with me."

I asked, "Chris, how did they show you that they loved you?"

"My father, well ... he ... I don't think he loved me very much. He provided for me, but he isn't a very loving man—at least not to me. My mother occasionally told me that I'd done well in sports or in school, but when my father shouted at me, she never defended me." He concluded: "It's my fault. I just wasn't the kind of son they could be proud of."

I explained to Chris that he was not responsible for making his parents happy. That responsibility belongs to parents, not children. Parents have the God-given responsibility of loving and protecting their children. But Chris would not accept this argument. His sense of guilt and responsibility prevented his seeing that he was a victim of a form of abuse. He showed no emotion at all during the conversation. He had become emotionally numb.

Chris and I had several more opportunities to discuss his family. Gradually, Chris started to see the light: "You mean ... they were supposed to love me unconditionally ... and it's not up to me to make them happy?" He raised his arm and slammed his fist on the desk! His eyes widened, and then he glared in anger. "I can't believe they did that to me! What would my life be like now if they had loved me?"

✎ Chris' story may be your story as well, or your story may be very different. Put yourself in Chris' place. How might you feel about the way your parents related to you?

❑ They did nothing wrong.
❑ If I had been a better child, my life would have been different.
❑ I am furious! What right did they have to treat me like that?
❑ I am so sad. I missed so much.
❑ It was terribly painful, but I have worked through my past. I have forgiven and now see that God brought good in my life through it all.

When we get in touch with our past, we sometimes experience painful emotions.

Chris' story is not an isolated incident, even among people who are in the ministry. When we get in touch with our past, we sometimes open a Pandora's box of painful emotions, such as anger, fear, anxiety, shame, guilt, sadness, and bitterness. You may have given any of these responses to the activity. The responses follow the general pattern of the grieving process, reflecting denial, bargaining, anger, sadness, and acceptance. Chris, and possibly you, may have given different responses at different times during the healing process. Tomorrow you will examine the grief process more closely.

If you repress anger over a period of time, it festers into resentment and bitterness. These feelings often find their outlets and expressions in revenge. Or a person may try to compensate by driving himself as a workaholic or by escaping through substance abuse or other compulsive behaviors.

Fear is less volatile but just as damaging. It promotes the kind of numbness and withdrawal that can amount to emotional, spiritual, and social paralysis. Most people who have repressed their emotions have repressed some combination of anger and fear. The fear of rejection and failure can cause a myriad of painful symptoms.

Three principles can help us experience and express our emotions, whether they are mild or the products of long-term repression. These principles are to be honest with yourself, to be honest with God, and to be honest with others.

Principle 1: Be Honest with Yourself

The first step toward coping with repressed emotions is, of course, to recognize that they exist. When one woman began to understand how her father's outbursts of anger had driven her into an emotional shell, she became angry with him. But she caught herself: "I can't be angry. I'm a Christian." She started to confess her anger to the Lord as if the anger itself were wrong. Had she stopped there, she never would have been able to deal effectively with her past. She would have continued to repress her emotions.

✎ Describe what you would say to this woman if she asked you how to deal with her anger.

_____

_____

_____

Emotions, in and of themselves, are not sinful.

After receiving encouragement and patient instruction, she realized that Christians do not have only happy feelings. They get angry, too! An emotion like anger does not always result from our sin. It may be a response to others' sins, the neglect or abuse others have inflicted. Willful disobedience is sin; but emotions are products of many factors, including our sins, the sins of others, circumstances, our backgrounds, hormones, and other causes. Emotions, in and of themselves, are not sinful. You may have said that you would encourage this woman to acknowledge and express her anger appropriately. When we realize that we are angry or fearful, the correct response is to be honest about those feelings, to try to understand their root cause, and then to grieve the loss and to forgive the offender.

Unit 9 163

Sometimes Christians say, "I'm really frustrated!" We use statements like this to avoid saying that we are angry, because we feel that anger is less acceptable than frustration. These statements attempt to downplay our emotions and to rationalize their severity. Rick once said, "I'm frustrated!" fairly often. A friend who realized that more emotion than mild frustration lay behind Rick's words decided to ask him: "Rick, is it possible that you are a little more than frustrated . . . maybe even angry?" Rick thought for a moment. Then he thoughtfully responded, "Yes, you're right. I guess I'm mad. Saying that I'm angry just doesn't sound spiritual."

Some people call this practice—not saying what we really feel—using weasel words. We rationalize a lot of anger by saying that we are frustrated. We need to be honest so that we can analyze the source of our anger and find a healing solution from the Lord.

✎ Below describe a time or a situation in which you use "weasel words"—words you use when you refuse to be honest with yourself about your painful emotions.

_____

_____

You may have described situations in which you seek to minimize your feelings. In certain situations many of us say, "It isn't important" when we really care very deeply; or we say, "I'm a little nervous" when we are filled with anxiety. Emotional healing requires that we become more honest with ourselves about our feelings.

Principle 2: Be Honest with God

The Lord never is surprised by our emotions. He is omniscient, or all-knowing. He knew everything about us before the world was created; and He is our understanding, loving, and trustworthy Confidant. We can tell Him everything about how we think and feel—and we should tell Him. David wrote today's Scripture verse which appears in the margin.

> Trust in Him at all times, O people; Pour out your heart before Him; God is a refuge for us.
> –Psalm 62:8

Pour out your heart to the Lord. Mark is deeply emotional. When he feels something, he feels it deeply! On a few occasions when he has been very upset, Mark has gotten into his car and has driven down the highway screaming at the top of his lungs! Who knows what other motorists have thought? But Mark says that screaming enables him to tell the Lord, without any inhibitions, how angry he feels.

Few of us will go to this extreme (highways are crazy enough as they are!), but all of us need to express our thoughts and emotions to the Lord. Learning to express your feelings takes time. A couple of minutes will not suffice. We need to get into the habit of instant honesty and quiet, prolonged communication with the Lord so that we can reflect on our feelings and situations and His truth about them.

We need to get into the habit of instant honesty and quiet, prolonged communication with the Lord.

David was an excellent model for pouring out one's heart to the Lord. The Book of Psalms, which reflects his deeply personal relationship with God, includes a full range of emotions.

✎ Read the following verses from Psalms that reflect David's honest expression to the Lord. Circle the words or expressions in the verses that seem extreme to you or that you would have difficulty saying to the Lord.

> O that Thou wouldst slay the wicked, O God;
> Depart from me, therefore, men of bloodshed.
> For they speak against Thee wickedly,
> And Thine enemies take Thy name in vain.
> Do I not hate those who hate Thee, O Lord?
> And do I not loathe those who rise up against Thee?
> I hate them with the utmost hatred;
> They have become my enemies (Psalm 139:19-22).

> Rescue me, O Lord, from evil men;
> Preserve me from violent men,
> Who devise evil things in their hearts;
> They continually stir up wars.
> They sharpen their tongues as a serpent;
> Poison of a viper is under their lips.
> Keep me, O Lord, from the hands of the wicked;
> Preserve me from violent men,
> Who have purposed to trip up my feet.
> I said to the Lord, "Thou art my God;
> Give ear, O Lord, to the voice of my supplications.
> O God the Lord, the strength of my salvation,
> Thou hast covered my head in the day of battle."
> I know that the Lord will maintain the cause of the afflicted,
> And justice for the poor.
> Surely the righteous will give thanks to Thy name;
> The upright will dwell in Thy presence (Psalm 140:1-4,6-7,12-13).

> O Lord, I call upon Thee; hasten to me!
> Give ear to my voice when I call to Thee! (Psalm 141:1).

As you honestly express yourself to the Lord, remember to listen to Him, too. His Spirit will remind you of passages of Scripture and will prompt you to think about the Lord and His desires for you. Focus on His character, His promises, and His commands so that you can understand how He wants you to respond to your circumstances. If you circled many words because they seem extreme, remember that God desires honesty rather than nice, "cookie-cutter" answers.

Principle 3: Be Honest with Others

After you have expressed your emotions to God, you will need to be appropriately honest with persons who have hurt or offended you. But you do not need to tell them everything you have thought or felt—that should be reserved for the time when you pour out your heart to the Lord.

What should you say? The answer comes from another question: What will help that person? The goal of expressing yourself is to benefit the other person. Loving confrontation can be a stepping stone for that person's growth and maturity and, ultimately, for strengthening your relationship.

Think about that person's maturity level and his or her ability to apply what

The goal of expressing yourself is to benefit the other person.

you would say. A reproof that would be digestible to a mature person may devastate a weaker one. You will need God's wisdom to know how much to say and, just as importantly, how much not to say.

A prudent man conceals knowledge, But the heart of fools proclaims folly.
—Proverbs 12:23

✏️ Write your own paraphrase of Proverbs 12:23, which appears at left. What principle does the verse illustrate about how much we say to others?

_____

_____

You might have paraphrased the verse something like this: "A wise person does not tell everything he knows; but a fool tells everything, no matter how much it hurts someone else." You could have stated that we need to base our honesty on the other person's benefit.

Should we talk to someone who has hurt us? Generally we should because honesty provides the opportunity for understanding, repentance, and reconciliation. However, if we have confronted someone and he or she has responded by denying or blaming us, then it may be wise to not confront that person again. In that case we need to grieve yet another loss.

On rare occasions we should not confront the other person at all if to do so would harm that person or others. If your father is on his death-bed and talking to him would only create turmoil with no hope of reconciliation you would achieve nothing through confrontation.

Continued repression is not the solution to your pain and anger.

Getting in touch with repressed emotions may seem almost unbearable at times, but continued repression is not the solution to your pain and anger. In later lessons you will explore the process we often experience when we begin to feel and experience repressed pain and anger.

✏️ Begin to memorize this unit's Scripture memory verse, Proverbs 10:25. Below write the verse three times.

_____

_____

_____

_____

SUMMARY STATEMENTS

- The first step toward coping with repressed emotions is to recognize that they exist.
- We need to get into the habit of instant honesty and quiet, prolonged communication with the Lord so that we can reflect on our feelings and situations and His truth about them.
- Loving confrontation can be a stepping stone for someone's growth and maturity and, ultimately, for strengthening your relationship.

DAY 2

Why the Suffering?

Behold, I will do something new, now it will spring forth; Will you not be aware of it? I will even make a roadway in the wilderness, rivers in the desert.
—Isaiah 43:19

God can use even the most neglectful or abusive parents to produce strengths in your life.

When you think about your relationships with your parents, what thoughts and emotions emerge: pain or thankfulness, cursing or blessing, or some combination of these feelings? If you experience pain when you think about your parents, remember that God can use even the most neglectful or abusive parents to produce strengths in your life. God's words above to the prophet Isaiah are as relevant to us today as they were to the Israelites then.

We know that God causes all things to work together for good to those who love God, to those who are called according to His purpose.
—Romans 8:28

No, the pain of being unloved, unaccepted, and unprotected as a child is not God's design for the family; but He can use even our most trying difficulties to produce good. Many of us find comfort in Romans 8:28, which appears in the margin. We need to apply this promise to our most sensitive situations: our relationships with our parents.

Before we look at the various strengths God can build through the ordeal of a painful childhood, we need to ask this question: why did God let this happen? Could not a loving God have given me nurturing, affirming parents?

The issue of suffering is a complex one. We need to understand that our sovereign God has allowed—not caused—evil in the world. Let us examine three causes of suffering: the fallen nature of humanity, the consequences of sin, and the Lord's work of pruning for greater fruitfulness.

The Fallen Nature of Humanity

You were dead in your trespasses and sins, in which you formerly walked according to the course of this world, according to the prince of the power of the air, of the spirit that is now working in the sons of disobedience.
—Ephesians 2:1-2

When Adam and Eve sinned, humanity's innocence ceased. Humanity and all creation fell from perfect union with God. When a person enters this world, he enters a system dominated by the prince of evil. In Ephesians 2:1-2, which appears in the margin, the apostle Paul described our natural state as fallen beings. The cross of Christ enables fallen humans to be reconciled to God, but He does not remove us from this fallen world. We have the responsibility and privilege of representing Him to others who are fallen and who desperately need His grace. Even as we do so, however, the fallen and evil forces in the world still affect us.

✎ Check the statement that best reflects the teaching of the previous paragraph.

❏ 1. Even when we are Christians, the results of sin in the world and in the lives of others affect our lives.
❏ 2. Because we are His children, God protects believers from the evil of the world's system.
❏ 3. Satan no longer has the power or opportunity to harass those who belong to Christ.
❏ 4. God will only allow Satan to bother you if you sin and willfully reject God's plan for your life.

Although we have been re-created in Christ Jesus, Christians are still a part of this fallen world. Jesus stated the principle clearly. God sends "rain on the righteous and the unrighteous" (Matthew 5:45). The first answer is the correct choice.

The Consequences of Personal Sin

Personal sin causes a great deal of suffering. Galatians 6:7-8 clearly states the issue. Our actions, which arise from our nature as fallen beings, bring painful results. On television we see happy endings at the end of almost every program, no matter how grave the characters' problems may be. These programs provide a very misleading picture of real life, for they do not depict the tremendous, prolonged pain of adultery, alcoholism, selfishness, jealousy, and hatred. That would not sell the sponsors' products! The truth is that these sins destroy families, create deep bitterness, and crush the lives of those who are most vulnerable—the children.

> Do not be deceived, God is not mocked; for whatever a man sows, this he will also reap. For the one who sows to his own flesh shall from the flesh reap corruption, but the one who sows to the Spirit shall from the Spirit reap eternal life.
> –Galatians 6:7-8

Pruning

A third source of suffering, of many that could be listed, is pruning. This kind of suffering differs from the other two because it results not from sin but from honoring Christ. In John 15 Christ used the metaphor of a vineyard to describe this phenomenon. If we are serious about honoring Christ, we will bear fruit. And if we bear fruit, Christ says that He will prune us so that we can bear even more fruit. His purpose in this action is very positive, but it is painful! Whether the cause of suffering is sin or pruning for fruitfulness, God can use our pain for good. Even when a family member inflicts excruciating pain, God still can use it for good.

> Every branch in Me that does not bear fruit, He takes away; and every branch that bears fruit, He prunes it, that it may bear more fruit. I am the vine, you are the branches; he who abides in Me, and I in him, he bears much fruit; for apart from Me you can do nothing.
> –John 15:2,5

Joseph: A Biblical Example

The Book of Genesis records the story of Joseph, a great example of a person who made the most of suffering. Joseph's brothers wanted to murder their upstart little brother (Genesis 37:18-20); but 2 of the 12, Reuben and Judah, persuaded the others not to kill him (Genesis 37:21-22,26-27). Instead, his brothers sold Joseph as a slave. After many years and as a result of divine intervention, Joseph rose to prominence in Egypt and became the prime minister under the Egyptian pharaoh.

Years later Joseph's father and brothers, experiencing a severe famine in Canaan, traveled to Egypt to buy food. They came to Joseph, not knowing that he was their long-lost relative. As the functioning ruler of all Egypt, Joseph had complete power over them.

✎ Imagine for a moment that you are Joseph. For the time being, forget what Joseph actually did. Describe two examples of what you would like to do. First, describe yourself doing your worst and venting years of pent-up anger on your family members.

_____

_____

Second, describe yourself dealing in a forgiving way with your family. What would you like to happen?

_____

_____

You could have described—with considerable glee—making your brothers suffer and seeing them beg for your forgiveness. In the second scenario you may picture a scene of reconciliation in which they recognize their mistreatment of you, they beg your pardon, and you graciously forgive them.

> "As for you, you meant evil against me, but God meant it for good in order to bring about this present result, to preserve many people alive. So therefore, do not be afraid; I will provide for you and your little ones." So he comforted them and spoke kindly to them.
> –Genesis 50:20-21

Notice the subtle difference from either of those possibilities in Joseph's response. He could have had his brothers executed instantly, but he did not. Joseph believed that God had a purpose for allowing him to suffer bitter rejection and brutal treatment by his own brothers. Instead of cursing them, he spoke to his brothers the words in the margin.

Joseph did not see himself as a victim of injustice—even though he was. He saw himself as an extension of God's care for his family—even though they had wanted to murder him. He believed that God had a purpose for his suffering, and this sense of purpose enabled him to see himself as God's servant instead of as a victim. Did you notice in Joseph's reply the lack of self-concern? His brothers apologized, but that does not seem to have been Joseph's goal.

Perhaps you have been a victim of neglect, abuse, or manipulation by your parents or other family members. Do you see yourself only as a victim? Or do you see that God has a higher purpose and that you can participate in that purpose as an extension of His love and power?

A victim mentality limits our focus to our own pain and needs. Believing that God has a higher purpose enables us to take our eyes off ourselves so that we can serve Him and help others. Our pain probably will not evaporate as we focus on God's purposes, but we will have a new sense of contentment when we realize that God can turn even our greatest pain or weakness into strength (2 Corinthians 12:9-10).

> He has said to me, "My grace is sufficient for you, for power is perfected in weakness." Most gladly, therefore, I will rather boast about my weaknesses, that the power of Christ may dwell in me. Therefore I am well content with weaknesses, with insults, with distresses, with persecutions, with difficulties, for Christ's sake; for when I am weak, then I am strong.
> –2 Corinthians 12:9-10

↪ Spend some time in prayer. Talk with God about the painful situations in your life. Ask Him to help you not to deny or ignore the events of your life but to see them as Joseph and Paul saw theirs. Note that the apostle said he was "well content" with his sufferings. Ask God to develop in you genuine contentment, based on His presence and purposes in your life.

SUMMARY STATEMENTS

- If you experience pain when you think of your parents, remember that God can use even the most neglectful or abusive parents to produce strengths in your life.
- We have the responsibility and privilege of representing God to others who are fallen and who desperately need His grace.
- Believing that God has a higher purpose enables us to take our eyes off ourselves so that we can serve Him and help others.

DAY 3

Turning Problems into Strengths

Man is born to trouble as surely as sparks fly upward.
—Job 5:7, NIV

The Lord can and will use your past to develop strengths in your life. Because of your difficulties you will be able to understand others and help them more than if you never had suffered. In the previous lesson we challenged you to pray that God would enable you to see the difficulties of your life differently. You can begin to see them as events God is using to develop strengths in your life. In this lesson you will examine five of those strengths.

Compassion for Others

Have you ever been really hurting and told someone that you needed his help, only to have him look at you strangely and say, "What's the matter with you? Just trust the Lord"? That helped a lot, didn't it?

Simplistic answers do not satisfy hurting people. But how do we develop understanding and compassion? Usually by experiencing pain ourselves. Our ability to comfort others is more or less proportional to the degree that we have experienced comfort in our own times of pain. Paul wrote to the Corinthian believers the words that appear in the margin.

Mary experienced the pain of her father's death. People sent expensive floral arrangements to the funeral, and she received many sympathy cards, but one note meant more to her than any other. A friend whose mother had died of cancer several months before wrote that her emotions and sense of stability had been fractured. She described the comfort the Lord had provided. She did not give advice or preach. She just let Mary know that she understood. That was the greatest comfort Mary could receive.

If you have experienced the pain of neglect, abuse, or manipulation, you can understand and comfort others who are experiencing the same kind of pain in their families. God can use you deeply and profoundly in their lives.

Dependence on the Lord

When the prophet Samuel came to Jesse's house, he invited Jesse and his sons to a ceremonial sacrifice (1 Samuel 16). At this intense, exciting moment Jesse's family undoubtedly wondered, *Why has the prophet come to our home?* The Lord had directed Samuel to go to Jesse's home to anoint a new king of Israel. "Bring your sons to me," Samuel instructed. One by one Jesse's seven sons passed in front of the prophet, but the Lord said to Samuel, "No, not this one … not this one … not this one." Soon no one was left.

"Are these all of your sons?" Samuel asked. Jesse replied, "I have only one more son, the youngest, but he is tending the sheep" (v. 11).

Samuel ordered Jesse to bring David to him, and the Lord instructed, "anoint him, this is the one" (v. 12). David was to become the king of Israel, but his

---

Blessed be the God and Father of our Lord Jesus Christ, the Father of mercies and God of all comfort; who comforts us in all our affliction so that we may be able to comfort those who are in any affliction with the comfort with which we ourselves are comforted by God. For just as the sufferings of Christ are ours in abundance, so also our comfort is abundant through Christ.
—2 Corinthians 1:3-5

father did not even count him among his sons! When Samuel had instructed Jesse to bring all of his sons to him, Jesse had left David in the field with the sheep. David was a reject in his father's eyes.

✎ Describe how you think you would feel if you were in David's shoes—if the prophet said to your parents, "Bring all of the children" and they brought all except you.

___

___

> Why have you come down? And with whom have you left those few sheep in the wilderness? I know your insolence and the wickedness of your heart; for you have come down in order to see the battle.
>
> –1 Samuel 17:28

You may have answered, "I would feel shamed and slighted, as if I were worth less than my siblings in my parents' sight." You may have experienced the same pain David suffered. His brothers also ridiculed him. After all, that is how their father treated him. When David took provisions to his brothers while they were in Saul's army, the eldest, Eliab, spoke the sarcastic and shaming words that appear in the margin.

Rejected by his father and scorned by his brothers, David spent many lonely nights watching the sheep. A deeply sensitive young man, he needed to be accepted and understood. No one else cared about him—no one but the Lord. So day after day and night after night, alone with the Lord while tending sheep, David developed a close, rich relationship with God. His psalms reflect a depth of intimacy, honesty, and understanding probably unparalleled in history. Yet we must not fail to recognize that rejection was the crucible that developed this intimacy and dependence. David had nowhere else to turn, so he turned to the Lord.

Somehow David recognized that God was not like his father. Maybe David memorized the Scriptures and realized that God is loving, kind, and powerful instead of harsh, demeaning, and neglectful, as Jesse was. David's realization of the contrast between the Lord and his father enabled him to experience the love and power of God's presence.

You can depend on God even if you can depend on no one else.

Perhaps you have experienced rejection. Perhaps you have no one but God to depend on. He is faithful and kind and powerful. You can depend on Him even if you can depend on no one else, and you can draw strength from the awareness that God can bring good out of your pain.

Perception

Children need love and acceptance to experience stability. Without these provisions they have to fend for themselves. Some try to do so by building emotional walls. "If I don't get close to people, then I won't get hurt," they surmise.

Others develop a different defense mechanism. They become acutely aware of the mood and intentions of those around them and then change their behavior to win approval. Their "antennae" are always up as they analyze every word, expression, and action. *Does that look mean she's upset with me? Why did he raise his voice? His words say that he cares about me, but the tone of his voice tells me that he's faking. What can I say to make her like me?* It is a cat-and-mouse game, and the children are the poor mice.

The ability to "read" others is a tremendous strength.

This ability to "read" others is a tremendous strength, even if learned through great anguish and painful introspection. Bill is a friend who is very perceptive. His parents, who fought a lot when he was young, were so involved in their own selfishness and bitterness that they often neglected him. His defense was to try to please them in every way so that they would notice him and approve of him. He learned to read their every mood.

As a result, Bill can now sense the attitudes of others long before most people can. One friend says: "I often ask Bill how he thinks another person is doing. I may sense that something isn't quite right; but Bill usually has the problem pinpointed, described, and illustrated with several examples. He is so perceptive that I sometimes walk into his office and jokingly say, 'Hi, Bill, how am I doing?' " Bill's sense of perception is a great strength, but he acquired it through pain.

Have you learned to read others because you felt that you had to respond perfectly as a child to gain approval? Perception is a wonderful strength.

Reflection

Some people respond to perceived rejection by becoming very cautious. These people are characterized by the thought, *I have to be right before I act.* This fear of failure and rejection can paralyze, but it can also have the positive result of developing an ability to reflect. This strength is similar to that of perception but centers more on ideas, problems, and issues than on people.

The fear of failure and rejection can develop an ability to reflect.

Patty has learned to analyze issues to a great degree. She often asks questions no one else thinks to ask. She likes to cover her bases to avoid mistakes. Some of us are risk-takers. We blindly rush ahead without being willing (or able) to take a hard look at the facts. We need someone like Patty, who is cautious and willing to ask difficult questions.

Are you a cautious person? Do you analyze problems well? Are you so cautious that you are afraid to make a decision even when all of your questions have been answered? Or is your reflection a strength that enables you to ask questions, reach solutions, and proceed with success?

Effectiveness

Lyle's story

Growing up in an alcoholic family, Lyle received very little attention. Often, the attention he received was condemnation. He developed a defense mechanism of excelling in school and sports in order to blunt the pain. He drove himself to do well because he thought that good grades and involvement in athletics would earn the respect and approval he longed for.

No matter how well he performed (as an honor student and an all-star in three sports), he felt like an outcast from his family. When he made 95 on his exams, his mother would ask him why he did not make 100. When he went four for four on his baseball team, it still was not enough to win his parents' approval.

When Lyle graduated from college, he focused his finely tuned skills on the business world. Soon he became a vice-president—the best employee in the company. He made a lot of money, married a beautiful woman, and continued to advance in his career. *Maybe if I get to the next position*, he reasoned, *then my parents will approve of me*. But they did not.

Some people, like Lyle, have learned how to focus their attention and abilities to accomplish almost any given task. Are you exceptionally effective but feel that nothing you do is quite good enough? Have you experienced God's unconditional love and acceptance, so that you can channel your drive to be effective for His glory?

✎ Review the five strengths we can develop because of a difficult childhood. Rate on a scale of 1 to 10 how much your past has helped you develop each quality, with 1 being lowest and 10 being highest.

___ Compassion for others
___ Dependence on the Lord
___ Perception
___ Reflection
___ Effectiveness

Which of the five has developed as your greatest area of strength? Why?

_____

_____

Which continues to be your greatest area of need? Why do you think this is the case?

_____

_____

God will use your difficulties to develop depth, character, and skills.

When we are in the midst of the agony of rejection, we often have difficulty seeing the strengths God is building in us. We just want relief! Yet God is there, building and developing strengths in us that will enable us to honor Him and help others. No matter how difficult your past has been, God has a divine purpose for you; and He will use your difficulties to develop depth, character, and skills so that you can have a great impact on other people. He can produce hope from despair, compassion from pain, joy from bitterness, and strength from weakness.

✎ Practice repeating Proverbs 10:25 until you can say the verse from memory. Read the paraphrase of the verse that appears in the margin.

The storm passes by, the wicked disappear, but the character that God builds in my life through my hardships will stand firm forever.

SUMMARY STATEMENTS

- The Lord can and will use your past to develop strengths in your life.
- If you have experienced the pain of neglect, abuse, or manipulation, you can understand and comfort others who are experiencing the same kind of pain in their families.
- No matter how difficult your past has been, God has a divine purpose for you; and He will use your difficulties to develop depth, character, and skills so that you can have a great impact on other people.

DAY 4

Overcoming Roadblocks

My eye has also grown dim because of grief, And all my members are as a shadow.

–Job 17:7

People who contract terminal diseases like cancer usually experience several stages of emotional response. Elisabeth Kübler-Ross described these stages in her very helpful book *On Death and Dying*. Those who have experienced severe emotional trauma pass through similar stages.

✎ The following paragraph summarizes the stages of the process for dealing with strong emotions. Write the stages ***denial, bargaining, anger, grief***, and ***acceptance*** in the margin beside the appropriate words or phrases. The first is already written for you.

denial

Many of us who have experienced neglect, abuse, or manipulation either suppress our pain and pretend it is not there or blame ourselves. We assume that we caused our own problems. When we finally confront our problems and our repressed emotions begin to flow, we often try to bargain with God or with the person who has hurt us. We ask, in effect: *How can I make that person love me? What can I do to be accepted? I'll change! I'll do anything!* Sooner or later we realize that bargaining will not work. We have not been able to win that person's approval in the past, and we cannot win it now. We then may experience deep anger toward the one who has hurt us. At that point we should express our anger fully to God. This stage of anger may last for several months. Often, a period of grief follows the anger. A life has been damaged. The past cannot be relived. A sense of loss about what never was or what might have been leads to the experience of grief. Grieving is healthy and positive, even if it is painful. After we have fully experienced grief, we find relief and acceptance. Life can go on.

If you are patient, you can work through the painful emotions.

This process does not happen overnight. Some people may take a prolonged period of time just to uncork their emotions and move from denial to anger. The time frame is not as important as is the process itself. Be patient and allow the process to take its course. If you try to hurry, you will be disappointed and possibly will experience even more pain because of your unrealistic expectations. But if you are patient, you can work through the painful emotions, and God will provide you healing and hope. No matter how painful our emotions may be, we need to be honest about them. Used wisely, such transparency will lend itself to healing—in our lives and in the lives of others.

✎ In the following discussion underline words or phrases that reflect thoughts or actions you have experienced or are experiencing.

Denial

Denial: A defense mechanism demonstrated by an inability or unwillingness to recognize our problems. In denial we tend to rationalize conflicts and justify either our own behavior or someone else's. We also attempt to avoid painful emotions by suppression, diversion, and/or withdrawal.

Bargaining

Bargaining: Usually, our first response to the reality of any hurt, neglect, and condemnation we have experienced is bargaining. We try to make a deal: *What can I do to make him love me?* But we still lack objectivity in this stage.

✎ As you have become aware of the pain of your past, how have you tried to make your parents give you the love and acceptance you have wanted? What have you said or done to win their approval?

_____

_____

People tend to drift back and forth through these stages as they continue to gain new insights.

An initial awareness of hurt and anger may trigger bargaining; but because it usually precedes a deeper awareness of those emotions, bargaining is in effect sandwiched between pain and anger. The entire process, as you may recall, does not follow a rigid schedule. People tend to drift back and forth through these stages as they continue to gain new insights.

Anger

Anger: When we begin to feel the pain we have suppressed—often for many years—we usually become very angry. Our anger may be directed toward God or toward the one(s) who hurt us, including ourselves.

Grief

Grief: After a time of anger our indignation abates, and a sense of loss prevails. We realize that we have lost the chance to have a happy childhood, a close relationship with our parents, or other important and meaningful experiences in life. We experience deep sorrow over the qualities of life we have never had—like love, intimacy, and security.

Acceptance

Acceptance: Sooner or later the process of grieving for these losses ends. Though we may have periods of anger and grief from time to time, we can accept the concept that a loving and sovereign God has a perfect plan for our lives. Now we can begin to experience the intimacy and warmth of God and of other people that our defense mechanism(s) had previously blocked.

You may have underlined sections of all of the stages or only a few. You do not have to experience the grieving process in the same order that another person does. We never totally complete this process; but if you feel more identification with the earlier stages than with grief and acceptance, you probably have some significant work to do.

This lesson and the next present an introduction to the grieving-healing process described above. For many people, doing the work in these lessons is a pivotal step that may provide the framework for the healing they so desperately need from the Lord.

Before you begin to apply the principles that will help you through these stages, these additional ideas can aid you:

Do not rush the process. You will experience gradual healing throughout these stages.

1. Do not rush the process. Digging through the defense mechanisms you have put up over the years will take more than an hour or a day. You may have suppressed hurt and anger for 20, 30, 40, or more years. Do not expect too much too soon. Take time to reflect and to experience the hurt and anger you have suppressed. Then take time to feel sorrow in the grief process. You will experience gradual healing throughout these stages. The entire process may take months—or even years—but it is worth it.

2. Throughout the process you will become aware of a growing sense of objectivity. Defense mechanisms may protect us from pain, but they blind us to the truth. Some people realize that they experienced guilt instead of hurt

when their parents shouted at them. Because these people felt responsible for their parents' happiness, they believed they were at fault when their parents were not happy. Some people realize that, apart from divine intervention, their parents never will love and affirm them, no matter how hard they try to please them. Such objectivity often brings with it a new sense of identity. The truth is a means of breaking one's bondage to parental approval and for beginning to develop a healthy sense of independence.

Objectivity often brings with it a new sense of identity.

3. As you begin to experience and express your new identity, your parents and siblings may not like it. As long as you play your role in the family, they are in control. Your new identity may pose a threat to their control, and they may respond with more condemnation and manipulation than ever! Be prepared for more conflict, not less.

4. Many of us may associate grieving with the loss of a loved one at death. However, the death of a child's identity through neglect, manipulation, or condemnation is a very real loss, even though no corpse is present to prove it. Still, grieving over this kind of loss is unusual because it is intangible and because you may have to continue relating to the person(s) who caused the hurt. These subsequent experiences of grief will slowly diminish if going through the stages initially is a deep, profound, and cathartic process.

5. Learning to respond with a new identity (especially to those who have hurt you deeply) is much like learning to ride a bicycle. No six-year-old can get off his tricycle, hop onto a 26-inch 10-speed, and ride around the neighborhood successfully. A person learns to ride a bike by trying ... and falling ... and trying again, going a little farther and falling again. Turns and hills present new challenges ... and new falls.

Be realistic about your progress. Do not expect perfection! Responding within the framework of a new identity is at first as awkward and scary as getting on a bike for the first time. After a while and after a lot of practice, it gets easier and begins to feel normal.

Work to learn what is true about the Lord and your new identity.

6. Be prepared for the battle ahead by fortifying your mind and heart with the encouragement of the Scriptures. Review unit 7 on the names of God. Work to learn what is true about the Lord and your new identity. Take time to study, reflect, and memorize. It will be well worth the effort.

7. The process of overcoming denial and experiencing hurt, anger, and grief is a painful ordeal. A loving, faithful friend can help you endure it. At times you will need a fresh perspective, objective wisdom, strong encouragement, or a warm hug of reassurance. Find someone who understands what you are going through and who will be a true friend to you.

✎ Review the seven principles you have read. Underline the two or three statements that you believe best apply to you. Below write your statement of commitment to work through the grieving process.

_____

_____

One person wrote: "I have lived many years in denial, and the results have been more pain. I now commit myself to work through my denial to the point of acceptance. I know the process will be painful, but the result will be better than staying where I have been."

↪ Review your Scripture-memory work for this week and for the previous weeks of *Breaking the Cycle of Hurtful Family Experiences*.

SUMMARY STATEMENTS

- If you are patient, you can work through the painful emotions, and God will provide you healing and hope.
- Digging through the defense mechanisms you have erected over the years will take more than an hour or a day.
- The truth is a means of breaking your bondage to parental approval and for beginning to develop a healthy sense of independence.

DAY 5

You can identify and then process the emotions connected with experiences of hurt, anger, and guilt.

Dealing with Hurt and Anger

Trust in Him at all times, O people; Pour out your heart before Him; God is a refuge for us.

–Psalm 62:8

This lesson may be the most difficult and demanding in *Breaking the Cycle*. We are presenting the plan as a daily study, but the process may take you months or years. The exercises in this lesson will lead you first to identify and then to process the emotions connected with experiences of hurt, anger, and guilt. We recommend that you first apply the exercises to a limited number of incidents so that you will learn how the process works. Then we urge you to take all of the time you need to work more thoroughly through the healing process.

To complete this exercise, you will need to find a quiet place where you will not be disturbed. Ask the Lord to remind you of specific instances in your past, particularly in your childhood, when you experienced hurt, anger, or guilt because of your parents. Some of these events probably will come to mind very quickly, but others may not. You may have a lull of 20 or 30 minutes or even several days before the Lord reminds you of an instance or two, followed by another period of time before you remember another one. Make a list of these events until your memory's "well" has run dry.

✎ List below and on the following page instances when you experienced hurt, anger, or guilt because of your parents. Use additional sheets of paper as necessary.

1. _____

_____

2. _____

_____

3. _____

4. _____

5. _____

6. _____

Describe as many incidents as the Lord brings to your memory.

✏️ Using the following list of topics as a guide, further describe each instance in greater detail. Because of the nature of this inventory you will need to use separate sheets of paper. We have given you two examples to follow.

Event:
My feelings then:
My actions:
What a healthy response would have been:
How I feel now about the event and people involved:
Lie(s) I've been believing:
God's truth:
Steps I need to take now:

Example #1

1. Event: My mother made me wear a new dress to school. It didn't fit. I felt ugly, and the other girls laughed at me.

My feelings then: I felt humiliated and ashamed. I was angry with my mother.

My actions: I tried to avoid people all day. I went to the restroom to cry. I didn't say anything to my mother because she would have laughed at me and then would have been angry.

What a healthy response would have been: I think most girls could have told their mothers that they didn't want to wear a dress that didn't fit properly because the other girls would laugh at them. Their mothers would respond by being reasonable and loving. They wouldn't demand that they wear a dress like that.

How I feel now about the event and people involved: I am really angry with my mother. She wasn't reasonable or loving. She wanted only her way. She didn't care about my feelings at all.

Lie(s) I've been believing (see chart on p. 152): Those who fail are unworthy of love and deserve to be blamed and condemned. Fear of punishment.
God's truth (see chart on p. 152): Christ satisfied God's wrath by His

178   Unit 9

death on the cross; therefore, I am deeply loved by God. As I experience God's love and forgiveness in my life, I will be able to extend His love and forgiveness to others, including my mother.

Steps I need to take now: I need to forgive my mother. I also need to be more honest in my relationships with others; therefore, it would be wise for me to seek relationships with persons who value and affirm honesty.

Example #2

2. Event: I was hit in the head with a baseball bat, and my forehead bled a lot; but I refused to cry because my father never let me cry about anything.

My feelings then: I was afraid that I might have a concussion or that I would pass out, but I was also afraid that if I cried, everyone would think I was a wimp.

My actions: My friends tried to persuade me to go home, but I stayed in the game even though blood got in my eyes and all over my uniform.

What a healthy response would have been: I would have cried, and hoped my father would have comforted me and put a bandage on the cut.

How I feel now about the event and people involved: I'm hurt. My father was always tough with me. He never cried, and he wouldn't let me cry. Now I don't feel emotions very much. I've blocked my feelings all my life.

Lie(s) I've been believing (see chart on p. 152): I must meet certain standards to feel good about myself. I must be approved by certain others to feel good about myself.

God's truth (see chart on p. 152): I would like to have the approval of others; but even if I don't, I'm fully pleasing to God and totally accepted by Him despite my performance. Therefore, I can be vulnerable with God and can afford to take the risk of being rejected by others.

Steps I need to take now: I need to forgive my father. I also need to ask God to help me experience my emotions so that I can have healthier relationships.

↪ Follow the pattern in the examples. Use as many sheets of paper and as much time as you need. As you go through this exercise, remember to relive the event, but this time do not suppress the emotions or try to change them. Express them fully to the Lord.

Trust in Him at all times, O people; pour out your heart before Him; God is a refuge for us.

–Psalm 62:8

Grief

After several weeks or months of experiencing and expressing repressed hurt and anger, you may begin to grieve. Repeat the writing process with the following exercise to help you to experience and deal with your grief.

✎ Look at each event that you described on pages 177-178 and answer the following questions, using additional paper as needed.

Unit 9   179

1. What did you lose?
2. What would a child in a healthier situation have had that you did not have?
3. What do you wish you had received from your parents?
4. How have your parents affected your view of God?
5. How have your parents affected your relationships?
6. How have your parents affected your self-concept, identity, and confidence?
7. How do you feel about what you have lost?

Acceptance

As you continue to experience feelings of hurt, anger, and grief, you will begin to see that you can have a relationship with God that is warm, intimate, and powerful. You also will begin to see that God can build strength in your life through pain.

You can have a relationship with God that is warm, intimate, and powerful.

✎ After you have completed the earlier phases of this process, answer the following questions.

1. How has your concept of God changed as you have gone through this process?

   _____
   _____
   _____
   _____

2. What strengths has God built into your life through your painful family experiences?

   _____
   _____
   _____
   _____

3. How might God use these strengths to help you and others?

   _____
   _____
   _____
   _____

4. What do you need to know, feel, and do when your parents and siblings do not understand your new identity, attitude, independence,

or actions?

Unit Review

✎ Review the five lessons in this unit. Find one statement that helped you better understand the importance of relationships. Circle this statement and rewrite it in your own words.

✎ Review your written work and prayer responses throughout the unit. What exercise was most meaningful to you during this week? Identify the exercise and explain your choice.

✎ Review the Scripture-memory verse. Find it in your Bible and check your memory. Then close your Bible and write the passage in the left margin. How have you applied this passage during your study of this unit?

UNIT 10

Modeling God's Character

Case in point

MISDIRECTED ANGER

Kerin left the church building with a new spring in her step. "I never dreamed that a sermon where the pastor talked about the Hebrew language could be life-changing," she said.

Kerin had been angry at God for a long time about Exodus 34:7: " 'He will by no means leave the guilty unpunished, visiting the iniquity of the fathers on the children and on the grandchildren to the third and fourth generations.' " Kerin explained: "The thought of God's punishing children for their grandparents' sins seemed unfair. How could I love a God like that? But tonight when we studied the passage, I discovered that I have been wrong.

I had thought that God was arbitrary and mean to punish children for their parents' sins, but I learned that it isn't God's fault at all. We create the process. The truth is that our God is too gracious to leave us in the mess we get ourselves into." (You will read more on p. 183 about what Kerin was learning.)

What you'll learn

This week you will
- make plans to grow in four areas of your life;
- describe the need for and the difficulty of achieving a changed self-concept and a changed purpose;
- identify a plan for dealing with children's disobedience through grief instead of anger;
- evaluate your schedule and identify changes you can make to model God's character in your family;
- identify actions you can take in five areas to share the blessing with your children.

What you'll study

Modeling God's Character	Self-concept and Purpose	Changing Affections	Changing Schedules	Changing Actions
DAY 1	DAY 2	DAY 3	DAY 4	DAY 5

Memory verses

This week's verses of Scripture to memorize
As you therefore have received Christ Jesus the Lord, so walk in Him, having been firmly rooted and now being built up in Him and established in your faith, just as you were instructed, and overflowing with gratitude.
–Colossians 2:6-7

DAY 1

Modeling God's Character

Thus says the Lord, "When seventy years have been completed for Babylon, I will visit you and fulfill My good word to you, to bring you back to this place."
–Jeremiah 29:10

We can model God's character for our children.

Can the cycle of family dysfunction be broken? Can the destruction and pain of reproduced sin be stopped? By God's grace and power, yes, they can; but the process is neither quick nor simple. To the degree that we understand and experience God's love, forgiveness, and power, we will be able to express these characteristics and to model them for our children. This unit is designed to help you model God's character for your children. (If you do not have children, you may want to apply the principles you learn this week to your other relationships.)

We began Unit 1 with Exodus 34:7 (page 10). For many weeks you have studied the process of how families work and how they transmit either health or dysfunction.

The Lord is slow to anger and abundant in lovingkindness, forgiving iniquity and transgression; but He will by no means clear the guilty, visiting the iniquity of fathers on the children to the third and fourth generations.
–Numbers 14:18

✎ Numbers 14:18, in the margin, expresses the same truth you read in Unit 1 from Exodus 34:7. How do you feel now about the passage? Is God fair to allow the effects of sin to be reproduced in our families?

❑ 1. No, I still don't think it is fair for parents' sins to affect their children and grandchildren.
❑ 2. It makes me angry. God should do something about this cycle of sin and suffering in families.
❑ 3. The cycle grieves me, as I know it grieves God; but I see that He has given us the opportunity to break the cycle.
❑ 4. How great God's love is to cover our sin and still work to save us from ourselves!
❑ 5. Other: _____

Compare Numbers 14:18 with Jeremiah 29:10, which appears at the top of the page. What word is common to each verse?

_____

The Numbers passage, along with Exodus 34:7 and several others, speaks of God's dealing with our sin. They are verses of judgment. The Jeremiah passage speaks of God's promise to restore His people after they had been exiled in Babylon for 70 years. The passage is one of promise and blessing. You may have selected the word *visit* (and *visiting*) as common to the passages. The definition of the word that Moses and Jeremiah used, which is translated *visit*, appears in the margin.

visit–v. (Hebrew *paqad*) attend to, pay attention to, observe (with care, practical interest) for different purposes: to search, test, punish (Brown, Driver, and Briggs)

Notice that *to visit* means *to pay attention to*. God does not choose to cause the cycle of family dysfunction. We humans cause that ourselves. God refuses to ignore and do nothing about the cycle. He refuses to leave us alone with our sins. You may have chosen any of the feelings the activity describes. Your feelings are uniquely your own. Honesty about our feelings is a sign of progress. We believe that responses 3 and 4 represent a growing understanding of God's loving and just work in our lives.

Unit 10   183

Breaking the Cycle

> He who conceals his transgressions will not prosper, but he who confesses and forsakes them will find compassion.
> –Proverbs 28:13

Proverbs 28:13 describes the process necessary for changing the course of family dysfunction. We usually conceal our transgressions either by denying that our actions are wrong or by feeling so guilty for them that we cannot face them. To break the cycle of sin, we must bring our transgressions into the light of God's Word and confess them. We can be confident of His forgiveness. And we must model this lifestyle of confession before our children.

To confess means *to agree with*. When we confess our sins, we agree with God that our attitude and/or actions indeed are sin. Sin is not relegated only to the more blatant varieties of wrongdoing like murder, rape, and stealing. Sin is an attitude that communicates to God: *I want to run my own life. You go Your way; I'll go mine.* At its most fundamental level sin is selfishness; and it can be expressed in many ways, some subtle and some blatant. When we confess to God, we also agree with Him that Christ's death is the complete payment for sin; consequently, we are completely forgiven.

After having agreed with God that we have sinned and that we are forgiven as a result of Christ's death on the cross, we must take a third step: to forsake that sin. *To forsake* means *to renounce, to leave altogether, to desert, to abandon*. When we forsake a sin, we go to any length to reject a wrongful attitude or behavior and replace it with that which honors Christ.

In his letter to the Ephesian believers Paul described the process of rejecting sin and replacing it with godliness.

> You did not learn Christ in this way, if indeed you have heard Him and have been taught in Him, just as truth is in Jesus, that, in reference to your former manner of life, you lay aside the old self, which is being corrupted in accordance with the lusts of deceit, and that you be renewed in the spirit of your mind, and put on the new self, which in the likeness of God has been created in righteousness and holiness of the truth.
> –Ephesians 4:20-24

✎ Read Ephesians 4:20-24, which appears in the margin. As you read, circle Paul's instructions. What specific actions did the apostle Paul describe that apply to modeling God's character for your children?

_____

_____

You may have noted that Paul instructs us to lay aside the old self, to be renewed in the spirit of the mind, and to put on the new self. "Laying aside" is a parallel of confession. To lay something aside, you first have to recognize that it exists and that it can harm you and/or others. Being renewed in the spirit of our minds occurs as we reflect on the truth of the Scriptures—especially the deep implications of the gospel—that we are deeply loved, completely forgiven, fully pleasing, and totally accepted by God because of the cross of Christ. Putting on the new self means making choices to spend time and effort doing what honors the Lord and encourages others.

No Magic Pill

Breaking the cycle happens through a combination of powerful, God-given forces.

The process of genuine change does not occur by magic. Breaking a cycle of family sin happens not by waving a wand or by reading a verse but through a combination of powerful, God-given forces: the Scriptures, the Holy Spirit, the body of believers, and the human will.

The Scriptures are our only source of truth about God, about ourselves, and about the process of restoration that God can perform in our lives. The Holy Spirit is the Agent of change. Self-effort is not enough. Real, lasting growth in

We choose to depend either on ourselves or on Christ to produce change.

a person's life requires the transforming power of the Spirit of God. The body of Christ needs to model and affirm the truth of the Scriptures and the work of God's Spirit corporately and individually. And finally, God has given each of us a will so that we play a role in the process of change. We choose to depend either on ourselves or on Christ to produce change. We choose either to continue living the reproduced sin pattern in our family history or to begin acting in a way that honors Christ and helps our children, even when every fiber of our hearts and emotions seems to tug at us to continue in a familiar but destructive cycle of behavior. If all of these ingredients operate, then eventually and gradually, the transformation we long for will happen!

✎ To aid your memory and to drive home the reality of the task, write four ingredients you need to break the cycle.

1. _____ 3. _____

2. _____ 4. _____

You could have answered the activity with more than one set of words, but you need these elements: the Scriptures, the presence and power of the Holy Spirit, the support and guidance of the church, and your own wise choices.

✎ How do you feel about the statement that no magic pill exists—that you face a lifelong task of discipleship and obedience?

_____

_____

You are nearing the end of this book. You probably are beginning to realize that this course is only a beginning. The truths you are learning can make a tremendous difference in your life, but you will not be completely healed at the conclusion of this study. Sometimes we feel discouraged and depressed when we realize that no simple solution exists. Remember that God provides genuine hope for change and restoration.

✎ Read Joel 2:24-26 in the margin. Does this passage give you hope about your relationships with your children? Why or why not?

_____

_____

The threshing floors will be full of grain, And the vats will overflow with the new wine and oil. "Then I will make up to you for the years that the swarming locust has eaten, the creeping locust, the stripping locust, and the gnawing locust, My great army which I sent among you. And you shall have plenty to eat and be satisfied, And praise the name of the Lord your God, Who has dealt wondrously with you; Then My people will never be put to shame."

–Joel 2:24-26

Even if you have failed miserably at modeling God's character for your children, you can take hope in the prophet Joel's words. We can apply this promise to our need to change the way we treat our children: " 'I will make up to you for the years that the swarming locust has eaten.' "

✎ What specific plans do you have to grow in each of the four areas? Describe your plans to grow in relation to:

The Scriptures: _____

_____

Unit 10   185

The presence and power of the Holy Spirit: _____

_____

The support and guidance of the church: _____

_____

Wise choices: _____

_____

We do not want to supply simplistic answers for you. Your plans to grow as a disciple are uniquely your own. You might think of actions like joining a Bible study through your church, enrolling in a Christian college or seminary, reading books on the subjects in which you need to grow, or studying the Book of Proverbs every day. The key to growing is to do something. Consistent, small steps will take you where dreams of giant steps never will go. You can give your children only what you have. The best thing you can do for them is not to help, rescue, teach, or fix them. The best thing you can do for them is to grow so that you can model health and discipleship for them.

Consistent, small steps will take you where dreams of giant steps never will go.

✏️ Begin to memorize Colossians 2:6-7 and review the passages you have been learning in this study.

SUMMARY STATEMENTS

- To the degree that we understand and experience God's love, forgiveness, and power, we will be able to express these characteristics and to model them for our children.
- To break the cycle of sin, we must bring our transgressions into the light of God's Word and confess them, confident of His forgiveness. And we must model this lifestyle of confession before our children.
- The best thing you can do for your children is to grow so that you can model health and discipleship for them.

DAY 2

Self-concept and Purpose

Behold, the Lord's hand is not so short that it cannot save; Neither is His ear so dull that it cannot hear.

—Isaiah 59:1

In his book, *You and Your Child*, Charles Swindoll wrote: "The locust of parental neglect and insensitivity may have taken its toll on your children's lives years ago. The swarming insects of indifference or ignorance or impatience or a host of other famines brought on by your failures ate away at your relationship with those precious children, resulting today in barrenness and perhaps even bitterness and resentment on their part. Now they are grown. You cannot relive those years. That's a fact. But God can renew them. That's a promise. That's hope!"[1]

Through the rest of this unit we will look at five principles for learning to model God's character for our children:

1. A changed self-concept
2. A changed purpose
3. Changed affections
4. A changed schedule
5. Changed actions

A Changed Self-concept

As we have mentioned several times before, most of us try to gain our security and significance by performing to win others' approval. This pursuit is a hopeless rat race because God has created us in such a way that only His love, forgiveness, and acceptance can truly satisfy us.

God has created us in such a way that only His love, forgiveness, and acceptance can truly satisfy us.

We need to change the way we see ourselves. If we are driven to perform, we may use others to get what we need and then condemn them when they fail. If we seek others' approval, we may alter our behavior to please them without being ourselves at all. Or we may use our approval as a tool to manipulate others to make us happy.

Robin is a young mother who realized that her perception of herself radically affects how she treats her children. As she has become more and more convinced that God loves her unconditionally, she has become more patient and affectionate with her children.

✎ Describe your self-concept. What do you think of yourself? What is the basis of your self-worth?

_____

_____

_____

We often base our self-worth on our own efforts. If we perform well on a given day or at a certain task, we feel good about ourselves. If we perceive that we have done poorly, we feel bad. Therefore, our self-concept—and, as a result, our behavior—depends not on the grace and faithfulness of Jesus Christ but on our own actions.

✎ What is your purpose in life? If a friend observed your attitude and activities, what would he or she see as your purpose in life?

_____

_____

_____

We need to understand our purpose and be able to communicate it.

Many of us have never taken the time and spent the energy to write our purpose in life. An old saying states that he who aims at nothing probably will hit it. We need to understand our purpose and be able to communicate it.

Unit 10   187

✎ Do you need to change or modify your purpose? If so, how?

_____

_____

A Changed Purpose

Our culture glorifies the triad of selfish purposes: success, pleasure, and approval.

Our culture glorifies the triad of selfish purposes: success, pleasure, and approval. Practically every television commercial, billboard, and magazine ad tells us that a product or a service will give us success, pleasure, or others' approval. Then we will be really happy! An excellent theological term exists to describe such thinking—hogwash!

Dan Hayes, a speaker for Campus Crusade for Christ, illustrates our fruitless pursuit of happiness with this dialogue:

Q: "What do most people want out of life?"
A: "They want the American dream: a nice car, a nice home, a nice job, a nice boat, nice vacations, nice neighbors, a nice husband or a nice wife, and nice children. They work like crazy to get these things; but after a while, they get bored with them."
Q: "Then what do they want?"
A: "They want a bigger car, a bigger house, a better job, better vacations, better neighbors, bigger and better children, and a better spouse. People are never satisfied with 'things'!"

In fact, God has made us so that things cannot satisfy us. No matter how we pursue them, they leave us empty. Jeremiah wrote the verse appearing in the margin, which describes the emptiness of pursuing selfish goals in the vain hope that they will satisfy us.

Cisterns are underground water tanks. In Jeremiah's day cisterns were carved out of rock. If the rock was fractured, the cistern could not hold water. The effort was wasted chasing a foolish dream.

My people have committed two evils: They have forsaken Me, the fountain of living waters, to hew for themselves cisterns, broken cisterns, that can hold no water.

–Jeremiah 2:13

✎ Can you describe one "broken cistern" you have carved for yourself? It might be any goal that you once pursued in hopes that it would make you happy.

_____

If you achieved your goal, how did you feel after you reached it?

_____

_____

Most people never think about their purpose in life. They merely adopt whatever purpose someone else gives them. Many companies demand that their employees put the company at the top of their priority list. As Brian was interviewing with an electric company, he was told: "If you come to work for us, we'll pay you well. You'll have excellent benefits. And in return, we'll expect you to eat, breathe, sleep, and work for our company. If you work for us, we'll expect you to place our company above anything else in your life." They wanted to own him, but Brian did not want anyone to own him except Christ. He resisted the urge to carve a broken cistern for himself.

↪ Take a few minutes to pray. If possible, take a walk as you visit with the Lord. Ask Him to show you the purpose He has for you or to reaffirm the purpose you already recognize.

Our compelling purpose in life should be to honor Christ in everything we think, say, and do.

Our compelling purpose in life should be to honor Christ in everything we think, say, and do. If our purpose is to seek as much success, pleasure, and approval as we can get, we will pass our selfishness to our children (in the little time we have left with them). If our purpose is to honor Christ, we will use every opportunity to model and teach God's character and truth to our children. Either way, they will be profoundly affected!

✎ In the margin write this week's Scripture-memory verses three times.

SUMMARY STATEMENTS

- God has created us in such a way that only His love, forgiveness, and acceptance can truly satisfy us.
- We need to understand our purpose and be able to communicate it.
- Our compelling purpose in life should be to honor Christ in everything we think, say, and do.

DAY 3

Changing Affections

Restore to me the joy of Thy salvation, and sustain me with a willing spirit.
—Psalm 51:12

David's words in Psalm 51 communicate to us powerfully because we identify with his pain. Struggling with his affections, David asked God to restore the joy of salvation. Once David had felt real joy in his relationship with God. Now he felt alienated and numb.

Some of us have affections that have been numbed by years of withdrawal. Others have replaced their affections with hatred, and their anger has a hair trigger. Some avoid any intimacy with others because they fear being hurt. Can our fear and sense of distance be overcome? Can anger be changed? Can we choose how we feel?

✎ Suppose a friend asked you that question: "Can we choose how we feel?" How would you respond?

_____

_____

Trust in Him at all times, O people; Pour out your heart before Him; God is a refuge for us.

–Psalm 62:8

You might tell your friend that the answer is yes and no. (How's that for a clear answer?) We should not try to deny how we feel. If we try to suppress negative emotions, they will build and, sooner or later, cause either depression or an explosion. We need to be honest about our emotions and to pour out our hearts to the Lord (Psalm 62:8). We need to ask: *Why am I fearful? Why am I angry? What do I believe about God or about myself that is producing these emotions?* Then we can examine our thoughts and beliefs and can choose to change what we think about instead of trying to change how we feel. If we think properly about the Lord and about ourselves and if an affirming relative or friend models these concepts for us, then our emotions slowly will change, too.

From Destructive to Productive

We can shift our emotions from being destructively negative to being productively negative.

Although we cannot change our emotions from negative to positive, we can shift them from being destructively negative to being productively negative. Instead of anger, we can experience grief, especially when our children disobey. *Search for Significance* LIFE® Support Group Series Edition includes this helpful insight:

> *Our worth is totally secure in Christ, so our children's success or failure doesn't affect our value in the least. If they shine, make the dean's list, or throw tantrums in the grocery aisle, it doesn't affect our self-worth. We need to see our children the way our heavenly Father sees us: deeply loved, completely forgiven, fully pleasing, and totally accepted. Then, when they disobey, our discipline will be like the Father's discipline of us: in love, not anger. If we approach our children with an attitude of sadness about their misdeeds rather than anger when they disobey, it will make a tremendous difference! We will be amazed at what happens if we always go to our children with the attitude and words, "It's sad that you disobeyed. It was harmful to you, and I love you so much that I don't want you to harm yourself. I will need to discipline you to help you remember not to do it again. Remember, the reason I am disciplining you is that I love you so much!" We can respond this way instead of with words like these: "You've done it again, and I'll make sure you regret it! I wonder if you'll ever amount to anything."*[2]

✏ How might responding to your children's disobedience with grief instead of anger affect your relationship with them?

_____

_____

_____

_____

✏ How would being thankful for your children affect your relationships with them?

_____

_____

List at least 10 things about your children for which you are grateful. If you have no children, list things about your relatives or close friends for which you are grateful. You may want to use an additional sheet of paper.

_____

_____

_____

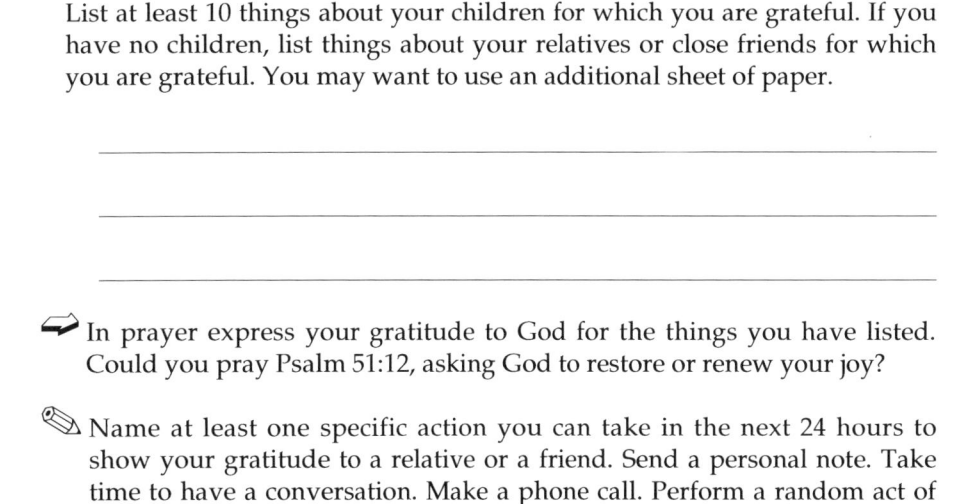

↪ In prayer express your gratitude to God for the things you have listed. Could you pray Psalm 51:12, asking God to restore or renew your joy?

✎ Name at least one specific action you can take in the next 24 hours to show your gratitude to a relative or a friend. Send a personal note. Take time to have a conversation. Make a phone call. Perform a random act of kindness. In the margin describe what you will do.

↪ Practice your Scripture-memory verses for the week.

SUMMARY STATEMENTS

- We need to be honest about our emotions and to pour out our hearts to the Lord.
- If we think properly about the Lord and about ourselves and if an affirming relative or friend models these concepts for us, then our emotions will slowly change, too.
- Although we cannot change our emotions from negative to positive, we can shift them from being destructively negative to being productively negative.

DAY 4

Changing Schedules

You shall teach them diligently to your sons and shall talk of them when you sit in your house and when you walk by the way and when you lie down and when you rise up.
—Deuteronomy 6:7

Many parents are too busy to spend time with their children. They work outside the home—sometimes for many extra hours each week. In their spare time they become involved in activities that do not allow much time with their family. Some people even become so involved in their church activities that little time is left for family togetherness. Sometimes people work excessively not just to provide necessities for their family but so that they can acquire more material goods. Their purpose is self-centered. They want more.

What is more important: more possessions or an emotionally healthy family? What is more important: a string of civic, community, and church

Excessive work and outside activities take time that parents could devote to nurturing and developing children.

involvements, or quality family time? The acquisition of things and excessive involvement in outside activities take time and energy that parents could devote to nurturing and developing children. Helping children progress through the developmental stages of bonding, separateness, adolescence, and maturity requires concentrated attention and affection; but it is well worth the effort, both for the parents and their children.

To change your established schedule so that you have time with your children takes courage and planning. As you begin, be sure to schedule and protect your time. Do not let anything steal the precious moments you have allotted for interaction with your children and spouse.

✎ What physical and/or emotional stage of development (bonding, separateness, adolescence, or maturity) do you think each of your children

Child's Age	Physical Stage of Development	Emotional Stage of Development
_____	_____	_____
_____	_____	_____
_____	_____	_____

is in? Why do you think so?

✎ How much time do you spend each week giving undivided attention to your children?

_____

What activities could you plan with your children that would meet their developmental needs?

_____
_____
_____

Do you need to change your schedule to spend more quality time with your children? If so, what specific changes will you make?

_____
_____
_____

Many families have developed special traditions that give every member something to look forward to and enjoyable memories later. One father makes chocolate-chip pancakes or waffles for his wife and children every Saturday morning. Another couple spends three hours every Sunday afternoon with the children. The family takes the phone off the hook and has a picnic (on the living room floor if it is raining), reads books, and plays games together.

Family traditions can be weekly, monthly, or seasonal; many center on holidays. Tomorrow's lesson contains a list of suggestions for family traditions. As you study that lesson, think of some family traditions that could be meaningful to you and to your family.

⇨ This lesson has asked you to take an objective look at your schedule. Most of us feel extreme amounts of guilt when we consider the gap between the type of parents we want to be and the type of parents we perceive ourselves to be. Take a few minutes to give thanks to the God who overcomes our mistakes. Read the following story and include the lesson you learn from it in your prayer time.

Pam's story

Pam came to her group meeting looking haggard and exhausted. Obviously, she had been grieving. She explained that as she studied how families work and how dysfunction passes from one generation to the next, she was encountering major difficulty in two areas. First, Pam said: "I am grieving over my childhood. I pretended for many years that we had a perfect home, that my parents loved me, and that everything was wonderful. Now I am coming to grips with the fact that it was all a dream world I had constructed because the reality was so bad. Then when I began to look at my present family, I realized that I have done many of the same things to my children that my parents did to me."

Rhonda, another member of the group, began to weep. "Pam," Rhonda said, "I remember when you shared with this group about your struggle to apologize to your son and when you told about listening to your daughter without telling her what to do. Pam, I am so grateful for you. I could never even imagine my parents being able to do those things. Could you imagine your parents treating you with that respect?" Pam shook her head.

✎ What message of hope can you learn from Pam's story?

_____

_____

Recognize how far you have come.

You might have written that the story reminds you of the reality of life. Pam has not completely broken free of the cycle of hurtful family experiences. We will probably struggle all of our lives with issues related to the ingrained patterns we have learned. Pam, however, has made genuine progress. Instead of feeling like a failure, she can recognize how far she has come.

✎ In the margin write this week's Scripture verses from memory. Review your previous memory verses.

SUMMARY STATEMENTS

- The acquisition of things takes time and energy that could be devoted to nurturing and developing children.
- To change your established schedule so that you have time with your children takes courage and planning.
- Do not let anything steal the precious moments you have allotted for interaction with your children and spouse.

DAY 5

Changing Actions

Prove yourselves doers of the word, and not merely hearers who delude themselves.

–James 1:22

The four principles of change we have examined focus on why and when you can model God's character for your children. The final principle centers on what to model. Good intentions are not enough. Our children need affirmation through our words and our deeds.

Our children need affirmation through our words and our deeds.

In their award-winning book, *The Blessing*, Gary Smalley and John Trent examine the way Isaac blessed his children.³ We can follow the same example with our children. The elements of the blessing are

- a meaningful touch;
- a spoken message;
- attaching high value to the one being blessed;
- picturing a special future for the one being blessed;
- an active commitment to fulfill the blessing.

✎ As you explore each of these five elements, underline words or phrases that you may want to apply in your family life.

Touch

• Touching someone can communicate warmth and a sense of intimacy. Giving a hug, patting someone on the shoulder, or holding a person's hand tells the person that you care about and accept him. John, whose family had avoided touching one another, determined to give his wife and children meaningful touches each day. He decided to touch each one 10 times a day until it became a habit for him. Most of us do not have to be this mechanical, but we would do well to adopt this kind of determination.

✎ What actions will you take to model God's character for your children this way? How will you express meaningful touch?

_____

_____

Spoken words

• A spoken message of affection and affirmation also is important. Condemnation and sarcasm are tremendously destructive. An estimate is that 20 positive messages are required to overcome every negative one. Some of us have experienced the reverse ratio: 20 negative to 1 positive! Simple statements have a powerful effect: "I love you." "You're a wonderful son." "You really did that well."

✎ What actions will you take to model God's character for your children this way? What specific things can you do to develop a habit of expressing affection and affirmation to your children?

_____

_____

• Attaching high value is another dimension of affirmation. When we

High value communicate that we value a person, we show him that he has a secure place in our eyes.

Tom asks his daughter, "If all of the little girls in the whole world were lined up, do you know which one I would pick?" She always smiles and says, "No, which one, Daddy?" Tom waves his finger as if deciding, then points to her and exclaims: "You! You're the one I'd pick!" He is communicating high value.

✎ What actions will you take to model God's character for your children this way? How will you express to your children that you value them highly?

_____

_____

A special future

• Picturing a special future involves observing a child's strengths and abilities. One parent might say, after observing his child's drawings, "You might become a great artist! You are so good at drawing monsters!" Or a parent might say to a child, "You are so loving and kind that the Lord will use you in hundreds or thousands of people's lives someday!"

✎ What actions will you take to model God's character for your children this way? How will you express your vision of a special future to the one being blessed?

_____

_____

An active commitment

• Finally, we need to demonstrate an active commitment to fulfill the blessing. Taking time to observe children and expending the physical and emotional energy to affirm them are important. But we also need to provide whatever is necessary to help our children develop and reach the special future we have described to them. Baseball practice, piano lessons, crayons, paper, and whatever else we provide for them communicate that we are actively committed to their welfare and development.

✎ What actions will you take to model God's character for your children this way? How will you show an active commitment to fulfill the blessing?

_____

_____

As we trust God to change our self-concepts, purposes, affections, schedules, and actions, we will be able to model His character to our children more consistently, regardless of the modeling we received as children. Our children do not have to experience what many of us have experienced. We have hope for change!

Our children do not have to experience what many of us have experienced.

One of the ways you might have completed the previous activity was making a commitment to develop family traditions. What do your children enjoy doing? What can you do together? What traditions do you already have?

What traditions will you begin?

→ Pray before you read the following suggestions for special traditions. Ask God to show you what traditions—large or small—you can begin or continue that can model affirmation and value for your children.

✎ As you read the suggestions, write in the margin your ideas for special traditions.

Christmas Traditions

A Birthday Box for Baby Jesus
Wrap a Bible in a box with the Christmas story marked. Make this the most beautiful present under the tree. Open this present first and begin gift-giving time by reading the Christmas story.

Decorate Your Children's Doors
Put wrapping paper and a big bow on each door. Then place a gift tag on it with a message like this: "Meagan, you are God's gift to our family; and God's gift to you is Jesus."

"You are God's gift to our family, and God's gift to you is Jesus."

Give Coupons to Family Members
Designating gifts of time you will spend with family members, these coupons can be special ways to tell others how much you love them.

Valentine's Day Traditions

Baked Valentines
Bake a cake in a heart-shaped pan. Write on small strips of paper Bible verses that speak of love. Fold them and wrap them in small squares of foil. Place as many verses as you would like in the batter before baking. After serving the cake, let family members who find the pieces of foil open them and read the verses aloud.

Valentine's Day Dinner
Have a candlelight dinner for your children. Choose a specific country for the theme of this special time together, and serve the appropriate ethnic food. Talk about God's love and the need to take His love to the world. Pray together after giving everyone a specific prayer request for that country.

Easter Traditions

Celebrate with a Romanian Custom
In Romania an Easter tradition for Christians is to place red eggs on the dinner table, one in front of each person. Before the meal each person picks up his or her egg. The person at the head of the table starts by turning to the person on his right and saying, "He is risen." That person responds by saying, "He is risen indeed" and then turns to the person on his right and repeats the process until the message has gone around the table.

"He is risen."

Passover Meal

Many Christian families acknowledge the Passover to connect with their

Jewish roots. You can obtain information about the Passover meal from the book *Hebrew Christian Passover Haggadah* by Arnold G. Frucktenbrus; c/o Beth Bar Shalom Fellowship; 460 Sylvan Avenue; P. O. Box 1331; Englewood Cliffs, NJ 07632.

Birthdays

VIP Chair
Decorate a special chair for the birthday person. If it is for your child, tell the story of his or her birth and how much you wanted him or her.

Give thanks for special people.

Celebrate Spiritual Birthdays
For children, give Christian books, tapes, games, and so forth to acknowledge the anniversary of when each family member became a Christian.

Thanksgiving

Talk about the people for whom you are especially thankful. Write them letters expressing your feelings for them.

At your Thanksgiving meal, read the story of the 10 lepers (Luke 17:11-19). Of the 10 Jesus healed, only 1 came back to thank Him. Talk about the man who expressed thanks and the lack of thankfulness exhibited by the other 9.

Weekly

Have special breakfasts on Saturday mornings featuring family members' favorite breakfast foods.

Schedule a family-fun night with games and snacks.

On a Sunday afternoon, have a family picnic that includes reading and games.

Daily

Read together before bedtime.

Conduct family devotions in the morning or evening.

Keep a chart of responsibilities (based on age and ability) for each person and award treats for jobs well done.

Other

Develop the practice of doing things with the children. Suggestions for possible activities are endless.
- Canoeing, hiking, rafting, fishing
- Working on hobbies together; building or making things together
- Saving children's clothes or other heirlooms
- Keep a scrapbook together; add pictures and mementoes year around, and on their birthday write a page or a letter telling about special memories from that year. Include the front page of the newspaper.

Unit Review

✎ Review the five lessons in this unit. Find one statement that helped you better understand the importance of relationships. Circle this statement and rewrite it in your own words.

_____

_____

_____

✎ Review your written work and prayer responses throughout the unit. What exercise was most meaningful to you during this week? Identify the exercise and explain your choice.

_____

_____

_____

✎ Review the Scripture-memory passage. Find it in your Bible and check your memory. Then close your Bible and write the passage in the margin. How have you applied this passage during your study of this unit?

_____

_____

_____

Notes
[1]Charles R. Swindoll, *You and Your Child* (Nashville: Thomas Nelson Publishers, 1977), 158.
[2]Robert S. McGee, *Search for Significance* LIFE® Support Group Series Edition (Houston: Rapha Publishing, 1992), 139.
[3]Gary Smalley and John Trent, *The Blessing* (Nashville: Thomas Nelson Publishers, 1986), 24.

UNIT 11

Responding to Your Parents

Case in point

NUMB ABOUT DAD

Lynda's father seemed to have a split personality. Most of the time he was quiet and unassuming, even passive. But occasionally, he would explode in a profane fury. Deeply scarred by her father's mixed signals, Lynda was fearful and insecure.

When her counselor asked her about her father, Lynda could describe his behavior very accurately. But when asked how she had felt when he was in a rage, she could not respond. "I ... I'm not sure how I felt," she stammered. The counselor asked, "Did you feel afraid of him?" Lynda responded, "I don't know." Then the counselor asked, "Lynda, how would you feel if you saw a man in your neighborhood treat his daughter the way you were treated?" She quickly responded, "I'd be angry." "You would?" he asked. "Yes, I'd be really angry with him!" Lynda responded, her eyes and voice intense.

"How would a little girl normally feel about a father like yours?"

"Well, I guess she'd be afraid of him. I guess she'd be very hurt and afraid." The lights began to come on in Lynda's mind. "I guess I'm just numb about my father." (You will read more about Lynda on p. 205.)

What you'll learn

This week you will
- explore the meaning of honoring your father and mother;
- analyze your views of yourself and of your parents;
- develop your sense of independence;
- describe some godly choices to make in relating to your parents;
- identify some preparation you need to make to relate properly to your parents.

What you'll study

Determining Your Response	Your Viewpoint: Self and Parents	A Sense of Independence	Make Godly Choices	Be Prepared
DAY 1	DAY 2	DAY 3	DAY 4	DAY 5

Memory verse

This week's verse of Scripture to memorize

See how great a love the Father has bestowed upon us, that we should be called children of God; and such we are. For this reason the world does not know us, because it did not know Him.

–1 John 3:1

DAY 1

Determining Your Response

Honor your father and mother (which is the first commandment with a promise), that it may be well with you, and that you may live long on the earth.
—Ephesians 6:2-3

You may find this unit very challenging but rewarding if you approach it with honesty and sincerity. It is challenging because responding to one's parents in a godly way, especially if they have been abusive or neglectful, can be extremely painful.

This subject also is challenging because everyone's situation is different. Because many relationships are complex, "cookie-cutter" answers do not fit individual situations. But this chapter is necessary because our relationships with our parents are God-given. The Lord wants us to respond to them in a way that honors Him. To do so, we need His wisdom and strength.

Our relationships with our parents are God-given.

Rick's story

Rick talked about his relationships with his parents. His father left when Rick was nine years old. Three years later his parents divorced. His mother had to work to support him and his sister. When she got home each day, she was too tired to give the children much attention and affection. Unresolved bitterness toward her husband also sapped her energy for giving. Throughout his childhood Rick received no emotional support from his father and very little from his mother. After talking about how his family situation had affected his view of God and how he could change those misconceptions, he eventually began to focus on how he could respond to his parents now. Rick's expression became intense as he leaned forward in his chair and said, "It would be easier for me if they were dead!"

✎ How would you respond to Rick's statement?

_____

_____

Have you ever felt the way Rick did—that it would be easier not to deal with your parents at all? Describe your feelings.

_____

_____

If you share Rick's emotion, remember that feelings are just that—feelings. You will do neither yourself nor your family any good by shaming yourself because of your feelings. We can learn to acknowledge our feelings in appropriate ways and then to respond in a way that honors Christ. One good response to Rick's statement might be to validate his feelings by saying something like: "I feel sad that you feel so hurt and alone."

Some of us have had relatively good relationships with our parents all of our lives, and we need to make only minor adjustments in our attitudes and actions toward them. However, some of us need a major overhaul. We cannot overcome years of withdrawal from our parents or bitterness toward them in

We must apply God's Word and follow His Spirit to respond properly to our parents.

a day. Rather, we must apply God's Word diligently and follow His Spirit closely to learn how to respond properly to our parents.

✎ The next two paragraphs describe two very different but typical models for relationships between parents and their grown children. As you read, circle the phrases that best describe your relationships with your parents.

Our parents have dominated some of us to the extent that we feel that they want us to say and do exactly as they wish all the time. Otherwise, we fear that they will criticize and reject us. If this is the case for you, you will need to develop objectivity in your relationships with your parents. You will need to escape the domination (without completely breaking your relationships with your parents) and to develop your own identity.

Some of us have coped with painful family relationships by moving in the other direction. We have withdrawn, either emotionally or physically, to protect ourselves from the pain of parental neglect or disapproval. We need to pursue the relationships with our parents as we extend to them the love and forgiveness we have received from Christ.

✎ Check the method of relating to your parents with which you most clearly relate.

- ❑ Domination: my parents seek to control my thoughts, feelings, and behaviors.
- ❑ Withdrawal: I have withdrawn from my parents to protect myself.
- ❑ Good boundaries: our relationships are based on neither domination nor withdrawal; they respect my boundaries, and I can be open with them.
- ❑ Other: _____

Explain why you answered as you did. How do you feel about your response?

_____
_____
_____

The Meaning of *Honor*

Both Old and New Testament Scriptures direct us to honor our parents. What does honoring our parents mean? Many people have misconceptions about this teaching.

Honor your father and your mother, that your days may be prolonged in the land which the Lord your God gives you.
–Exodus 20:12

Honor your father and mother (which is the first commandment with a promise), that it may be well with you, and that you may live long on the earth.
–Ephesians 6:2-3

People who are overly responsible believe that if their parents are not completely happy with everything they say and do, they have not honored their parents. If you are one of those people, you probably answered the above question with the domination response—unless you are so excessively loyal that you cannot admit the truth about your relationships. For overly responsible people, the burden of making their parents happy is oppressive!

You are not responsible for making your parents happy. They are responsible for themselves. Their happiness is between them and the Lord. Their contentment should not rest on your shoulders. They need to depend on the Lord, not on you, for their security and significance.

✎ Have you thought and felt that you are responsible for making your parents happy? ❑ Yes ❑ No

Although you are not responsible for your parents' happiness, you are responsible for developing your own separate identity and for extending your respect and love to them. At that point, let them respond in any way they choose. Sometimes they will appreciate what you say and do. Sometimes they will not, but you need to do what the Lord wants you to do, whether or not they appreciate it.

You are responsible for developing your own separate identity and for extending your love to your parents.

A statement in *Search for Significance* LIFE® Support Group Series Edition gives objectivity and perspective to honoring our parents. As we develop our own identity and seek to honor them, we should remember: *It would be nice if my father and my mother approved of me, but if they don't, I'm still deeply loved, completely forgiven, fully pleasing, and totally accepted and absolutely complete in Christ.*[1] Remember, you are responsible not for your parents' happiness but for acting in a way that pleases God. If your parents are happy with you, that is fine. If not, be content that you have obeyed and pleased God. After all, He is the Lord, and He deserves our primary affection and obedience.

✎ Describe your reaction to the previous two paragraphs.

_____

_____

Am I now seeking the favor of men, or of God? Or am I striving to please men? If I were still trying to please men, I would not be a bond-servant of Christ.
–Galatians 1:10

In Galatians 1:10 Paul wrote that we can be bond-servants either to people or to God but not to both. We are responsible for treating our parents in a way that pleases the Lord. Our parents' response is their decision.

As we develop our own identity and learn how to express God's love and grace to our parents, they may well notice a difference in us, and they may not like it! If we have been withdrawn, they may not know how to deal with our expressions of gratitude and acts of love. If we have been virtual puppets, doing anything and everything to make them happy, our new identities and healthy independence from them will likely threaten their domination of us. In that case even our loving actions and words may be misunderstood because in their jaded, self-preoccupied view, they will see our new independence as dishonoring them. Any change in the status quo can disturb our parents, and the transition to new relationships with them often is awkward and sometimes painful.

The transition to new relationships with our parents is often awkward and sometimes painful.

Not to Change Them

Many people expect that treating their parents differently will cause their parents to change and to treat them differently. That may happen after a while, but it may not. In fact, no matter how much you change, your parents may not change at all! You can pray for their response. You can love them and accept them unconditionally. Yet they still may not change their behavior toward you. Do not fall into the trap of believing that you are responsible to

Your parents may never change— but you can!

change the way they evaluate and respond to you. That is bargaining (see page 174). They have their own free wills and make their own choices. Be content that you are doing all you know to do, learning by trial and error, and depending on the Lord for His love and His strength. Their response is their decision. They may never change—but you can! This week you will learn principles that will help you respond to your parents in a way that honors the Lord.

✎ Begin to memorize this week's Scripture-memory verse, 1 John 3:1, by writing it in the margin.

SUMMARY STATEMENTS

- We can learn to acknowledge our feelings in appropriate ways and then to respond in a way that honors Christ.
- Although you are not responsible for your parents' happiness, you are responsible for developing your own separate identity and for extending your love to them.
- Your parents may never change—but you can!

DAY 2

Your Viewpoint: Self and Parents

No, in all these things we are more than conquerors through him who loved us.
—Romans 8:37, NIV

Some people have experienced extraordinarily tragic family situations in which they have been emotionally and physically abused, neglected, abandoned, or manipulated to accomplish their parents' selfish goals. Relationships like these cause indescribable anguish and trauma.

✎ Do you see yourself as a conqueror or a victim in your relationships with your parents? Why?

_____

_____

When people have been deeply hurt by their parents, the normal response is either withdrawal to avoid pain or revenge to inflict pain (or some combination of these). Neither withdrawal nor revenge honors Christ. One of the greatest needs of those who have severely repressed their emotions is to move from denial to honesty and to begin to experience the hurt and anger they have repressed. For a while these people need to see themselves as victims of the neglect and abuse they have experienced.

Christ can give us hope and confidence because His grace is bigger than our pain.

Regardless of our backgrounds, Christ can bring light from darkness and purpose from pain. He can give us hope and confidence because His grace is bigger than our pain. Because we are His children, we can be conquerors instead of victims. Paul wrote to the believers in Rome about this perspective

> Who shall separate us from the love of Christ? Shall tribulation, or distress, or persecution, or famine, or nakedness, or peril, or sword? But in all these things we overwhelmingly conquer through Him who loved us.
>
> –Romans 8:35,37

in the midst of his most severe difficulties. Read the verse appearing at left.

If we see ourselves as victims, we always will be defensive–blaming others for the way we are. If we see ourselves as conquerors, we will have a deep sense of both purpose and thankfulness, realizing that God uses difficulties to build character strengths in us. And He will use our difficulties to help us relate to the needs of others so that we can comfort them in times of need.

See Your Parents as People, Not Villains

Children see their parents as god-like. What the parents say is truth. What they demand is law. How they act is the order of the universe. Sooner or later, we realize that our parents are not gods after all, and with that realization come two possible conclusions: we either understand that they are more or less ordinary people, or we believe that they are villains who have hurt us maliciously.

Most parents treat their children the same way their parents treated them.

The truth is that very few parents intentionally hurt their children. The vast majority simply live their own heritage. They treat their children the same way their parents treated them. Most of them, far from being evil villains, experience the deep pain of guilt and shame because they know they are not the parents they want to be.

✎ Describe your father's relationships with his parents.

_____

_____

✎ Describe your mother's relationships with her parents.

_____

_____

Paula's story

Paula's mother was kind and gracious to most people, but she was a demanding tyrant to Paula. No matter how well Paula performed, it was not good enough for her mother; and nothing escaped her jaundiced eye: Paula's grades, her appearance, her friends, her activities—every facet of her life. Paula tried everything to please her mother, but constant disapproval and criticism had caused her to become passive and withdrawn.

When she later realized that she had been her mother's pawn all of her life, Paula became bitter and resented her mother. A few months later, Paula, still angry, traveled to visit her mother's parents, who lived across the country. She had not seen them for a long time, but after only one day she had a startling revelation. Her grandmother was a harsh, demanding woman. Her mother had never received genuine love and affirmation, only criticism and disapproval.

Paula realized that her mother had treated her the same way she had been treated! Instantly, she understood that her mother was not the villain Paula had thought she was. Paula's mother was a person who had been hurt deeply all of her life by her own mother's condemnation. The pain Paula had felt from

204   Unit 11

her mother's constant criticism remained, but her bitterness turned to grief when she understood that both she and her mother had never experienced the love they needed.

✎ How does understanding your parents' families affect your attitude toward them?

___

___

Our parents are not gods, but most of them are not evil villains either. They are people who tend to treat us the same way they were treated. Many of them are deeply hurt themselves. They need our understanding and forgiveness, not our criticism and condemnation.

Our parents need our understanding and forgiveness, not our criticism and condemnation.

➪ Spend a few minutes in prayer. Tell God what you are feeling about your relationships with your parents. Ask Him to give you the wisdom to understand and to respond appropriately to them.

✎ To help you memorize 1 John 3:1, write your paraphrase of the verse. Then repeat the verse aloud until you can say it from memory.

See how great a love the Father has bestowed upon us, that we should be called children of God; and such we are. For this reason the world does not know us, because it did not know Him.
—1 John 3:1

___

___

SUMMARY STATEMENTS

- Christ can bring light from darkness and purpose from pain. He can give us hope and confidence because His grace is bigger than our pain.
- If we see ourselves as conquerors, we will have a deep sense of both purpose and thankfulness, realizing that God uses difficulties to build character strengths in us.
- Our parents need our understanding and forgiveness, not our criticism and condemnation.

A Sense of Independence

DAY 3

Each one shall bear his own load.
—Galatians 6:5

Some people base their whole identity on their parents' opinions of who they are. This is understandable for a child but devastating for an adult. As people mature, they need to develop their own identities.

Lynda's story

Lynda's father seemed to have a split personality. Most of the time he was quiet and unassuming—even passive. But occasionally, he would explode in a profane fury. Deeply scarred by her father's mixed signals, Lynda was fearful and insecure.

Her fear and insecurity did not diminish as she grew older. She married and had children, but she cowered at the slightest change in her husband's tone of voice. She needed help.

When her counselor asked her about her father, Lynda could describe his behavior very accurately. But when asked how she had felt when he was in a rage, she could not respond. "I ... I'm not sure how I felt," she stammered.

The counselor asked, "Did you feel afraid of him?"

Lynda responded, "I don't know."

Then the counselor asked, "Lynda, how would you feel if you saw a man in your neighborhood treat his daughter the way you were treated?"

She quickly responded, "I'd be angry."

"You would?" he asked.

"Yes, I'd be really angry with him!" Lynda responded, her eyes and voice intense.

"How would a little girl normally feel about a father like yours?"

"Well, I guess she'd be afraid of him. I guess she'd be very hurt and afraid." The lights began to come on in Lynda's mind. "I guess I'm just numb about my father."

✎ What would Lynda need to develop a healthy sense of independence?

___

___

Many of us can identify with Lynda's response to her father's behavior. Although we might be quick to agree that our parents have many faults, few of us would be able to name those faults and to describe their effects on us. We tend to shut out the negative aspects of our parents' behavior toward us, not just because we love them but because so much of our identity and security is invested in who they are. What we might perceive as loyalty toward our parents often is a defense mechanism that protects us from seeing behaviors that are disappointing and hurtful to us. The failure to establish objectivity (the ability to see both the good and the bad in our parents) prevents us from establishing a healthy sense of distance and independence from them. Instead, we focus on them and conduct ourselves according to their desires, hoping to secure their blessing and approval. Not only is this harmful to our human development, but it also blocks our spiritual growth. After all, when we allow our world to revolve around our parents, we effectually serve them instead of God.

When we allow our world to revolve around our parents, we effectually serve them instead of God.

You might have noted that Lynda needed several things. She needed to acknowledge her father's faults and the effects of his behavior on her. She needed to stop trying to get the blessing from her father—which he probably was not going to give anyway—and to seek it from her Heavenly Father.

Her counselor advised Lynda to think of her father as "that man in the neighborhood" for a while, until she could look at him and at herself more objectively. She allowed herself to feel normal emotions of hurt and anger as she thought about how she would feel if she saw him enraged at his daughter for no good reason. Soon she was able to transfer those objective perceptions to her own father.

As Lynda began to base her identity on the truths of God's Word instead of on the unreasonable fury of her unbalanced father, she was gradually able to develop a healthy sense of independence from him. This has been a long process, but it is making a world of difference for Lynda and her family.

A world of difference

✎ What would having a healthy independence, or a sense of objectivity, in your relationships with your parents mean to you?

_____

_____

How would having a healthy sense of independence help you?

_____

_____

✎ In the margin write from memory this week's Scripture verse. You may check your work on page 199.

SUMMARY STATEMENTS

- Before we gain insight, we tend to shut out the negative aspects of our parents' behavior toward us, not just because we love them but because so much of our identity and security is invested in who they are.
- The failure to establish objectivity prevents us from establishing a healthy sense of distance and independence from our parents.
- When we allow our world to revolve around our parents, we effectually serve them instead of God.

Make Godly Choices

DAY 4

Laying aside falsehood, speak truth, each one of you, with his neighbor, for we are members of one another.
—Ephesians 4:25

When your primary goal in life is to bring honor to the Lord, the goal of your every activity and relationship is to honor Him. As you begin to understand, believe, and live by the truths of Christ's unconditional love and acceptance, you then can begin expressing that love and acceptance to others. In fact, we can express God's love, forgiveness, and acceptance only in proportion to the depth to which we have experienced those qualities ourselves. We therefore need to drink deeply of these powerful truths so that our relationships can be characterized by them.

> ... bearing with one another, and forgiving each other, whoever has a complaint against anyone; just as the Lord forgave you, so also should you.
> –Colossians 3:13

> Wherefore, accept one another, just as Christ also accepted us to the glory of God.
> –Romans 15:7

Colossians 3:13 and Romans 15:7 are only two of many clear biblical teachings that our ability to love, forgive, and accept others is based on our own experience. Until we begin to develop our new identity in Christ, we have no choice but simply to defend ourselves as best we can and withdraw from or punish those who have hurt us. But when we realize that Christ is our protector and that He is the complete source of our security and significance, then we can choose to act in ways that are good for us and others and that honor Him. We can take our attention off ourselves and put it on Christ and others because *we are secure in Him.*

Sounds good, doesn't it? It is good; but the transition from self-defense and revenge to accepting unconditionally those who have hurt us deeply is awkward, long, and difficult. Our emotions run out of control. When our emotions tell us to fight back or hide and the Scriptures tell us to believe the truth about ourselves and love others, we need to have the courage to live by the truth instead of by our emotions. Many of us have been living by our emotions all of our lives; so the choice to live by the truth—in spite of our painful emotions—is difficult indeed. But seeing our emotions objectively and knowing that they are often based on our old identity are at least half of the battle.

We need to have the courage to live by the truth instead of by our emotions.

The transition may be difficult, and you may need the advice and encouragement of a friend or counselor to keep going in the midst of the battle; but realize that life is a series of choices. Will we choose to live by withdrawal and revenge or by the truth of the Scriptures and the power of God's Spirit?

After their parents have died, some people realize that they can choose to love, forgive, and accept their parents, but it is too late. The potential for a reconciliation with their parents is gone. This situation can be very disappointing; but instead of letting this disappointment lead to bitterness, they can realize that God is sovereign. He is aware of the situation, and He does not demand anything that is beyond reason. Those whose parents have died can thank God for what they have learned about His character and can share their newfound wisdom with those whose parents are still living. Then another family will have the potential for reconciliation.

↪ Review this lesson. Ask God to show you how you may apply the content by taking some specific actions in your life. Do not forget to thank Him for the things He is showing you through this process.

✎ List some ways you can communicate God's love, forgiveness, and acceptance to your parents—or to others if your parents no longer are living.

_____

_____

Remember what you read earlier: cookie-cutter answers do not work. Your list of actions is uniquely your own, but we hope one factor shows up on your list. You will be able to share and live the powerful truths of Scripture only to the degree that you have experienced them yourself. Your list needs to include actions to help you grow in your identity in Christ. When you appropriately take care of yourself by getting your security and significance from the Lord, you will build a better basis from which to relate to your parents. When you make godly choices that honor Christ, you will build yourself up in the faith so that you can better relate to others.

↪ Repeat this unit's Scripture-memory verse and review your previous memory passages.

SUMMARY STATEMENTS

- As you begin to understand, believe, and live by the truths of Christ's unconditional love and acceptance, you are then able to begin expressing that love and acceptance to others.
- When we realize that Christ is our protector and that He is the complete source of our security and significance, then we can choose to act in ways that are good for us and others and that honor Him.
- We need to have the courage to live by the truth instead of by our emotions.

DAY 5

Be Prepared

Put on the full armor of God, that you may be able to stand firm against the schemes of the devil.

–Ephesians 6:11

The idea that *if you change, your parents automatically will change too* may sound spiritual. However, your family developed certain behavior patterns over many years, and probably more than one conversation will be needed to rectify all of its wrongs and to develop new habits of relating. You may require years simply to change yourself, and your parents may never change.

Be prepared for your communication with your parents. Do not expect them to change quickly. They may, but they may not. Your new behavior may threaten them, and your desire for reconciliation may at first produce more bitterness.

Darren's story

Darren was from an alcoholic family. His father was neglectful and abusive, and his mother was a perfectionist. When Darren began to understand how his parents had affected him, he asked, "What should I tell my parents about what I'm learning?"

His pastor asked, "What would happen if you told them?"

Darren answered, "They would be furious!"
The pastor replied, "Then tell them only what would be positive and helpful

to them and to your relationships with them."

Darren changed his game plan from telling his parents everything to carefully planning his communication with them.

✏️ Compare Darren's story to Proverbs 29:11, which appears in the margin. Write a moral to Darren's story and to the proverb. What wisdom can you gain from the two?

> A fool uttereth all his mind; but a wise man keepeth it in till afterwards.
> –Proverbs 29:11, KJV

_____

_____

_____

You might have written that the moral is not automatically to tell all you know. We need to pour out our hearts to God; but in dealing with others learn to exercise wisdom and discretion. We can choose to speak only what helps ourselves and others grow. However, this does not mean returning to the habits of stuffing our feelings, using lies, or deception.

Fortify yourself with the truth.

Fortify yourself with the truth so that when you talk with your parents, you can remember that you are deeply loved, completely forgiven, fully pleasing, and totally accepted by the Lord, no matter what they—or others—think of you. Then you can make the difficult but right choice to love, forgive, and accept them, no matter what their response or your emotions might be.

Responding to parents can be very difficult. Do not be naive about the difficulties. Ask God for His wisdom and power, and be prepared.

✏️ What do you need to do to prepare yourself for your communication and interaction with your parents?

_____

_____

_____

What have you learned always to do?

_____

_____

_____

What have you learned never to do?

_____

_____

What is wise to avoid?

210   Unit 11

On what common ground can you build or rebuild your relationships with your parents?

Unit Review

✏️ Review the five lessons in this unit. Find one statement that helped you better understand the importance of relationships. Circle this statement and rewrite it in your own words.

✏️ Review your written work and prayer responses throughout the unit. What exercise was most meaningful to you during this week? Identify the exercise and explain your choice.

✏️ Review the Scripture-memory passage. Find it in your Bible and check your memory. Then close your Bible and write the passage in the margin. How have you applied this passage during your study of this unit?

Notes
[1] Robert S. McGee, *Search for Significance* LIFE₀ Support Group Series Edition (Houston: Rapha Publishing, 1992), 98.

UNIT 12

Toward the Future

Case in point

> MILES TO GO
>
> Ellen grew up in a large and very rigid family. She married from a desire to escape her parents more than from a commitment to her husband.
>
> Ellen was determined not to treat her children with the disrespect, anger, and abuse that she had experienced. From time to time, however, she was disturbed to hear her mother's voice coming from her own mouth and was disgusted to find herself acting out her father's patterns. When she heard that her church was offering a study called *Breaking the Cycle of Hurtful Family Experiences*, she enrolled with fear.
>
> Ellen felt both elated and fearful as she completed the discovery group. She had gained much understanding about herself and about her family. She had begun to understand the causes of the actions she had experienced. She was able to forgive and release painful memories and anger. But Ellen also realized that the job was far from completed. Understanding that genuinely breaking the cycle is a long-term project, she began to lay plans for how she could grow and could overcome the patterns that still operated in her life and family. (In this unit you will read about your options for continuing your growth.)

What you'll learn

This week you will
- review your study and describe how the cycle of family dysfunction has affected your life;
- describe how a person can achieve change and break the cycle;
- make deliberate choices to live life with purpose rather than simply react to events;
- identify your progress in the grief/healing process and determine your continued needs for growth and healing;
- survey options for additional study and growth.

What you'll study

Assessing Your Progress	Forming a Plan	Living Intentionally	Facing Problems	Where Do We Go from Here?
DAY 1	DAY 2	DAY 3	DAY 4	DAY 5

Memory verse

This week's verse of Scripture to memorize
You are from God, little children, and have overcome them; because greater is He who is in you than he who is in the world.

–1 John 4:4

DAY 1

Assessing Your Progress

It is not good to have zeal without knowledge, nor to be hasty and miss the way.
—Proverbs 19:2, NIV

The proverb above indicates two vital elements of effective living. We need zeal. *Zeal* means *passionate concern*. We also need knowledge. *Knowledge* means *the awareness of information*. Without accurate information about human development, about how family systems work, and about how to achieve life change, no amount of passionate concern will help us achieve our goals.

Anna's story

Anna realized that she had come from a long line of family dysfunction. Her grandparents', parents', and siblings' lives were marred by chemical dependency, divorce, and various types of abuse. She hated the trail of hurt and dysfunction she saw in her family. As a teenager Anna absolutely determined that she would not be like her family members. She did everything she knew to turn her back on them and their way of life. She left home, made new friends, became a diligent worker, became a Christian, and for the next 20 years stayed away from her family.

✎ Exercise your detective skills. Combine the message of the proverb above with what you have learned in this study. Describe what you think might be the outcome of Anna's attempt to break free from the cycle of family dysfunction.

_____

_____

As Anna neared her 40th birthday, she began to reflect on her life and made a discouraging discovery. Although the outward circumstances of her life differed greatly from those of her family of origin, very little had changed under the surface. She was a successful career woman, while her family of origin had been impoverished, but her home life was a wreck. Her mother had been an alcoholic. Although Anna used neither alcohol nor other drugs, she was a workaholic, and her children rebelled at her attempts to control their lives. Her family had been irreligious. Anna and her family were active members of a church, but her religious devotion seemed to drive people away rather than build deep relationships.

You might have suggested that although Anna had changed the outward circumstances of her life, the cycle of family dysfunction probably had continued uninterrupted. You might also have suggested that unless Anna learns and deeply applies knowledge about her identity in Christ and about family relationships, her children will be at great risk to repeat the cycle of hurtful family experiences.

A Beginning for a New Life

In the first 11 units of this study you built a foundation for understanding the cycle of hurtful family experiences. That understanding is the beginning point for lasting life change. We hope that you have gained knowledge about yourself and about your family. You may have faced some issues that have been difficult to admit. You may have experienced grief as you looked more objectively at your life. You may have become discouraged by the process.

✎ Reflect on this study. What has been the one subject or concept that has caused you the most personal difficulty?

_____

What has been the one subject that has given you the most help?

_____

We congratulate you for reaching this point in the study. We are sad to report—but you have probably figured this out by now—that no easy answers exist. No one has developed a magic pill to break the cycle of family dysfunction. The ability to delay gratification—to postpone immediate desires and focus on long-term goals—is a major mark of maturity. You have learned that repeating Anna's mistake will not solve the problem. You need a plan for deep, lasting life change.

You need a plan for deep, lasting life change.

In this final unit of *Breaking the Cycle* you will examine options for your personal life plan. We will challenge you to make some intentional decisions about how you will live life from now on. Will you live as a victim of the cycle? Will you apply a coat of paint to the cycle and declare the problem solved? Or will you make a commitment for the long haul to achieve deep, loving relationships and to engage in faithful discipleship?

A Look Backward

As you develop your long-range plans, you will review the material you have studied.

✎ Take a few minutes to review unit 1 of this study, titled "Identifying the Cycle." Summarize the ways the cycle of hurtful family experiences affects your life and family.

_____

_____

_____

You may have discovered that the cycle of family dysfunction has touched your life only to a minor degree, or you may have discovered that your entire life has been shaped by distorted perceptions and experiences.

✎ Review unit 2 of this study, titled "Substitutes for Relationships." Describe the substitutes with which you have tried to fill the void in your life.

_____

_____

Have you pursued one or more of the empty solutions described in day 3 of unit 2? If so, describe the experience.

_____
_____

How has the decision to make God your functional parent and role model affected your views of yourself, others, and God?

_____
_____

> You are from God, little children, and have overcome them; because greater is He who is in you than he who is in the world.
>
> –1 John 4:4

✎ Begin to memorize 1 John 4:4, this week's Scripture-memory verse, by copying it below. Repeat the verse aloud several times.

_____
_____
_____

SUMMARY STATEMENTS

- Without accurate information about human development, about how family systems work, and about how to achieve life change, no amount of passionate concern will help us achieve our goals.
- No easy answers exist. The ability to delay gratification—to postpone immediate desires and focus on long-term goals—is a major mark of maturity.
- You need a plan for deep, lasting life change.

DAY 2

Forming a Plan

He who tends the fig tree will eat its fruit.

–Proverbs 27:18

✎ Review unit 3, "Stages of Development." Describe the impact learning about the stages of development has made in your thinking and in your feelings about yourself.

_____
_____
_____
_____

If you identified one or more areas in which your development has been blocked, describe that area.

_____

✎ Review unit 4, "Emotional Healing." Describe actions you need to take or are presently taking to mature in the areas you identified above.

_____

_____

If you have difficulty determining actions you can take to grow and mature, review pages 76-79 in unit 4 for specific suggestions.

A Plan for Relationships

We need relationships characterized by love, objectivity, hope, and depth.

In day 3 of unit 4 you studied "The Role of Relationships." We need relationships characterized by love, objectivity, hope, and depth. As you draw close to the end of this study, you have a variety of options about developing relationships. You may determine that you already have healthy relationships. You may determine, however, that you need such relationships with people who understand and share your particular journey. If you recognize the need for deeper relationships, you have several options.

✎ A plan for developing deeper relationships could include one or more of the following options. Check the options that could help you in your growth or write your own plan.

❑ 1. Participate in a group study and discussion of this workbook (if you have studied it on your own).
❑ 2. Participate in another discovery group in which individuals meet, study, and share together to understand a life problem better.
❑ 3. Participate in a support group—a group of people who share the same problem and who meet with, share with, and encourage one another in their quest for change.
❑ 4. Pursue private counseling with a Christian counselor.
❑ 5. Participate in group therapy with a Christian counselor.

❑ 6. Other: _____

_____

If through this study you have uncovered some painful emotions and behaviors, thank you for having the courage and honesty to face them. The above actions are only a few options that can help you grow. Some people genuinely have no underlying problem. They complete a study like this one to understand better the hurts of others. Some people first need to concentrate on a critical issue like chemical dependency or to seek joint marriage counseling. They first need to gain a sense of stability before they begin to deal with underlying issues.

We urge you to avoid a common pitfall: if you recognize the need for growth, do not ignore the problem. Healing can be a messy, painful process, but it

216   Unit 12

Make a plan to grow emotionally, relationally, intellectually, and spiritually.

brings great rewards. Make a plan to grow emotionally, relationally, intellectually, and spiritually. Then begin slowly and steadily to work for life change.

↪ Spend a few minutes in prayer. Ask God to lead you as you consider additional work. Ask Him to show you areas of your emotional, spiritual, intellectual, and relational life that you can improve. Share with Him how you feel about these issues. Ask Him to give you the motivation to work toward growth.

✎ Continue to work on memorizing 1 John 4:4. Write it in the margin three times.

SUMMARY STATEMENTS

- We need relationships characterized by love, objectivity, hope, and depth.
- Healing can be a messy, painful process; but it brings great rewards.
- Make a plan to grow emotionally, relationally, intellectually, and spiritually.

DAY 3

Living Intentionally

Do you not know that when you present yourselves to someone as slaves for obedience, you are slaves of the one whom you obey, either of sin resulting in death, or of obedience resulting in righteousness?

–Romans 6:16

Have you played a video game in which you drive a race car or a speedboat? In the game you stand still, and the landscape rushes toward you. You are not really in control but only reacting to what comes next. You try to avoid crashing; you just try to stay alive. Have you ever felt that life is like that—that you were reacting to the forces around you and trying to hold your life together?

A huge difference exists between a video game and a drive in the country. Part of that difference is intentionality. When you drive in the country, you choose what you will do. You choose the course, within the limits of the roadway. You choose the speed, within the upper limit imposed by your automobile's engine and the lower limit imposed by the guy in the sports car who keeps honking his horn at you. You do what you choose rather than just reacting to circumstances.

We can work to make Christ-honoring and life-enhancing choices.

We all face difficult life choices and situations. We can apply Romans 6:16 to those situations. We can "present ourselves" to obey our life circumstances. As a result, we will go through life reacting, like puppets on a string. Or we can work to make Christ-honoring and life-enhancing choices. This study has been a doorway to some of those choices.

Unit 12   217

✎ Review unit 5, "Analyzing Your Family." Remembering that the purpose is not to blame but to understand ourselves, write a summary of what you learned about yourself from your family-of-origin work.

_____
_____

What impact has your family of origin made on your relationship with God?

_____
_____

What impact has your family of origin made on your adult relationships?

_____
_____

✎ Review unit 6, "Bonding with God." Your relationships with God and with healthy believers can help you repair the damage caused by a dysfunctional family of origin. Describe your feelings about the promises in the unit—that God wants you with Him, that He will not abandon you, that He accepts you as you are, and that you are precious to Him.

_____
_____

You may feel a positive response to the unit; or you may feel skeptical, frightened, angry, or numb. The important tasks are to identify your feelings and reactions and to begin to make purposeful choices. Remember the video game. By learning, making choices, and drawing support from others, you can live life rather than react to it.

By learning, making choices, and drawing support from others, you can live life rather than react to it.

✎ Review unit 7, "Getting to Know God," in which you studied the meanings of His names. Describe which of the names God used to reveal Himself means the most to you now and why.

_____
_____

Understanding that getting to know God is a major life task, what do you need to do to get to know Him better?

_____
_____

Try to avoid general answers like "I need to read the Bible more." Attempt to set realistic, specific goals to help you get to know God as He really is. If you are not already doing so, beginning to attend worship with a Bible-believing church family is a practical goal. Beginning to set aside a specific time to pray and read Scripture is practical. Participating in a Bible-study group is practical. In the last lesson this week we will suggest some resources that can help in your spiritual growth.

✎ Review unit 8. ***Metamorphosis*** means ***change.*** The four key actions necessary to achieve life change appear below. Beside each action write the percentage of effort you believe you need to dedicate to the action. For example, to a large degree you might have completed number 1 but need to concentrate on number 3; so you might write *5%* for 1, ***20%*** for 2, ***60%*** for 3, and *15%* for 4.

    ___ 1. Recognize the contrast between God's character and that of your parents.
    ___ 2. Choose God as your source of security and significance.
    ___ 3. Dwell on God's love, forgiveness, and power at any and every given moment.
    ___ 4. Be patient; develop a "siege" mentality.

You may have estimated the percentages above in any possible combination. Actually implementing the four actions is the critical issue.

In this lesson you have reviewed units 5–8 of this study. Can you relate them to the four actions above? Doing a family-of-origin study (unit 5) helps us recognize the contrast between the concept of God we constructed from our experiences with parents and who He really is. In unit 6 you described bonding with God, which means choosing God as our source of security and significance. Studying God's character as revealed through His names (unit 7) is a way to dwell on His love, forgiveness, and power. In unit 8 you brought these actions together with the awareness that patient, determined work will bring lasting change.

Studying God's character as revealed through His names is a way to dwell on His love, forgiveness, and power

↪ Take a few minutes to pray. Talk with God about what you have reviewed in this lesson. Thank Him for the insights you have gained as you have worked. Ask Him to continue revealing Himself to you.

✎ Below attempt to write this week's Scripture verse from memory. Check your work on page 212.

_____

_____

_____

SUMMARY STATEMENTS

- We can work to make Christ-honoring and life-enhancing choices.
- By learning, making choices, and drawing support from others, you can live life rather than react to it.
- Attempt to set realistic, specific goals to help you get to know God as He really is.

DAY 4

Facing Problems

The sluggard does not plow after the autumn, so he begs during the harvest and has nothing.

—Proverbs 20:4

We hate to end on bad news, but here comes the truth: no pain, no gain. Work is the only way to break the cycle. Today you will review three kinds of work. None of them are easy, but each is valuable. Unit 9 discussed healing as a grief process. Grief work is the first kind of labor. Unit 10 presented the second type of work—modeling God's character for your children. In Unit 11 you examined the third area—dealing with your parents.

Work is the only way to break the cycle.

✎ Review unit 9, "Grieving and Healing." Do you continue to experience difficulty in honestly expressing your emotions—particularly painful emotions—to yourself, to God, and to others? ❏ Yes ❏ No

Below you will find listed the elements of the grieving process. As both a review and a self-evaluation, write beside each part of the process at least one incident from your experience that illustrates that particular stage. We have given examples for the first two stages.

Denial: *I blamed my wife and children for the shame I felt whenever someone suggested that our family wasn't perfect.*

Bargaining: *I promised God that I would go to church every week if He would fix the problems I was having with my son.*

Denial: _____

Bargaining: _____

Anger: _____

Grief: _____

Acceptance: _____

Consider the possibility that you need to do further recovery work.

If you have problems remembering the stages of grief, review pages 174-175. If you can describe a personal experience for each element above, you are probably progressing through the grief/healing process well. If you have difficulty, consider the possibility that you need to do further recovery work in this area. You may want to spend some extended time working through the writing process proposed in day 5 of unit 9. Additionally, you may want to consider a support group or counseling.

✎ Review Unit 10 on modeling God's character to your children. What concrete, specific plans have you made or can you make to achieve each of the following?

A changed self-concept: _____

_____

A changed purpose: _____

_____

Changed affections: _____

_____

A changed schedule: _____

_____

Changed actions: _____

_____

✎ Review Unit 11, "Responding to Your Parents." Describe what you have learned about your parents through this process.

_____

_____

_____

Write your personal statement of purpose for your relationships with your parents. Clearly state your goals for the relationships.

_____

_____

_____

_____

Process your experiences until you can practice forgiveness.

Through studies like this some people make great progress in forgiving their parents. Having learned how the cycle of hurt has affected their parents, they are better able to understand and forgive the hurts they have experienced from their parents. Others, realizing how dysfunctional their home life was, become more angry. Your response may have been either of the two or some combination of the two. We encourage you to process your experiences until you can practice forgiveness.

Unit 12   221

➪ You now have completed an enormous amount of work. You have worked through 11 challenging units and have reviewed your work to prepare for your future growth. Take a few minutes to sit quietly. Thank God for the pleasant insights you have experienced. Thank Him also for being with you through the difficult times. Ask Him to give you wisdom, courage, and strength to know where to go from here.

As your fellow travelers on the road to build families that honor God and convey blessings, we thank you for the work you have invested. You may have skipped parts of this workbook. If you are in a group, you may have been unable to complete all the work all the time. If so, we do not want to shame you. We encourage you to set realistic, achievable goals and to complete the work you have missed.

You may have discovered some gaping holes in your personal and family life. In the last lesson we will present some options to help you meet those needs. All of us are pilgrims on the road of discipleship. Do not allow the length of the journey or past failures to keep you from moving forward to the joy that lies before you.

Do not allow the length of the journey or past failures to keep you from moving forward.

✎ Review this week's Scripture verse. Also review all of the memory passages you have learned in this study.

SUMMARY STATEMENTS

- Work is the only way to break the cycle.
- Process your experiences until you can practice forgiveness.
- Do not allow the length of the journey or past failures to keep you from moving forward to the joy that lies before you.

DAY 5

Where Do We Go from Here?

The name of the Lord is a strong tower; The righteous runs into it and is safe.
—Proverbs 18:10

We all need to grow. None of us has arrived. As you have worked through *Breaking the Cycle of Hurtful Family Experiences*, we hope that you have come to understand yourself better. We hope that you have come to understand and to love God more. We hope that you have also discovered areas in which you need to grow.

✎ Think about areas in your life in which you need to grow. On the following list check your top three priorities.

We all need to grow.

___ Understanding the Bible
___ Memorizing Scripture
___ Developing your prayer life
___ Building witnessing skills

___ Changing unhealthy relationships
___ Knowing God's will
___ Becoming a disciple maker
___ Caring for your physical needs
___ Other: _____

Character development and spiritual growth are not instantaneous.

Remember that character development and spiritual growth are not instantaneous. Worthwhile goals take time.

The following resources are written in the interactive format you have used as in *Breaking the Cycle of Hurtful Family Experiences*. These books are intended for group study along with daily, individual work. Choose one or more of these resources to help you continue your spiritual growth.

To build your self-worth on the forgiveness and love of Jesus Christ:
- *Search for Significance* LIFE® Support Group Series Edition by Robert S. McGee, Johnny Jones, and Sallie Jones (Houston: Rapha Publishing). This study continues your work of replacing the four false beliefs with principles of truth from God's Word. Member's Book, 0805499903; Leader's Guide, 080549989X.

To identify and replace codependent behaviors:
- *Untangling Relationships: A Christian Perspective on Codependency* by Pat Springle and Susan A. Lanford (Houston: Rapha Publishing). This course helps individuals understand codependency and learn how to make relationships more healthy. Member's Book, 0805499733; Leader's Guide, 0805499741.

- *Conquering Codependency: A Christ-Centered 12-Step Process* by Pat Springle and Dale W. McCleskey (Houston: Rapha Publishing). The learned perceptions and behaviors called codependency—the compulsion to rescue, help, and fix others—often add to our addictive behaviors. *Conquering Codependency* applies the Christ-centered 12 Steps to these habits. Member's Book, 080549975X; Facilitator's Guide, available for free download at www.lifeway.com/discipleplus/download.htm.

To help you grow in developing a healthy lifestyle:
- *Fit 4: A LifeWay Christian Wellness Plan* addresses all four areas of life—heart, soul, mind, and strength. This wellness plan blends taking proper care of your body, being devoted to God, and maintaining healthy relationships with family, friends, and others. For more information contact LifeWay Church Resources Customer Service at 1-800-458-2772 or fit4.com.

To understand God's will for your life:
- *Experiencing God: Knowing and Doing the Will of God* by Henry Blackaby and Claude V. King (Nashville: LifeWay Press). Find answers to the often-asked question "How can I know and do God's will?" This study helps Christians discover God's will and obediently follow it. Member's Book, 0805499547; Leader's Guide, 0805499512.

To help you develop your prayer life:
- *Disciple's Prayer Life, Revised* by T. W. Hunt and Catherine Walker (Nashville: LifeWay Press). This course helps adults learn to pray through

experiences based on prayers of the Bible. Its sessions offer practical experiences that strengthen and deepen prayer lives and help churches develop an intercessory prayer ministry. 0767334949.

To learn more about the Bible:
- *Step by Step Through the Old Testament* by Waylon Bailey and Tom Hudson (Nashville: LifeWay Press). This self-instructional workbook surveys the Old Testament, provides a framework for understanding and interpreting it, and teaches Bible background. Member's Book, 0767326199; Leader's Guide, 0767326202.

- *Step by Step Through the New Testament* by Thomas D. Lea and Tom Hudson (Nashville: LifeWay Press). This 13-unit self-instructional workbook surveys the New Testament, provides a framework for understanding and interpreting the New Testament, and teaches Bible background. Member's Book, 0805499466; Leader's Guide, 0767326210.

To help you learn to think the thoughts of Christ:
- *The Mind of Christ* by T. W. Hunt and Claude V. King (Nashville: LifeWay Press). This course is a serious study of what it means to have the thoughts of Christ and to renew the mind, as Scripture commands. Member's Book, 0805498702; Leader's Guide, 0805498699.

To help you learn how to disciple others:
- *MasterLife* by Avery T. Willis, Jr. (Nashville: LifeWay Press) guides both new and experienced believers to develop lifelong, obedient relationships with Jesus Christ. The series includes four studies which can be studied in sequence or separately. The Leader Kit includes all four Member Books, a Leader Guide, and three videotapes, 0767326407.

To order copies of these resources: WRITE LifeWay Church Resources Customer Service, 127 Ninth Avenue, North, Nashville, TN 37234-0113; FAX order to (615) 251-5933; PHONE 1-800-458-2772; EMAIL to CustomerService@lifeway.com; ONLINE at www.lifeway.com; or visit the LifeWay Christian Store serving you.

Life can be an exciting adventure. The options you have reviewed present some possibilities for a lifestyle of continued growth, health, and service.

Life can be an exciting adventure.

We heartily congratulate you for completing this workbook. Thank you for having the courage and tenacity to reach this point. This book ends, but the process of breaking the cycle of hurtful family experiences continues. It is the process of victorious Christian living. If you feel some discouragement, pain, or fear about the process, remember the nature of the grieving/healing process. Your feelings are normal. Typically, we feel worse before we feel better. You can draw strength from your final Scripture-memory verse:

> *You are from God, little children, and have overcome them; because greater is He who is in you than he who is in the world.*
> —1 John 4:4

Breaking the Cycle of Hurtful Family Experiences

Chain labels: stuffing, chasing empty solutions, denial, poor parental modeling, legacy of dysfunction, blocked human development, broken relationships, distorted concept of God, lic areness

BREAKING the CYCLE

- Contrast God and Parents
- Choose God
- Dwell on God's Love
- Develop a "Siege" Mentality

LEADS TO

- Modeling God's character to your children
- Working through the stages of development
- Realistic concept of God
- Grief process
- Forgiving
- Getting to know God
- Intimacy with God
- Relating to your parents
- Understanding family origin

Untangling Relationships: A Christian Perspective on Codependency $15.50
- volume discounts also available

Codependency is the:
• Compulsion to please others.
• Feeling responsible to make others happy, successful and good.
• Feeling guilty when you don do everything just right - all the time.

Untangling Relationships: Leader's Guide $7.00

Conquering Chemical Dependency $15.50
- volume discounts also available

Whereas most other 12 step programs simply use an undefined understanding of God, this program presents the only true God. The person will be led to understand the following:

• What their real perception of God is and how it was created in their childhood.
• God's process for setting a person free from the power of sin.
• The origin of the pain in their life and what to do about it.
• The warning signs of chemical dependency.
• Who they are in Christ and how to deal with shame and guilt... and many other issues. This is simply the most extensive, Christ-centered proven program in existence.

Conquering Eating Disorders $15.50
- volume discounts also available

Here is an effective, proven program for everyone who has experienced the debilitating disorders of anorexia, bulimia, and compulsive overeating.

This 12-Step Program for Overcoming Eating Disorders tackles the compulsive-addictive patterns in which a person uses food in an emotionally or physically abusive way. The reader will learn what eating disorders are... and are not, and why they occur.

Breaking the Cycle of Hurtful Family Experiences $15.50
- volume discounts also available

Learn how your parents shape the way you feel about yourself, how you relate to others, even how you form your ideas about God.

Breaking the Cycle of Hurtful Family Experiences Leader's Guide $7.00

Conquering Codependency: A Christ Centered 12-Step Process $15.50
- volume discounts also available

Conquering Codependency: A Christ-Centered 12-Step
Process helps you recognize the painful problems of codependency, the compulsion to fix everyone and everything. It offers sound biblical strategies that give
hope and promise healing from the damage codependency can do to your life.

Shelter From The Storm $15.50
- volume discounts also available

From beyond her own darkness, author Cynthia Kubetin leads others to freedom.
"This was one of the most eye opening books I have ever read. After I read the book, I realized I wasn't crazy."

Codependency: A Christian Perspective $15.50
- volume discounts also available

Codependency is the:
- Compulsion to please others.
- Feeling responsible to make others happy, successful and good.
- Feeling guilty when you don't do everything just right - all the time.

Rapha's 12-Step Program for Overcoming Codependency $15.50
- volume discounts also available

Rapha's 12-Step Codependency manual is a complete work that introduces the reader to the processes they must go through to find freedom from the lifelong pattern of codependency. This manual not only allows the person to identify the specific ways their life has been impacted by this deception but takes them through the steps that will set them free. This manual was part of Rapha's Treatment programs that treated over 30,000 patients. There are no other books that have demonstrated the effectiveness and the attention to spiritual issues as this one.

Rapha's 12-Step Program for Overcoming Chemical Dependency $15.50
- volume discounts also available

Includes what the other 12-Step programs leave out - how to deal with the foundational issues that allow the person to gain freedom.

The Search For Peace $12.50
- volume discounts also available

Forgiveness of others is the key to discovering your own forgiveness as well as stopping the reliving of hurtful experiences. More mistakes are made in the teaching of forgiveness than almost anything I know.- Robert S. McGee

Video CD Included

The Search For Freedom $15.50
- volume discounts also available

As children we create strongholds which greatly influence the way we perceive life, respond and relate to others. Find out how to identify the strongholds and destroy them.

Rapha's 12-Step Program for Overcoming Eating Disorders $15.50
- volume discounts also available

Here is an effective, proven program for everyone who has experienced the debilitating disorders of anorexia, bulimia, and compulsive overeating. This 12-Step Program for Overcoming Eating Disorders tackles the compulsive-addictive patterns in which a person uses food in an emotionally or physically abusive way. The reader will learn what eating disorders are... and are not, and why these disorders occur.

Discipline With Love $10.00
- volume discounts also available

A practical guide for establishing systematic discipline in your home. The principles offered here have helped many parents form a plan for discipline, so that their children can grow to be mature, responsible adults. These principles work because they are based on the truths of the Scriptures. With them, you can experience success in disciplining your children.

Rapha's Handbook for Group Leaders $10.00

This book helps any group wanting to begin or improve on small groups. It contains the following:

- The Goals and Expectations of a Group
- Organization and Selection
- The Mechanics of a Group
- The Dynamics of a Group
- How to Get Started
- And more!

Right Step Christian Recovery Program $50.00

In 1986, Rapha began. Over the next 12 years, over 30,000 patients were seen in this in-hospital program. During this time the presentations seen in this video series was presented to hundreds of thousands of people. This material comes from those who are in the best position to know what works and doesn't work. It contains the following video presentations:

- Functional & Dysfunctional Families
- The Addictive/Dysfunctional Personality
- Codependency
- Support Groups
- Leading Support Groups
- Getting Started/ Follow-Up Training

Would you like Robert McGee to speak to your group? Robert maintains a limited speaking schedule. However, if you would like to contact him about coming to your church or group, write to him at rmcgee@searchlife.org or call him at 1-800-460-4673.

To order call 1-800-460-4673 or go to www.searchlife.org

Made in the USA
San Bernardino, CA
24 November 2018